CRIME, VALUES, AND RELIGION

Editors:

James M. Day
University of Pennsylvania

William S. Laufer
Temple University

Ablex Publishing Corporation
Norwood, New Jersey

Copyright © 1987 by Ablex Publishing Corporation

Printed in the United States of America

Library of Congress Cataloging-in-Publication Data

Crime, values, and religion.

Bibliography: p.
Includes index.
1. Crime and criminals—Religious aspects.
I. Day, James M.   II. Laufer, William S.
BL65.C7C75   1987   291.1′7833   86-28783
ISBN: 0-89391-411-8

ABLEX Publishing Corporation
355 Chestnut Street
Norwood, New Jersey 07648

About the Editors

James M. Day is a graduate of Oberlin College and Harvard University and has done additional work at Yale University Divinity School and Union Theological Seminary. He is Staff Psychologist at St. Joseph's University, and a doctoral candidate in professional psychology at the University of Pennsylvania. Author and co-author of numerous articles, national and international conference presentations, his first book, edited with William S. Laufer, was *Personality Theory, Moral Development, and Criminal Behavior* (D.C. Heath: Lexington Books 1983).

William S. Laufer is an Assistant Professor of Criminal Justice in the Department of Criminal Justice, Temple University. He received the Ph.D. in Criminal Justice from the Graduate School of Criminal Justice, Rutgers University, the J.D. from Northeastern University School of law, and the B.A. in social and behavioral sciences from the Johns Hopkins University. His research on criminal and asocial behavior has appeared in the *Journal of Research in Crime and Delinquency, Journal of Personality and Social Psychology, Journal of Clinical Psychology, and Journal of Vocational Behavior*. Dr. Laufer is currently Editor of the periodical *Advances in Criminological Theory* (Criminal Justice Press). He co-edited *Personality Theory, Moral Development, and Criminal Behavior* (Lexington Books, 1983) with James M. Day.

Contents

Introduction

James M. Day
William S. Laufer

In recent years much has been made of what has been called the alarming, even epidemic frequency with which crimes are committed against American citizens. Writers in popular and scholarly journals have examined various dimensions of the criminal phenomenon, legislatures, courts, and justice systems have experimented with methods for managing it, and individuals have found confrontation with its effects unavoidable.

At the same time, observers have noted an increase in the numbers of Americans who actively associate with religious institutions, ideas, and practices. Growth of churches, the rise of non-traditional religious groups —sometimes called cults, increasing numbers of students in religious schools at every level, Moral Majority participation in political debates and campaigns, and highly public discussions by Roman Catholic, "Mainline" Protestant, and Jewish clergy over the role of religion in the nation's affairs are some cases in point. Public figures "gone religious," from prominent politicians to popular music stars, add to the list.

For all of the commotion, few have gone beyond simplistic formulations regarding relations between these two phenomena. In this book the editors consider the long-neglected factor of religion in criminology and criminal justice. Every chapter here has as its aim the integration of knowledge about religion, values, and crime. Together they go beyond the constraints of those who have neglected one or another of those phenomena, as well as the limitations of theorists whose assertions have not been tested by research, and researchers whose evidence has not been theoretically elaborated.

The reader will find chapters expositing the social dimension of the crime-religion relationship, from religious foundations of American jurisprudence and involvement of religious organizations in public policy on crime, to sociological analyses of religion-crime connections and theological treatments of crime and personality. Other chapters present work that empirically test and delineate religion as a factor in the personalities and group psychology of criminals and as a variable in the prevention and reduction of crime.

Thus religion is construed here to mean, on the one hand, organized religions and, on the other, the various value, attitude, and belief systems held by individuals and groups. Both conceptions of religion are important for those who would understand religion's place in criminology. Western legal and intellectual institutions have their source in those of the Judeo-Christian tradition, as do the ideas of justice, mercy, truth, and responsibility that, in theory, guide their activity. At the same time, psychology derives at least in part from religious philosophy and is informed by the same tradition's conceptions of human nature.

It is surprising, but not since the Franciscan Herald Press published Kalmer, Weir, and Meyer's *Crime and Religion* in 1936 has a project like this been undertaken. That admirable volume consisted in three sections, describing religions in criminal populations, Roman Catholicism and offenders, and religions in comparison and contrast with other factors such as race, education, and socio-economic status. Chief among its shortcomings were its equation of religion, qua religion, with Roman Catholicism, and its failure to clearly defend the claim that religion is at once the best guarantee against and cure for criminal behavior.

Most recently, within the very small body of literature on the subject, the trend has been toward reporting measures of offenders' religious attitudes and examining possible differences between the religious attitudes of those who are and are not offenders. Little attention has been paid to the relation of religious and moral values, even less to the relation of those attitudes, and religious practices to the actual behavior of criminals; religion within offender populations, and the use of religion as a means of delinquency insulation.

This volume revives longstanding questions, and poses new ones through the integration of previously distinct disciplines and modes of analysis, toward a more comprehensive understanding of criminal behavior.

Chapter 1

Crime and Sin in Puritan Massachusetts

Clyde A. Holbrook

William H. Danforth Professor of Religion, Emeritus
Oberlin College

The word "crime" in typical modern dictionary definitions lends itself to a variety of meanings. First, it has a legal meaning. It is "an act. . forbidden by a public law of a sovereign state" as injurious to the public welfare, which, after indictment and trial, may be punishable by the judgment of a court. But a moral ingredient is also involved in the definition when it is regarded as any grave or aggravated offense against or departure from moral rectitude (*Webster's 3d*, 1976). In this way the tension between the legal "ought" and the moral "ought" creates a problem for jurisprudence (see Olafson, 1961, p. 435 ff). An even more confusing problem appears when an offense against morality is defined as sin (*Webster's College ed.*, 1960). If crime be taken in its strictly legal sense, inclusive of immorality, and sin is then equated with immorality, the word "crime" would also encompass the meaning of sin. But when sin is defined as the breaking of a religious law by a willful act or, as it turns out, any act or impulse against God, immorality then is no longer an adequate term. A religious dimension has thereby been added to the legal and moral significance of crime. In modern circumstances courts may tend to tread cautiously in the area of crime where moral considerations are at stake in criminal cases, but try to avoid, so far as possible, recognition of crime as a sin. However, in seventeenth century Massachusetts, although efforts were sometimes made to distinguish between crime, immorality and sin, the distinctions were often overridden, and even seemingly petty offenses were treated as crime under the rubric of law. This state of affairs was largely due to the unique nature of the community which the Puritans set out to establish. The analysis offered here is an examination of some of the ways in which their religious purpose impinged upon and molded their ideas of law and crime, immorality and sin, but no attempt is made to sort out exhaustively the misdeeds which fell under each of these categories.

1

I. THE COMMUNITY, LAW, AND SIN

In the Puritan setting it is important first to recognize the distinction made between morality and piety. A vivid example of this distinction is offered in the description of the moral man and his destiny by the Puritan preacher Thomas Hooker. The moral man, he said, was one who was "outwardly just, temperate, chaste, careful to follow his worldly businesse, will not hurt so much as his neighbour's dog, payes every man his owne, and lives his owne. . . ." He was "no drunkard, adulterer, or quarreller" and "loves to live peaceably and quietly among his neighbours." Yet, concluded Hooker, such a man was on the way to Hell (cited in Morgan, 1966, p. 1; cf. Niebuhr, 1937, p. 31). The exemplary behavior described by Hooker no more fulfilled the high aim of a grace endowed life than did overt immorality. The love of sin which still worked in such a person stained his incontrovertible virtue. And thus love of sin could not be extinguished by any law imposed on conduct, since only the gift of the Holy Spirit could nullify this misplaced affection. Indeed, asked Niebuhr, "What definite counsel could be given to the man who sought perfection when perfection was defined not as a matter of behavior, but as an affair of faith and love, neither of which was subject to man's control?" (Niebuhr, 1937, p. 31). Sin was not simply immoral acts, but a profound distortion in the very soul of a person which no law of state could remedy. By the same token, true piety was not to be sought in mere conformity to human or divine law, important as these were to the Puritan consciousness. The Puritans certainly believed in the rule of law, but to understand this legalistic tendency we look in the wrong direction at the outset if emphasis is placed only upon this aspect of the Puritan experience. In at least the ideal sense, Puritanism in the New World, as seen through the eyes of its earliest leaders, was not founded in law, but upon a deep awareness of organic community organized around a common purpose. The rigorism of enacted law, which we attribute to these Puritans, was not at root the central feature of their community, but as realists about the ever present danger of sin, they regarded law as a means by which their common purpose and community was to be protected against the ruination the Devil intended to bring upon them. Hence the rule of law was necessary, although not all misdeeds could be caught in its toils. "Every Puritan who really believed the basic tenets of his faith expected lawbreaking and a good deal of conflict and friction that was ungodly but not formally illegal (Foster, 1971, p. 6). Yet without laws the whole Puritan experiment would founder. But having admitted this much, we must affirm that it was not law alone that could guard the Puritan experiment; God alone at last could insure its survival. The sense of sin might teach the Puritan that laws per se, enacted by sinful men, might never be the perfect law, yet the laws that passed were to be as binding as natural laws to the degree that they reflected divine law (Haskins, 1960, p. 159).

Certainly, however, one cannot gain a balanced view of the Puritan colonies if only the records of their lawsuits, reports or crimes and compendia of laws are consulted. Litigious as these Englishmen were, and strenuously as they pursued the ethical and religious life, nevertheless a great deal of the support for the rule of law, civil and ecclesiastical, sprang from the sense of a shared community purpose as well as from traditional family and social custom brought with them from England. Daily life was as much carried on and stabilized by these familiar patterns as it was by constant recourse to legal proceedings or incessant regard to duty. Nor does the enactment of myriad laws against specific crimes or sins signify that these people dwelt in a constant state of wrongdoing.

Obedience to law presupposed, as it must today, a community which willingly supports and accepts law. Without a shared sense of community, law would lack any basis for acceptance. It was acquiescence in the over-riding purpose of the Puritan enterprise that ideally bound these people together in a common venture. The vision of that purpose entailed a driving conviction that God intended them to build a society in obedience to His Kingdom, a society which in John Winthrop's words would be "as a city upon a Hill" with the "eies of all people upon them (Morgan, 1965, p. 93). These Puritans did not come to the New World to build the Kingdom or, in distinction from other settlements, to establish a theocracy (cf. Haskins, 1960, p. 62–63; Niebuhr, 1937, p. 45; Miller & Johnson, 1963, p. 191). Rather they planned to constitute a community bent on practicing the pure, unfettered Word of God, a society which held the Kingdom as "a rule which having been established from eternity, needed to be obeyed despite the rebellion against it which flourished in the world (Niebuhr, 1937, p. 56). The seal of this engagement with God and His Kingdom, as Winthrop saw it, was not first of all a body of laws, but a covenant between these wayfarers and the deity. "Thus stands the cause between God and us," proclaimed Winthrop to his hearers on the Arabella, "wee are entered into covenant with him for this worke, we have taken out a Commission, the Lord hath given us to drawe our owne Articles... if the Lord shall please to heare us, and bring us in peace to the place we desire, then hath hee ratified this Covenant and sealed our Commission, and will expect a strikt performance of the Articles contained in it..." Failure to observe these Articles, he added, will cause the Lord to "breake out in wrathe against us" and "make us knowe the price of the breache of such a Covenant" (Morgan, 1965, pp. 91–92). On this Covenant, with Articles not yet formulated as laws, rested the sanction for the laws yet to come. In spite of the quasi-legalistic tone of his remarks, Winthrop by no means envisioned life in the New World to be one lived only by legal restriction.

True, he spoke of the two laws of Justice and Mercy, but these were not yet formulated into specific enacted laws, and he made clear that at times the two concurred and merged as he spelled out their application and meaning.

Covenant language may have sounded legalistic, but Winthrop put much weight on "the Bond of brotherly affeccion" which was to unite the community. It was to be one where "every man" was no more honorable than another, although he maintained that the difference between rich and poor was established by divine providence. However, this difference was not to be regarded as due to any dignity self-conferred by high economic status (Morgan, 1965, p. 77).[1] The traditional Christian concept of Christians as the body of Christ was used by Winthrop when he spoke of love as the "ligaments" of this body. From this love came "a sensibleness and Sympathy of each others Condicions" which would "necessarily infuse into eache parte a native desire and endeavour, to strengthen defend preserve and comfort the others (Morgan, 1965, pp. 85, 89, 90–91). Love therefore, not law, was to knit together Puritan society.

This love was not expected to give way to religious antinomianism and civil disorder. A hierarchical social, political and ecclesiastical system was presupposed, which guaranteed order for the whole community. Just as families, inclusive of servants and apprentices, were to be bound in love, so society at large would also in love exhibit a hierarchical structure (cf. Haskins, 1960, p. 79; Breen, 1980, p. 49–50). Thus by love uniting the people "in a unitary organism" each part was to be contributary and subordinate to the welfare of the whole (cf. Haskins, 1960, p. 59; & Foster, 1971, pp. 15, 21). Superordination and subordination, whereby mutual responsibilities could be apportioned, was necessary for the good of all and the glory of God. Winthrop had explained the divine ordering of economic distinctions among men. And he reminded his fellow Puritans that by conscience and public interest they were to allow governance to "oversway all private respects" since the welfare of "perticular estates" depended on it (Morgan, 1965, p. 90). Thomas Hooker took up the refrain in respect to societal and ecclesiastical unity. "The power is in the whole firstly," he wrote, "but each part knows its rank . . . every part is subject to the whole" ("A Survey of the Summe of Church Discipline," cited in Levering, 1980). Or as he put it elsewhere, "Mutual subjection is as it were the sinewes of society, by which it is sustained and supported (cited in Foster, 1971, p. 16).

Winthrop may have waxed enthusiastic about love as the "ligamentes" of the community, but he was far from being a romantic about the prob-

---

[1] In Winthrop's company the meaner sort as well as the better believed in inequality, and the few who refused to accept it did so only in the same sense as we refuse to accept it did so only in the same sense as we refuse to accept sickness and death" (Foster, 1971, p. 7).

lems facing man's corrupt nature. He let it be known that by mutual consent and a special overruling Providence these people had ventured abroad "to seeke out a place of Cohabitation and Consortship under a due forme of Government both civil and ecclesiastical." In this phraseology Winthrop was simply repeating the long held principle of religious uniformity, which maintained the necessary joint partnership of religion and civil government within a political unit. By the same principle, it was reckoned that toleration of more than one religion within a state could only lead to social disorder. One established religion was therefore necessary to uphold good government and the security of the entire society. Government, "civil and ecclesiastical," signified the presence of laws, legislators, judges, courts, penalties and executors of the law. Thus civil and church law, conceived as the orderly arrangement of the affairs of the whole community, naturally developed, feeding, as it were, on itself to cover more and more exigencies, until the area of human conduct free from legal definition greatly diminished. The result was a concatenation of laws, many of which from this distance look pathetically picayune or morally repulsive and certainly far from the "affection" about which Winthrop had rhapsodized. The character of this body of laws is described by Haskins as "a syncretization of biblical precedent and a complex English heritage which included not only the common law and the statutes, but practices of the church courts of manors, of the justices of the peace, and of the local courts of manors and towns from which the colonists came" (Haskins, 1960, p. 4i). But it is also important to recognize that many legal prescriptions found in the Bible and the English law were rejected or adapted to the new conditions confronted by the Puritans.

If a government of laws was intended to protect the covenanted aims of the Puritan community, it followed that the resultant society was to be no mere aggregation of atomistic individuals, each freely and randomly pursuing his or her own ends. The Protestant tradition which Puritanism exemplified did not hold to the idea of human freedom as the presupposition of the moral and religious life. Human beings, they were convinced, were not by nature free, but locked into an inheritance of original sin. Once Adam and Eve fell from their original innocence, they forfeited freedom for themselves and all their progeny. Freedom therefore could not be taken as the inherent endowment by which mankind lived. It was rather the goal of the religious life. "The actual starting point," Niebuhr observed, "from which to understand freedom was the free God" not the free person (Niebuhr, 1937, p. 24). So persistently and subtly did sin work in men, even with the freedom brought by the Holy Spirit, that some vestiges of the "old man" remained, to which temptation could appeal. The English Puritan Thomas Goodwin was so taken up with this theme that he insisted that "a regenerate man...is guilty of more human sin than an unregenerate man (cited in Kevan, 1964, p. 102). If those supposedly "saved" courted so perilous a state, then clearly evidences of human freedom in the social and religious life should be structured by laws, lest there be an anarchist outpouring of ungodly acts. And these, by law, were adjudged to be crimes.

For the Puritan a government of laws was essential, not simply because, as Aristotle thought, all men were political beings, but because as individuals and social beings they were sinners. The original Eden could not be reproduced in Massachusetts. The Epistle which introduced the Code of Laws of 1648 made this clear when it explained that government was made necessary because of human corruption (cf. Haskins, 1960, p. 138). Yet, as we have seen, enacted law, the product of sinful men, could only imperfectly mirror the supreme law of God. Nevertheless, it was to be obeyed as the best these creatures could formulate. True, law, either civil or ecclesiastical, could not root out pride and inordinate self-interest. Nor could the punishments entailed in it establish one in a state of grace. The Puritan leaders, Morgan observed, "would have been the first to acknowledge that sin could not be extinguished by punishment alone, for they knew that only the Holy Spirit could destroy man's love for sinful ways (Morgan, 1966, p. 173). However, laws could place a hedge around human life and prevent sin's overt expression. It provided a space within which human behavior could at least exhibit outward conformity to law and the practice of external virtue. This legalistic bent of Puritanism had, almost unwittingly, seized upon the psychological fact that external conformity carried on over a period of time has a way of transforming and molding inner motivation. Of course, in this direction also, as critics of Puritanism have been quick to point out, lies hypocrisy. But John Cotton, making the best of things, can be heard to say, "Hypocrites give God part of his due, the outward men, but the prophane person giveth God neither this outward nor inward man." (Hutchinson, 1769, p. 405).

The laws enacted by the Puritans appear to be exceedingly oppressive, yet their purpose was not in all cases punitive. Reform and education in virtue was as much a part of their purpose as was the exaction of punishment. Once Winthrop himself was charged with "over much laxity and remissiveness" in the administration of law, and in consequence he promised "to take a more strict course hereafter" (Morgan, 1965, p. 106). He, at least, apparently did not want to press matters to the extreme if it could be avoided. And he argued stoutly against any attempt to attach prescribed penalties to every law because "Prescript penaltyes take away the use of Admonition. . ." (Morgan, 1965, p. 151). On numerous occasions, including those of Anne Hutchinson and Roger Williams, prolonged counseling, argument and admonition preceded punishment, thus showing the reluctance with which judges and magistrates moved to severity. "Reform and regeneration" concludes Haskins, "were among the magistrates' chief objectives, but when neither proved possible they did not hesitate to apply the most serious sanctions at their command (Haskins, 1960, p. 47). Strictness of observance was necessary, but often failure in observance was first met by the ministration of mercy rather than coercion.

The Puritans' fascination with law owed something to the inherent dynamic by which laws tend to multiply, seemingly of their own accord. More importantly, the Puritans' acute sense of sin called for control by law. But insofar as they followed the Bible, they found there an even more important reason for a life lived under law. The laws in scripture were viewed as a gift of a beneficent deity who not only desired to curb the errant tendencies of his people, but to train them up to walk in ways of righteousness. Only a God who cared for his people's welfare would issue laws. They were evidence of his graciousness. While reading the First Psalm, then the devout Puritan, at least in hope, could see himself as the one who delighted in the Law of the Lord, meditating on it day and night. Gratitude mingled with awe was therefore the proper attitude in which to receive God's law, not that of a sullen bearing of a burden. In the Bible three kinds of law were to be found. There was the judicial or civil law of Israel, the ceremonial, ritualistic law pertaining to worship, and the moral law most obviously seen in the Decalogue. If the Puritans had been strict literalists and legalists, all three types of law would have had equal validity for the guidance of their lives. However, the New Testament dispensation with the coming of Christ, the Incarnate Word of God, was seen as abrogating the ceremonial and judicial laws and having brought the law of love. In practice, as worked out in Massachusetts, some parts of the judicial law as well as the moral law were enacted into laws of the Bay Colony. (cf. Kevan, 1964, p. 43; Haskins, 1960, p. 159). Even so, the Puritans distinguished among laws in both categories, following some and putting aside others as need dictated. In general, biblical laws pertaining to what the Puritans regarded as the most heinous immoralities or repudiations of God's authority were enacted into laws, thus making them crimes deserving of capital punishment. But some civil laws were less traceable to biblical influence.

This selectivity in the use of biblical law suggests that there were differences in attitude toward the Bible, even among those who never doubted that it contained the Word of God. John Cotton, for example, seems to have leaned to a stricter application of biblical law than did Winthrop. He saw the Bible as providing an immutable constitution not only for the right ordering "of a private man's soule" but also "for the right ordering of a man's family, yea, of the commonwealth, so farre as both of them are subordinate to spiritual ends. . ." (Miller & Johnson, 1963, p. 209). Or as he tartly snapped, "the more any law smells of man the more unprofitable" (Haskins, 1960, p. 180). Winthrop, on the other hand, emphasized "the dependence of all civil laws upon natural law, and implied that a test of the law of nature was its agreement with the needs of the society to which it is applied" (Haskins, 1960, p. 180). Or, in his own words, "the matter of the scripture be always a Rule to us, yet not the phrase" (Haskins, 1960, p. 157). In this respect Winthrop retained the Bible's revelatory character without yielding to literalism. This conviction was not unique in Winthrop, for many Puritans were reluctant to carry over biblical prescriptions wholesale into civil and ecclesiastical law. The Bible itself taught that God had acted immediately through his Holy Spirit and spoke through his prophets. And had not Jesus Christ severely criticized the worship of the letter of the law? True, antinomians like Anne Hutchinson went wide of the mark when they appealed to the immediate promptings of the Holy Spirit, but saner Puritan minds believed they could draw a line between the inspiration of the Holy Spirit found in the Bible as of ancient days and what was happening in their own day, when control of such fancies was called for. They had before them the horrid example of England, where immediate inspirations were exploding riotously in sects like the Quakers, Familists, Levelers, Diggers, Ranters, and Anabaptists. Enthusiasts like these had never founded or attempted to govern a state as the Puritans were trying to do. Nevertheless, the tension between following the exact words of scripture and allowance for the free, immediate worship of God's Spirit haunted the Puritan experience. If the Bible as a whole and in every detail was to be equated with divine revelation, then God's present living presence and watchful guidance would be endangered. God, as it were, would have retired from the world's affairs after having delivered his truths in the past. This conclusion could not be wholeheartedly embraced by devout Puritans because they also believed that God had his eye upon their daily lives, directing their fortunes by signs of his pleasure and displeasure. This conviction tended to temper the Puritans' attitude toward biblical law, although it did not prevent a high degree of legalism. One of Puritanism's defenders even denies this charge of legalism by insisting that "any criticism of Puritanism which is based upon its alleged 'legalism' must be dismissed as uninformed. . ." It is "a bogey" concocted out of prejudice and ignorance (Kevan, 1964, p. 259).

With all due consideration given to differing estimates of Puritan attitudes toward biblical law, hardly had they stepped ashore before problems of government entailing law confronted their leaders. The Charter under which the Massachusetts Bay Company acted gave absolute authority over the government to the governor, his deputy-governor, assistants and freemen of the company meeting in a general court. In the first year of their coming, Winthrop, then governor, and the assistants granted freemanship to almost all free adult males then in the colony. These freemen once a year were to elect their rulers and the assistants, and the rulers, in turn, would make the laws and choose officers to execute them. When this arrangement was accepted by a general vote of those qualified, a commonwealth was established, based on a limited popular consent. In 1631, after this establishment, the General Court required all future freemen to belong to one of the colony's churches (cf. Foster, 1971, p. 74).

In 1636 John Cotton and several other ministers were asked to assist the magistrates in drawing up "a body of fundamental laws," but the result was not supported by the General Court. In 1639 Winthrop noted in his Diary that "the people had long desired a body of laws" because they believed too much power was vested in the magistrates (cf. Morgan, 1965, p. 114). At this point Nathaniel Ward, sometime pastor of the Ipswich church, was asked to prepare another body of laws. In his work, containing one hundred laws, he included a part of John Cotton's previous efforts, and the final document came to be known as "the Liberties of the Massachusetts Colonie in New England." After being publicized in all the towns and undergoing some revisions and alteration, "the Liberties" were adopted as law by the General Court in 1641 (cf. Morgan, 1965, p. 122). In view of the popular image of Puritanism as repressive, it is remarkable that a document bearing in its title the word "Liberties" should have been passed. A few examples of these liberties may suffice to show the direction in which this early representation of the Puritans' legal mind moved. One of the principal concerns expressed was that of the inviolability of a man's life and honor. "No man's person shall be arested, restsrayned, banished, dismembered, nor in any wayes punished. . . unlesse it be by vertue or equitie of some expresse law of the country waranting the same, establalished by a generall Court and sufficiently published, or in case of the defect of a law in any particuler case by the word of God." Every person "whether inhabitant or forreiner shall enjoy the same justice and law. . . ." Every person "inhabitant or forreiner, free or not free" can come before a public court, council or town meeting to move "any lawfull, seasonable, and materiall question" or present complaints or information. "No man's person shall be restrained or imprisoned by any authority whatsosever, before the law hath sentenced him thereto." A person could not be sentenced twice for the "same Crime, offense, or Trespasse"—the last phrase being suggestive that there were degrees of offenses. The document also tried to clarify the jurisdictions of civil and church powers. The civil authority had the power and liberty to see that "the peace, ordinances and Rules of Christ" were observed in every church, and the same authority was to have power to deal in a way of civil justice with church members, regardless of their standing as church members. On the other side, no church censure "shall degrade or depose" a person holding office in the commonwealth.

The section on capital crimes did not depend upon common law, but was annotated with scriptural passages, all of them from the Old Testament. The only crime deserving of capital punishment that lacked a scriptural basis was that of conspiracy, insurrection or public rebellion against the commonwealth (cf. Morgan, 1966, p. 179 ff). With the exception of this section of "The Liberties" no penalties were attached to the laws as accepted. Apparently Winthrop and some other leaders were reluctant to see this code developed and passed lest it hinder future adjustments to be made in the light of new circumstances, and perhaps more importantly, because it might expose the colony to interference from England if it did not conform to English law as the Charter provided. The years after 1641 saw more laws developed, and by 1648 another code was adopted, which in a sense was the final rendering of "The Liberties" (cf. Haskins, 1960, p. 131).

In the same year of 1648, ecclesiastical government was stabilized, at least in theory, by the adoption by the churches of "The Cambridge Platform of Church Discipline," largely composed by Richard Mather. The synod which created the Platform was established by both state and church. The Platform expressly stated that "Magistrates have power to call a Synod," but insisted nevertheless that the constituting of a Synod "is a church act & may be transacted by the churches, even when civil magistrates may be enemies to churches & to church assemblies" (*The Cambridge Platform of 1648*, n.d., ch. xvi inc 3.30). The Platform, inclusive of the Westminster Confession, was developed with a sensitivity equal to that of Winthrop toward the situation in England, to avoid provocation of jealousy between the Presbyterian and Independent wings of the English Puritan movement (cf. *The Cambridge Platform of 1648*, 1949, p. 28).

As the years passed, changes took place that threatened the cohesion of the Puritan community. New arrivals whose motivations were often out of accord with the original purpose of the New England settlement poured into the towns. Economic advantage jostled religious commitment for pride of place. Escape from neighborhood squabbles and family quarrels, England's political turmoil, as well as love of adventure proved to be more important than the pious hopes of a Winthrop for living under a due form of civil and ecclesiastical government (Breen, 1980, p. 56). There was always the danger that high fliers of the enthusiastic sort, Quakers and others, might penetrate and disturb the peace and security the leaders hoped for. In fact, as early as 1637 the General Court had passed an order forbidding the entertainment of strangers for more than three weeks without the magistrates' consent, to fend off these undesirables. The controversy that ensued moved Winthrop to defend the order by writing, "If we heere be a corporation established by free consent, if the peace of our cohabitation be our owne, then no man hath right to come to us etc. without our consent (Morgan, 1965, p. 145). But by 1648 John Cotton, making the best of matters, could look back on the coming of those who "came over hither not only out of respect to conscience, or spiritual ends, but out of respect to friends, or outward enlargements" as having had unforeseen benefits. They "have here found that grace, which they sought not for ("The way of the Congregational Churchs cleared," cited in Breen, 1980, p. 58). However, the increase in religious persecution of the late 1650's onward has been interpreted by some observers as the frantic attempts of the religious and political minority to retain its authority lest the whole society be torn apart by religious disaffection and worldliness.

The increased resort to legal actions shows that the convenental purpose and "ligaments" of brotherly affection had sadly frayed. Oppression and persecution for the sake of conformity in belief and conduct was increasing in proportion to the failure in the sense of an organic community. Mere law could not make right what divine influence so far had not done. The inherent contradiction of the Puritan way of conceiving the social and religious order was yielding a bitter harvest. One scholar, reviewing the deterioration of the Puritan communal vision, summed up the matter in this way: "Advocates of political hierarchy would do well to base their franchise on something other than church membership; governors who rule by God's ordinance should not make their offices dependent on popular elections; ministers who preach that every man should remain in his calling should not call upon every man to increase his estate; above all, anyone who maintains traditional concepts of social relationships should not found them on voluntary contracts (Foster, 1971, p. 7).

II. CRIME OR SIN?

One of the principal problems in distinguishing crime from sin in the Puritan Commonwealth lies in its adherence to the principle of religious uniformity. This principle, accepted by Protestants and Catholics alike, was part of the political theory the Puritans took for granted. According to it, the church and state were to be in a symbiotic relation. Membership in the established church was expected of all inhabitants within the state's jurisdiction, and the state in turn would support the church in its efforts to raise up a God fearing population. In this way each person was subject to the discipline of two governing bodies. Theoretically this discipline was to be exercised by each body independently of the other, but herein lay part of the problem of distinguishing crime from sin. Crime could not simply be identified as an act forbidden by the law of a sovereign state when the church had a hand in deciding that sin was a crime and the state treated crime as a sin. Even the language used by both clergy and civil magistrates betrayed the slippage from one category to the other. Winthrop, for example, called Roger Williams's attack on the colony's claim to the land they occupied "a great sin," although Williams's charge was in this respect a purely political or civil charge. Winthrop could also speak of the right of magistrates to excuse a "sin" on the grounds that some acts were secrets of state of which the church need not be notified (Morgan, 1965, pp. 101, 108). John Cotton, in Perry Miller's opinion, thought that bad men were criminals "whether their offense was theft or a belief in the 'inner light,'" and therefore fit to be punished (Miller & Johnson, 1963, p. 186).

So strange did the Bay Colony's exercise of the principle of religious uniformity seem to Lord Say and Seal that from England he questioned whether he and others of superior social standing should come to America, where as members of the church they would lose their status. Cotton in a letter to the Lord explained that neither church nor state usurped the authority of the other. These two institutions of God, he pointed out, "may be close and compact, and coordinate one to another, and yet not confounded." He hastened to remove his correspondents' fear that the church dominated everything by stating "that magistrates are neither chosen to office in the church" nor govern by directions from the church, "but by civil laws." With these, the courts and the execution of laws, "the church (as the church) hath nothing to doe." Its task is only to prepare people to rule and to choose rulers. Nor in all this was there the slightest hint of a democratic spirit. "Democracy," he wrote, "I do not conceyve that ever God did ordeyne as a fitt government eyther for church or commonwealth (Miller & Johnson, 1963, p. 209 ff: cf. Foster, 1971, p. 19). Lord Say and Seal had nothing to fear. Nevertheless he did not come to New England.

As we have seen in his contribution to "The Liberties," Cotton had spelled out the liberties which the Lord Jesus had given to the churches, again striving to show their status as both co-ordinate and independent of the state. Interestingly enough, the church liberties he recited were part of a document which had been initiated by the authority of civil magistrates as well as by church leaders. But behind these liberties loomed the authority of the General Court, which had the right to prevent and remove error and offense from creeping into the churches. Meetings of the churches to weed out dangerous opinions were to be allowed and ratified "by the Authoritie of this Generall Court as a lawful libertie of the Churches of Christ (cf. Morgan, 1965, pp. 200, 201). This view was consistent with Cotton's suspicion of sin's influence to run power to extremes, "It is necessary," he claimed, "that all power that is on earth be limited, Church-power or other . . ." And he added, "It is counted a matter of danger to the State to limit Prerogatives, but it is a further danger, not to have them limited (cf. Morgan, 1965, p. 175). Winthrop could also draw the line on the church's jurisdiction. When the Boston church called him to account for his part in the General Court's treatment of Anne Hutchinson and her followers, he blandly explained that magistrates, although they were church members and hence subject to church discipline, were accountable to the church only "when they are out of their calling." He clarified this sharp distinction by illustration. "If a magistrate shall, in a private way, take away a man's goods. . . the church may call him to account for it, but if he doth this in pursuing a course of justice (though the thing be unjust), "yet he is not accountable" (cf. Morgan, 1965, pp. 109–116). This argument would seem to place public officials outside the range of church discipline so long as they pursued their calling, but in that direction lay the possibility of unraveling the whole texture which the principle of uniformity was supposed to guarantee. One might commit a crime as an official, but not be counted a sinner by the church.

This tangle over church and state jurisdictions, with its implicit distinction between civil wrongdoing and sin, was scarcely reduced to order by the Cambridge Platform, which gave the orthodox answer to the problem. That document attested that church government "stands in no opposition to civil government" and in no way infringes upon the authority of the magistrates. Rather church government strengthens the hands of civil officers and "furthereth the people in yielding more hearty & conscionable obedience to them." On the other hand, the magistrates should not restrain or obstruct the church in its work, as it is unlawful for church officers to meddle with the sword of the Magistrate, so it is unlawful for the Magistrate to meddle with the work proper to church officers." What could be fairer than a division of labor in which religion and politics were to be kept in separate compartments, with sin in the province of the church, and crime in the civil bailiwick? But matters were not so evenly and neatly balanced. The Platform conceded that the state could correct the church if it went astray, but it did not claim an equal authority for the church, nor did it have the power to correct the state. Finally it allowed that if any church grew schismatical and walked "incorrigibly or obstinately in any corrupt way. . . in such case the Magistrate is to put forth his coercive power as the matter shall require. . . ." (*The Cambridge Platform of 1648*, 1949, pp. 31, 32). On numerous occasions the clergy's advice was sought by the civil authorities, and it carried much weight. And we have the examples of pastors Cotton and Ward drawing up "The Liberties" for the whole colony. But Cotton was correct when he informed Lord Say and Seal that the church did not direct and dominate all.

In a society arranged in the pattern of religious uniformity it becomes almost impossible to find a crime that is not a sin, or a sin that cannot be counted a crime as designated by law. One major source of this confusion lay in the Puritan's usage of the word "sin." On the one hand, as earlier suggested, sin was conceived in radical terms as an inherent distortion or warp in the soul, only expungeable by the gift of the Holy Spirit. As such, no simple conformity to moral or civil law could touch it or correct it. Pride and a sense of human self-sufficiency before the great and glorious God could seep into every thought, motivation, purpose and act separating men from God. In this radical sense it was "original" in humankind, and therefore systemic. Humans did not happen to sin; they were sinners. On the other hand, Puritans spoke of sins as discrete, specific acts of defiance of God's established order. Erroneous belief, immoral conduct, obstinacy shown in disobedience to church and civil rulers—these were public manifestations of the radical sin for which people could be held accountable by civil, legal and judicial means, because they threatened the peace and security of the social and political order. Thomas Hooker can be heard again, this time showing how radical sin breaks out in specific sins. "This [sin] makes crooked servants in a family, no man can rule them, crooked inhabitants in towns, crooked members in congregations, there's no ordering nor joynting of them in that comely accord and mutual subjection" (cited in Foster, 1971, p. 19). Where public order is essential and sins bring disorder, sins easily become crimes.

When sins were cast in the form of crime, the question arose as to appropriate punishment which should be meted out. The church might discipline its members for sins that disturbed church order by admonishment, denying the ordinances, or casting them out entirely. But the sins which were treated as crime lay in the jurisdiction of the state. A drawn out debate at one time had been carried on over the question as to whether every crime listed in the codes should bear a specific penalty. One Mr. Hathorn set off the debate by insisting that laws against lying, swearing, etc., should include stated punishments. Winthrop argued against this proposal on the grounds that it would strip the judges of their authority to measure out justice according to circumstances and the severity of the crime. "Justice," he affirmed, "requireth that every cause should be heard before it be judged, which cannot be when the sentence and punishment is determined before hand." He went on to say that "God hath not confined all wisdom etc. to any one generation, that they should set rules for all others to walk by" (Morgan, 1965, p. 122 ff). But some laws, fashioned after biblical precedent, were to carry specific penalties. These were found in the Code of 1648 as capital crimes, and included idolatry, witchcraft, blasphemy, bestiality, sodomy, rape, stealing, treason, false witness to endanger another's life, cursing, smiting a parent, stubborn rebelliousness of a son, and homicide with malice aforethought. In fact, however, there was a great difference between enacting these capital laws and their execution. It appears that Winthrop's more lenient position in practice often won over the draconian intent of the laws, as they were seldom enforced. As Haskins points out, "Despite the Puritans' dependence upon the word of God, and the close connection that they saw between sin and

crime, they were demonstrably reluctant to prescribe death for every offense that the Bible ordered so punished (Haskins, 1960, p. 145 ff). Moral
persuasion as often ruled the magistrates and court officers as did retribution.

This weakening of the severity of Biblical as well as other laws is borne
out by Foster's observations on the execution of laws during the seventeenth
century. Laws dealing with contempt of authority, he noted, were enforced most of the time, while others having to do with dress or prices or
wages were only sporadically or rarely enforced by the latter part of the
century. The long list of criminal charges found in the Essex County
records of 1680–1683 showed how closely the personal lives of persons were
supervised, but, Foster concludes, not all these charges resulted in convictions (cf. Foster, 1971, p. 23, n. 25). Excessive legalism seems to have
broken down of its own weight.

By the end of the 17th century, a community ideally founded on a
covenantal basis, bound together by the "ligaments" of love, mutual sympathy and a common purpose, had become a law-ridden society, defensive
against external and internal dangers. Between church and state discipline
the initial dynamic had drained away, to be largely replaced by legal prescriptions. The perfection once glimpsed had eluded the Puritans as the
sense of an organic community faded in a welter of laws wherein crime
and sin were inextricably confounded. In the churches the conflict over
the Half-Way Covenant was taking place, and the ranks of churchmen
were being filled by those too honest perhaps to attest that they had been
savingly wrought upon by the Holy Spirit. The early generation had passed
away, to be forever enshrined in New England mythology as "our forefathers."

III. FROM HOLINESS TO SECULARITY

Thomas Prince looked back on the religious and moral temper of Massachusetts and saw only creeping disaster. The lament he sent up was to echo
many a pulpit. "A little after 1668," he wailed, "there began to appear a
Decay: and this increased to 1670...and yet much more to 1680, when
but few of the first generation remained" (cited in Dexter, 1880, p. 476).
Cotton Mather in 1706 hoped to stem the decline by summoning people
back to the example of the forefathers' "Good Old Way." Undoubtedly the
civil and religious orders were in disarray when viewed from the perspective of earlier standards. However, some exception should be taken to the
excessively gloomy pronouncements that filled the air as the eighteenth
century opened. People still attended church, often to be treated to a fare
of condemnation for their apathy and shortcomings. They were as morally

upright as circumstances and human nature permitted. Some of them would admit that they were sinners, but still lived within the law. There was no deluge of criminality among the populace at large, although court cases were still being decided on the basis of some laws passed in the preceding century. What was lacking was a zeal and enthusiasm for a holiness of life which apparently the exertions of pastors could not bring about. Clearly some drastic and vigorous remedy was needed to stir people from their lethargy, and it was to come with the outbreak of revivals in the 1730s and 1740s.

One of the principal promoters and defenders of these revivals was Jonathan Edwards, pastor of the Northampton church. He too could refer to "the state of things in New England. . . and the way we had been so long going on in," but reckoned that revivals had brought a strange revolution which had changed the direction of the spiritual and moral life of New England (Goen, 1972, p. 344). In many ways Edwards was attuned to the theological and social ideas of the earlier generation of Puritans. He believed in the awesome, sovereign God of the Bible, although he could also revel in the sweet beauty that came upon the soul in loving consent to that Great Being. He believed in the doctrine of original sin, and wrote a major treatise to prove its truth. He believed in the power of the Holy Spirit, so evident to him in the revivals that rescued humans from the clutches of self-love and pride and gave a new spiritual sense unlike any natural inclination. He was sure that mere morality could not save, although at times he confused sin with immorality (cf. Holbrook, 1983). He vigorously protected the inviolability of the Christian community against the inroads of Arminians, Quakers, Familists and Wesleyans (Smith, 1959, pp. 250, 257, 341). He believed in the Bible as the rule, law and guide for Christian faith, although he was not a dogged literalist. Carried away with hope at the height of the revivals, he foresaw a new spiritual order that was to appear in America, supplanting that of the Old World. And he chided the civil rulers for not more zealously promoting "this great work of God." He asked "whether we hadn't reason to fear that God is provoked with this land that no more notice has been taken of this glorious work of the Lord. . . by the civil authority." At least, he suggested, they might set aside a day of public thanksgiving, fasting and prayer (Smith, 1959, p. 370 ff). Yet, he thought that ministers should not take it upon themselves "to dictate, direct and determine" how public matters should go, while at the same time in the name of a "free nation" and "the liberty of the press" he claimed for himself and other pastors the right to speak on the management of public affairs, the duty of the legislature, and to "those that are at the head of the administration, though vastly his superiors" (Smith, 1959, p. 291).

In these words he affirmed the authority of both clergy and civil officers, but he also revealed the potential tension between the two, which was to grow in the remainder of the century. The revivals were eventually to disrupt the relation between pastors and their flocks, church and state, and divide churches into factions. In principle as well as fact, the revivals were to weaken the symbiotic relation between church and state, with major consequences for the understanding of the difference between sin and crime. The principle of religious uniformity was finally to be breached by the coming of religious toleration, although the Congregational Church remained as the established church of Massachusetts until well into the nineteenth century.

Edwards praised highly what he regarded as the positive effects of the outpourings of God's spirit, but in all his written defenses of the revivals he was kept busy explaining and excusing the emotional excesses they engendered. His last major defense of revivals, the "Treatise on the Religious Affections," was a careful discrimination between false religion, on the one hand, and true heart faith on the other. But its publication unfortunately came too late to help restore order to a society riven by conflicts. Church order, as well as political structure, had been too badly fractured. In this work he affirmed good works to be the best available signs of true piety, but these works were couched in the generalities common to Puritan preachers. At the same time he asserted "what is commonly called an honest man, and a moral man. . . is no great evidence of the sincerity of his profession." What he sought was a sincere religion of the converted heart, and to that no one had access except God himself. How then could one pass judgment upon those who went off in an emotional frenzy or claimed for themselves the right to judge the validity of their ecstasies?

It is this freedom in religious matters which broke through the restraints of law, civil and ecclesiastical, and severed the bonds of authority that held together pastors and their people. When ministers like Edwards preached the untrammeled sovereignty of the free God, not unexpectedly it was matched by the freedom of the laity, until respect for pastors and civil rulers was jeopardized. One episode in Edwards's career may illustrate this breakdown of pastoral and civil authority, the so-called "bad book" case. Several young men had secured a copy of a midwife's manual. Its description of the female anatomy had led these youths to taunt young women. Edwards tried to discipline them with the help of a colonel, a deacon, a captain, and a lieutenant, all gentlemen of standing in the community. When the young men were brought before these figures of authority, instead of submissiveness, they expressed disrespect of their superiors. One swore he would not "worship a king" and vulgarly announced that he cared not a turd or a fart for their opinions. After all, these officials were "nothing but men, molded up of a little dirt" (see Tracy, 1980, pp. 160–163). Trivial as this episode may appear, it was symptomatic of the larger problem which the loosening of church and civil authority presented. Responsibility for it may not be laid directly at the door of revivalism, but it signified a legacy of freedom that revivalism had begotten. It also proved that piety alone could no longer sustain the community. The hierarchical order was tottering. In 1736, for example, the town had reestablished the office of tithingman to shore up conformity and seek out signs of sinful behavior, and in 1748 Edwards himself had called for a body of wise men to assist him "as agents of the people" to enforce discipline (see Tracy, 1980, pp. 124–125, 166).

In the aftermath of the revivals Edwards was finally expelled from his pulpit, in part because of the whirlwind of freedom he had sown, but could not control. And equally significant was the separation that grew between civil officers and church leaders. "Governors and divines," writes Tracy, "still respected each other in New England, but their spheres of power and strategies of dominance had been growing apart for at least a half a century (see Tracy, 1980, p. 152). As civil and church rulers grew apart, so also did the distinction between sin and crime. Increasingly, acts considered to be sins were left to the churches, and acts deemed to imperil the social and political order were considered as crimes, to be handled by civil authorities.

By intent Edwards was no social or political reformer in a modern sense. His eye was upon sin and the great God. Sins for him were at root disaffections of the soul, which had turned in upon themselves. Acts of sin, that is, sins were distinguishable from "heart sin" which went to the depth of the self. The former were to be met with the preaching of biblical law, threats of hell, promises of heaven and the community ethos upheld by civil authority. The latter succumbed only to God's forgiving grace. To change the former, the sharpest excoriation was needed; the latter might be reached by the preaching of forgiveness and hope. But in neither case could law as such accomplish the desired end.

Edwards' high reputation as a theologian and metaphysician rests primarily upon the major treatises he composed at Stockbridge after his ejection from Northampton. In these he stood back from the turmoil of the revival periods to contemplate the larger issues which agitated his mind. He was at a distance, by and large, from the practical problems which sin entailed. But during the revivals he had been at grips with concrete misdeeds he saw as sins. The list of these gives a clear notion of what he saw in Northampton. In 1735 one of his sermons included a catalog of sins which called for correction: failure to keep God's holy day, feasting one's lust, uncleanness, keeping company with the wicked, indecent carriage, wicked carriage toward parents, ill-will, revenge and malice, envy and hatred of one's neighbor, pride in knowledge and abilities, intemperance, drinking, time spent in taverns, lasciviousness, unclean imaginations, "things not fit to be named," a flighty frame of spirits, stupidity, sottishness and obstinacy (cf. Tracy, 1980, pp. 82–83). In the "Religious Affections" he added to this list nightwalking, unseemly mirth, company keeping, lax family government, quarreling, backbiting, extravagances and dancing schools (Smith, 1959, pp. 146ff, 326). He considered courtship by "bundling" an abomination when "young people of different sexes" lay in bed together. This was "one main thing that has led to that growth of uncleanness that has been in the land (Tracy, 1980, p. 130). This litany of sins, it will be noted, included what he considered to be immoral acts and motivations, the breaking of ecclesiastical regulations, specific religious shortcomings, unseemly social customs, and even the innocent accompaniments of a healthy life, such as mirth and dancing schools. But nowhere does he mention capital crimes. Undoubtedly he would have welcomed the support of civil authorities in suppressing the evils he mentioned, but the remarkable thing is that nowhere did he denominate them as crimes. Lost was that earlier tendency in Puritan New England to seek conformity by appeal to enacted law and the pronouncements of the court. Sins were to be eradicated by religious means, and the reformed life was to be lived by the gift of the Holy Spirit. Edwards seems almost to have glided above the techniques of social and political administration by which a society is governed. As he once remarked, the purpose of God's outpouring of his spirit was to make men holy, not politicians. True, in a few sermons he preached about government, economic ethics and personal charity, but he was not one to spend much time on these areas (cf. Holbrook, 1973, ch. V). His goal was holiness, which he saw as bringing with it reform throughout society as a whole. The treatment of crime was an affair for the magistrates and courts, and with these he did not dabble. His business was the rectification of sinful lives so far as human powers, with God's help, could achieve it. He lamented civil disorder, as his list of sins showed, but it was not his task to promote their expiration by law.

Insofar as Edwards in his major treatises distinguished between immorality and sin, he opened the way for an increase in making immorality a secular rather than a religious concern. Before the eighteenth century ended, his high aim of holiness was being reduced to a moderated, decent moralism, still vaguely imbued with religious overtones, but clearly moving in the direction of secularity (cf. Haroutunian, 1932). It was finally to be left to the state to set the bounds where immorality left off and crime began, and sin fell outside this perimeter, which still lacks clear definition.

IV. CONCLUSION

Today a secularized society scoffs at the Puritans of New England, and few there be who aspire to the holiness upon which Edwards set his eye. We congratulate ourselves on our enlightened breadth of mind, which no longer makes capital crimes of idoltry, witchcraft, blasphemy or the cursing of one's parents. But the heritage of Puritanism is not lightly cast aside. The statutes of the Code of 1648 in other forms survive in our laws against sodomy, rape, stealing, treason, homicide and perjury. Nor have we ever surrendered attempts to enforce an externalized righteousness by legal and judicial means. The state, for example, still interferes with the free practice of religion when, as in cases of child neglect arising from religious belief, it steps in to protect the welfare of minors. The courts may not recognize sins as a legal category, but they punish acts that some people count to be sins. In the 17th century the Puritan Samuel Sewall identified human slavery as a sin, but after the agitation of anti-slavery forces in the nineteenth century, and a great civil war, human slavery became a crime by the passage of the 13th, 14th, and 15th Amendments to the Constitution, followed in the 20th century by laws against racial discrimination. Today the Supreme Court wrestles with the problem of abortion, which in the eyes of some religious leaders is a sin and nothing but murder. As such, they seek to have abortion made a crime. If certain proposed amendments to the Constitution are passed, we would have another example of sin conceived as an immorality and finally passing by civil legislation into the area of crime. Attempts to put prayers into the public schools show that religious forces continue to try to enforce the outward forms of righteousness by resort to law, and at the other extreme a no less Puritanical zeal governs the American Civil Liberties Union, when in the name of the First Amendment, it opposes creches on public property, Christmas songs, or prayers in public schools. In this case a kind of civic virtue is to be enforced by strict adherence to laws reminiscent of the Puritan's dependence upon law to enforce conformity. The Puritans and Edwards knew that law could not save a person because it could not reach beyond external acts to the heart of human corruption. And in this sense sin at root could never lie within the jurisdiction of man made laws. But like them we strive to legislate in respect to overt manifestations of immorality and sin, though the latter term no longer has a place in legal vocabulary. The Puritans did not flinch from calling public misdeeds sins or crimes, but now what was once counted a sin or a crime in sociological jargon is called "deviational behavior," to be met with "enforcible deprivations." What was once flatly named as crime is now often treated as psychological and social maladjustment or a sickness to be cured. What were once counted to be unethical or sinful persons are now often judged to be suffering from misunderstanding. The murderer is given a lighter sentence or remanded for rehabilitation since he or she was mentally disturbed at the time of the commitment of the act. Whereas Puritans traced crime to the all-embracing category of sin, we now seem to turn to psychology rather than to ethics or sin for explanation and cure. But the Puritan conviction that outward acts were manifestations of a deeper level of the human psyche still shows up in modern courts when intent and motivation play a major role in the decisions made. And sometimes, like the admonishments of the Puritans of the past, religious counseling may play a part in penetrating these sources of criminal behavior. So as the Puritan knew, law could have only a limited effectiveness in curing the waywardness of human beings.

The lines between immorality, sin, and crime remain blurred, as they often were for the Puritans. The legal and the moral oughts are still entangled, and the religious ought in the face of sin may have no standing in a modern court, yet all three in their various ways affect the administration of justice. And so even in a vastly changed cultural and social milieu the Puritanical struggle with these three elements continues to enlist the efforts of our legislatures and courts. We cannot nor do we desire to return to Puritanism, but its mark has been irrevocably set upon our culture, even though it be in a secularized form. Church and state may be separate institutionally and theoretically, but religion still strives to influence public policy while the state strives to control moral behavior by legal means. And that is not too far removed from the Puritans' aim.

REFERENCES

Breen, T.H. (1980). *Puritans and adventurers*. New York, & Oxford: Oxford University Press.

The Cambridge Platform of 1648. (abridged from the 1st ed.). New York: The General Council for the Congregational Christian Churches.

Dexter, H.M. (1880). *Congregationalism of the last three hundred years as seen in its literature*. New York: Harper and Brothers.

Foote, H.W. (Ed.). (1949). *The Cambridge Platform of 1648*. Boston: Beacon Press, Pilgrim Press.

Foster, S. (1971). *Their solitary way*. New Haven & London: Yale University Press.

Goen, C.C. (Ed.) (1972). *The Great Awakening*. New Haven & London: Yale University Press.

Haroutunian, J. (1932). *Piety versus moralism*. New York: Henry Holt.

Haskins, G.L. (1960). *Law and authority in early Massachusetts*. New York: Macmillan.

Hill, C. (1972). *The world turned upside down*. New York: Viking.

Holbrook, C.A. (1973). *The ethics of Jonathan Edwards*. Ann Arbor: University of Michigan Press.

Holbrook, C.A. (1983). Jonathan Edwards addresses some modern critics of original sin. *Journal of Religion*, 63 (2), pp. 211–230.

Hutchinson, T. (Ed.). (1769). *Collection of original papers relating to the history of the colony of Massachusetts Bay*. London: Thomas and John Fleet.

Kevan, E.F. (1964). *The grace of law*. London: Carey Kingsgate Press.

Levering, D. (1980). *The language of Puritan feeling*. New Brunswick, NJ: Rutgers University Press.

Miller, P., & Johnson, T.H. (1963). *The Puritans* (Vol. 1 rev. ed.). New York, Evanston, & London: Harper and Row.

Morgan, E.S. (1966). *The Puritan Family* (rev. ed.). New York: Harper Torch Books.

Morgan, E.S. (Ed.). (1965). *Puritan Political Ideas.* Indianapolis, New York, & Kansas City: Bobbs-Merrill.

Niebuhr, H.R. (1937). *The Kingdom of God in America.* Chicago & New York: Willett Clark.

Olafson, F.A. (Ed.). (1961). *Society, law and morality.* Englewood Cliffs, NJ: Prentice-Hall.

Smith, J.E. (Ed.). (1959). *Jonathan Edwards, Religious Affections.* New Haven, CT: Yale University Press.

Tracy, P.J. (1980). *Religion and society in eighteenth century Northampton.* New York: Hill and Wang.

Webster's third international dictionary, Unabridged. (1976). Springfield, MA: Merriam-Webster.

Webster's new world dictionary of the american language (college ed.). (1980). Springfield, MA: Merriam-Webster.

Chapter 2

Punishment in the Scripture and Tradition of Judaism, Christianity, and Islam

Rev. Virginia Mackey

**National Inter-religious Task Force on Criminal Justice
Rochester, New York**

INTRODUCTION

The practice of punishment is often associated with religious roots. Consider how frequently the scriptural phrase, "an eye for an eye," is cited as justification for punishment in present responses to crime. Since the United States is recognized as among the most punitive of nations—having the highest incarceration rate of all the Western free world[1]—(Dale, 1980) it is important to try to determine whether our major religious traditions do or do not provide justification for the "American Way of Punishment."

To assess the influence of religion on the development and present enforcement of criminal law, the National Religious Leaders Council of the National Council on Crime and Delinquency commissioned this research paper on the Scripture and tradition of Judaism, Christianity, and Islam.

The religious approach to fundamental questions lies in the shaping of theologies—the Word (*logos*) about God (*theos*). Religions and theologies have emerged as certain human beings have claimed that portions of God's will have been revealed to them, or that God has acted in history in

---

[1] "Great Britain has 84 persons locked up per 100,000 population. West Germany has 60. Canada listed 95 per 100,000 in 1974. Sweden has 40; Denmark 54; the Netherlands 22. Are you ready for the U.S. rate? 212! Only Russia and South Africa have higher rates, because of their use of prisons for large number of political prisoners. . . . U.S. sentences are unusually *long*, also, as compared to other countries. For instance, in 1974, 75% of the people in the U.S. prisons were there for terms ranging from 5 years to life. In contrast, only .05% of Danish prisoners had terms of over 8 years." Frank Dale, Address to National Religious Leaders Consultation on Criminal Justice, New York City, April, 27, 1980.

specific situations in order to reveal the divine will. Hence, a theology entails the human perception of God's Word.

On the question of punishment, the basic methodology of this paper is to search the theologies of Judaism, Christianity, and Islam for the answer to a fundamental question: "Does God intend that human beings punish one another?" In other words, what do human beings think God "says" about punishment?

Punishment, as used in this paper, means to "subject someone to a penalty for a crime, fault, or misbehavior" (American Heritage Dictionary. 1971). It is important to remember that "punishment is never automatic. Rather, it is the judgment, presumably as an expression of the good or just decision, of personal agencies (acting persons)" (Flew, quoted in Beach, 1979, p. 7). Presumably, also, the punisher always has the force of superior power of authority, since it is unlikely that most persons would submit voluntarily to any but the mildest of reprimands.

The association with the concept of a penalty means that *a punishment is a deliberate act*. Within the criminal justice system, the current understanding of punishment is that it is a sanction, an act which deliberately inflicts pain—either psychic or physical. The superior power to apply the sanction is, of course, a given in jurisdictions with legally constituted criminal justice systems.

Without question, Judaism, Christianity, and Islam each depict God as having "the force of superior power or authority" and as sometimes taking "deliberate action" in human affairs. It is highly doubtful, however, that the God worshipped by each of the three faiths ever inflicts deliberate pain or desires that human beings inflict such pain on one another.

It is a conclusion of this paper that the scriptural portrayal of the actions of God are more closely associated with the *consequences* of countering God's moral law than they are with *punishment* for persons having disobeyed that law. It is a further conclusion that the scriptural accounts portray the intent of God's actions as saving and reconciling—in distinct contrast to an intent to punish.

It is difficult to make a convincing argument for these positions when so much of the scriptural language is cast in terms of judgment and punishment. The argument can be made but it requires taking into account the anthropological and historical contexts in which the Scriptures and traditions of each of the three faiths emerged, the literary forms used, and the theological substance of the Scriptures.

A search into the question of punishment reveals that two quite distinct and contradictory theologies have arisen from the Scriptures and traditions of each of the three faiths. One is a *theology of retribution*, which maintains that God punishes and expects humans to punish in order to dignify human nature or modify human behavior; the other is a *theology of restoration*, which maintains that God wills "to save and to reconcile" human beings who rebel or fail and that God expects human beings to exhibit saving and reconciling action toward each other.

When such contradictions exist, one is led to ask, "Where do truth and orthodoxy lie within each faith and within a broad religious perspective? How is a secular society such as ours to resolve the current debate about the relative merits of a punitive 'just deserts' (retribution) versus reconciliation (restoration)? Does religion have a contribution to make to the resolution of the debate, or only an obligation to clarify the reasons for its own conflicting theologies?"

Since the religious debate is as old as recorded history, it cannot be resolved with finality. This paper treats the subject in broad strokes and only points to some of the painstaking work which must be done if a theology of retribution is to be invalidated and a theology of restoration is to be given credibility. The paper explores some of the fundamental issues, makes a case for a theology of restoration common to the three faiths, and encourages further research and dialog on the part of religious communities as a means of diminishing the punitive nature of American society.

Just over one hundred years ago our nation was confronted with the same type of contradictions over the issue of slavery. Each person of faith had to decide "what God 'said' about slavery." This was the situation which Frederick Douglass, the noted abolitionist, faced. In a fascinating book, *The Paradox of Cruelty*, Philip Hallie says that Douglass' "following of the North Star and the ride on the freedom train" began when he decided:

> that God was good, and that God knew what was best for everybody...
> (Douglass, "The life and times of Frederick Douglass," quoted in Hallie, 1969, p. 149).

Hallie contends that because Douglass was a person with an irresistible desire to see facts fit together consistently, he started finding discrepancies between the slaveholders' images of slaves as inferior beings and his own understanding of all human beings as having been created in the image of God. The crucial "fact" for Douglass was the nature of God (Hallie, 1969, pp. 144–149).

This is the crucial question for us in a study of punishment. It makes all of the difference how we think about God and how we believe that God intends us to think about and act toward other human beings. Finally, this paper implies that our own answers to the questions about punishment will have to be consistent with our views of a God who loves unceasingly and unconditionally and who desires that human beings live together in harmonious community.

I. THE INTERACTION OF LAW AND RELIGION

The first "fact" common to the three faiths is that the monothestic Being whom they worship is the same God, a God of love. They ascribe to God the same attributes:

> tenderness, compassion, slowness to anger, rich in graciousness, ready to relent (*Joel 2:13; Jonah 4:2*)

> merciful is the Lord and just. Yea, our God is compassionate (*Psalm 116:5*)

> a gentle parent and the God of all consolation, who comforts us in all our sorrows, so that we can offer others, in their sorrows, the consolation that we have received from God ourselves (*2 Cor. 1:3–4*)

> without beginning, without end, omnipotent, omniscient, and omnipresent, God is *one* (*Qur'an 112*)

The Judaic conception of montheism is, of course, the earliest. The Hebrew idea of God emerged from the experience of their own and other tribal cultures of the Ancient Near East. It was the Hebrews who first conceptualized *the living God*, the God who is active in history as deliverer of Israel from bondage in Egypt, as judge and restorer during the periods of Exile and Restoration, and as saving and reconciling presence. Islam and Christianity share this biblical heritage.

Each of the religions emerged, however, in a different historical context. There are differences in emphases, striking differences in liturgical practices, and divergence in the conceptual frameworks of law and justice.

A. The Scripture and Tradition of Judaism

> Judaism is a theocracy whose code of laws is the Torah. (*Universal Jewish Encyclopedia*)

Jewish law is the sum total of the law laid down in the Scripture with the interpretations, the reforms and innovations added by Talmudic law, the post-Talmudic codes, the customary laws of the various communities in which Jews have lived, and last—but not least—the rational and ethical principles deduced from them (Cohn, 1971, p. xxx).

The Law of the Torah is not literal, because it is as momentous as the Mind of God, thus not totally comprehensible in human terms. On the other hand, it is not abstract, because it contains an ethic and has, for the nation of Israel, an element of jurisprudence and normativity.

For the Jew, law is not dictated by God but is revealed in a dynamic and ongoing process throughout history. According to Judaism, God first revealed the law to Moses—both the Written Law (Torah Shebektav) and the Oral Law (Torah Shebaal-peh). All actions pertaining to humanity's spiritual and physical welfare are said to be regulated by the Torah. Moses had biblical and traditional authority (*halakah*). It was through Moses that the Law was transmitted to Joshua and through the elders, kings and prophets (Universal Jewish Encyclopedia, 1942, p. 55).

Actually, the material in the Pentateuch (the first five books of the Written Torah, containing the bulk of the "legal material") is a collection of writings extending through several centuries. The dates of most of the sources were placed after David's time (c. 1010–970 B.C.); only fragments of the poetry are thought to be from the time of Moses in the 13th century B.C. (Rowley, 1962, pp. 74–87).

There are two different legal strains within the Pentateuch which should be noted. The first emanated from the legal-moral systems of the Near East. This material includes the Ten Commandments in Exodus 20 and the extensive regulations pertaining to daily life in chapters 20 through 24 of Exodus, as well as the codes in Leviticus, Deuteronomy and Numbers. All of the legal material in Jewish Scripture and tradition is *halakah*, pertaining to "conduct," the "way to go," hence "canon law."

In biblical times, religious leaders were responsible for the resolution of civil, criminal, and family disputes, as well as for matters of faith. In criminal cases, a defendant was brought before the king or judges, elders of the city, or the head of a household appointed by the king. There were no public prosecutors and no lawyers. The "judge" examined, the defendant testified and a witness to the act was required (in capital cases, two witnesses). Attempted crime or plotting was not punishable. Certain crimes, such as incest, blasphemy, necromancy, work on the Day of Atonement, were sometimes left to God to judge.

The Pentateuch included, as did the Hammurabic Code of Babylonia (c. 1750 B.C.), provisions for settling disputes on the basis of the *lex talionis* —the oft-quoted law of retaliation:

> Your eye shall not pity; it shall be life for life, eye for eye, tooth for tooth, hand for hand, foot for foot. (*Deut. 19:21; also Ex. 21:23–24, Lev. 24:20—RSV*)

Because this maxim is so frequently cited today, there are several things which need to be said about this concept. First, this form of "exact justice" was instituted as a *limit* on previous tribal practices of "blood revenge" against the tribe of the person who had committed an act which should be "revenged," or it was meant to limit the number of sheep a herdsman could seek as restitution if one of his animals had been killed.

Secondly, the *lex talionis* as used by the Hebrews could pertain to exact or proportional monetary restitution. The English word "restitution" is closer to the meaning of *talionis* than is the word "retaliation."

Thirdly, it is important to remember that the acts which most concerned the authors of Scripture were sins—conduct deemed evil in the eyes of the deity. "Temple sacrifices were the *usual* penalties for sins, but since the same act often constituted both a 'sin' and a 'crime,' such offerings must be considered part of the penal law (Horowitz, 1963, pp. 157, 159). If the act were thought to have been done inadvertently, the penalty imposed was lenient; if it were thought to have been done willfully, the prescribed punishment could—but seldom did—entail lashes or death.

According to Haim Cohn, when the *lex talionis* was part of the theocratic code, the primary application of it was whatever form of expiation (redress or atonement) would best "turn away God's 'blazing anger' (Deut. 13:17, Num. 25:4)" (Cohn, 1971, p. 63). Theologically, the message of the Torah was meant to convey what it was that God considered worth being angry about.

Any reference to criminal practices in the Torah must be set in the total context of the faith. Disputes did arise and had to be resolved. Vestiges of superstition and tribal tradition were blended with religious ritual and with "fair" judgment in the Hebrews' responses to the type of offenses now called crimes.

No matter what the transgression, there was an obligation to appoint responsible judges:

> You shall appoint magistrates and officials for your tribes, in all the settlements that the Lord your God is giving you, and they shall govern the people with due justice. You shall not judge unfairly: you shall show no partiality; you shall not take bribes, for bribes blind the eyes of the discerning and upset the plea of the just. Justice, justice shall you pursue, that you may thrive and occupy the land that the Lord your God is giving you. (*Deut. 16:18-20*. The Torah. *Jewish Publication Society of America*)

By the Talmudic period (c. 35 B.C.–500 A.D.), the rabbinic literature reflected attempts to temper the retributive tone of the language of judgment and punishment found in the Pentateuch. The *Mishnah*, a compilation of oral laws made at the close of the 2nd century A.D., and the commentary in the *Talmud* contain sections on *nesikin* (civil and criminal law). "In mercy is the world judged," insisted several of the rabbis engaged in tempering the retributive tone:

> The Lord's judgment of men is indeed a merciful one, it is not what strict justice requires (*Maimonides*)

> Even the wicked are judged by Him mercifully. (*Rabbi Jonah*)

> The Lord created the evil impulse, but He created Torah and repentance as its remedy. And the world is judged in mercy in that the sinner's repentance is found acceptable; and this is a merciful act of the Lord toward His creatures. (*Meiri*) (Goldin, 1957, p. 142)

After the fall of Jerusalem in 70 A.D., the rabbis in exile devoted themselves to study and interpretation. They attacked, head on, some of the thorny problems contained in the pentateuchal codes. One translator of the Babylonian Talmud, Michael Rodkinson, says that the *Tract Sanhedrin*

> distinguishes itself from all others in Halaka (legal material) as well as in Haggada (story telling). Aside from the many strange explanations of the verses of Scripture, which are not used in other extracts, it says plainly that there are numerous laws written in the Pentateuch which have never occurred, and never will occur, but they were written merely for study. (Rodkinson, 1918, p. v)

Through ingenious argumentation, the rabbis explained away some of the passages which seemed to contradict the image of a loving and saving God. Here are some examples:

(1) They noted in the Pentateuch the tendency to overstatement as a means of communicating feelings about the enormity of misbehavior. They cited examples of excessive laws. In addition to the synoptic references to the *lex talionis*, the Talmudists pointed out that the Bible provides also for the death penalty for Sabbath violators, for adulterers and for stubborn and rebellious children (Deut. 21:18-21). These overstatements, according to the rabbis, could be considered more homiletic than legal. They said that *hayyav mitah* (liable to the death penalty) was an example of overstatement because the procedural restraints attached to capital cases indicated how little intent there was to carry out a sentence of death.

(2) Strict proceduralism, then, was a means recommended by the rabbis of avoiding what they considered to be the injustice of too severe penalties. They virtually abolished "exact justice" for all but murder, and in murder cases they required the testimony of two witnesses. Not only did criminal convictions require eye witnesses, they required proof that forewarning (*hatra'ah*) had been given.

The Talmudists held that "judges must do everything in their power to avoid passing death sentences (Makkot 1:10), e.g., by rigorously cross-examining the witnesses long enough to have them contradict themselves or each other in some particular and, thus, render their evidence unreliable" (Encyclopedia Judaica, 1971, p. 1387).

There were so many restrictions to carrying out the death penalty in ancient Israel that it was said, "a Sanhedrin that effects one execution in seven years is branded a bloody court. Eleazar ben Azariah [said]: 'one in seventy years.' (*Mishnah: Makkot* 1:10)." Here is a description of the way one questioned a witness in a capital punishment case:

> How shall one impress witnesses in a criminal case with the gravity of their position? One takes them aside and charges them, "Be certain that your testi-

mony is no guess work, no hearsay, not derived at second-hand, nor by reliance on the observation even of a trustworthy person. Remember, you must face a severe cross examination." Know that a criminal case is by no means like a civil. In the latter, he who has caused an injustice by his testimony can make monetary restitution, but in the former, the blood of the accused and his unborn offspring stain the perjurer forever. Thus, in the case of Cain, Scripture says, "The voice of the bloods of your brother call to Me." Observe that the text reads in the plural, not blood, but bloods. For Abel's blood and that of his unborn seed were alike involved. (*Mishnah Sanhedrin 4:5*)

Witnesses were further cautioned about the consequences of their testimony. The import of the example of Cain is that "the witness is answerable for the blood of him [that is wrongfully condemned and the blood of his posterity]...if any man has caused a single soul to perish from Israel, Scripture imputes it to him *as though (ke-illu)* he had caused the whole world to perish" (Encyclopedia Judaica, 1971, p. 1484).

(3) The phrase *ke-illu* was also employed as a legal fiction in cases in which a penalty was established but not carried out—it was "as if" or "as though" it had been applied—and in releasing someone from a moral teaching which was unenforceable even though it was construed as legally binding (Encyclopedia Judaica, 1971, p. 1484).

(4) Substitution of penalties. The Talmudic law reformers pointed out that it was possible to substitute penalties even for the pervasive threat of divine punishment in many of the passages of Scripture. In Makkot 3:15, they made it clear that whoever underwent a judicial punishment such as flogging would not be visited with any further divine punishment. In Shevuth 21a, they asserted that, even though it said in Exodus 20:7 that a criminal would not be 'guiltless" and escape divine wrath, judicial authorities could impose a flogging in order to clear the wrongdoer.

Further, social penalties (*herem*) could substitute for flogging. Among the types of social penalties were the "donkey's burial" (interment by the fence of a cemetery); expulsion from the synagogue, from a trade guild, or from the country; military service; public confession and self-vilification (Encyclopedia Judaica, 1971, pp. 1389–1390).

The comparison of attitudes between biblical and Talmudic prescriptions for reform are of interest because the scholars were not limited, as are modern judges and penologists, by the contingencies of daily life. Their task was to interpret the will of God.

Many of the reforms spelled out in the Talmuds were never tested in practice because criminal jurisdiction by Jewish courts ended, for the most part, with the destruction of the Temple in 70 A.D. Civil jurisdiction was maintained through c. 586 A.D. Since the closing of the canonical law books, Jews have tended to live in ghettoized areas of urban centers in which they were a minority without political power.

Wherever Jews have settled, there has been a wariness about the secular laws of the nations in which they live because it is that law which has been used to persecute them. They have looked upon the secular law as "an evil which had to be accepted and lived with" (Cohn, 1971, p. 4).

Insofar as possible, Jews have sought to fulfill the spirit of the law and to arbitrate in their own tribunals their own civil and family matters. The *Beth Din*—a forum for arbitration—flourished in Europe throughout the Middle Ages and could be found in every self-contained Jewish community until the time of the Holocaust. While in the strictest sense these courts had no criminal jurisdiction, they are illustrative of the mode of peacemaking which can forestall the filing of criminal charges.

A model of the *Beth Din* was established in New York City in 1920. First named the Jewish Court of Arbitration, the name was changed because the word *court* carried an implication of sternness and implacability that it wanted to avoid. James Jaffe describes its method:

[judges] are constantly stating the principle to the litigants. One judge says, "We are not going to attempt to say who is morally or legally justified; we are interested in settling things."... *Shalom bias*—peace in the house—is the phrase most frequently to be found in the records of the court (Jaffe, 1972, pp. 23–24).

It is sobering to note that in the modern state of Israel, established in 1948, where the adherents of Judaism do exercise political power, there is a highly punitive character to the latest chapters of Jewish law. Justice Haim Cohn of Israel's Supreme Court explains that "as a matter of practical legislative policy, Jewish law is not as yet acknowledged as a source of Israeli law except in matters of marriage and divorce" (Cohen, 1971, p. xxxiii). Jewish law, Cohn explains, is quoted in official communiques submitted to Parliament to explain the "objects and reasons" of a bill; the Ministry of Justice has a special Advisor on Jewish Law; and a similar practice exists in the courts, particularly in the Supreme Court. But the positive law prevailing in Israel today is primarily Western—it derives not only from British, but from Roman, Ottoman and French sources.

The imprisonment rate in Israel is rising significantly. Israel Drapkin notes a drastic change in a 26-year period. When the government of Israel was instituted in 1948, it "decided to close immediately all the mandatory prisons. This was done on the conviction that there was no need for places of imprisonment, due to the insignificant rate of Jewish criminality in the Diaspora." On February 10, 1949, there were 29 prisoners in the only penal institution. By 1975 the number of prisoners, in a total population of 3,519,200, had reached 2,276—an imprisonment rate of 65 per 100,000 (Drapkin, 1979, pp. 129–131).

Hovav and Amir, a pair of researchers, explain the rate of imprisonment as follows:

[P]olice have to contend with the effects of the War of Independence, the absorption of millions of immigrants, cultural pluralism, urbanization and cyclical economic patterns. These developments take their toll on Israeli society: conflicts among groups, changing patterns of crime and more organized criminality, growing rates of recidivism, development of a drug culture, a counterculture and politically antagonistic groups. (Hovav & Amir, 1979)

Drapkin comments that in the nature of crime, "social environment and the political structure" proved more influential than ethnic origin (Drapkin, 1979, p. 127). He deplores the fact that there are few initiatives to adopt a criminal justice policy in line with rabbinic reform or with the most humane practices of modern nations:

When one considers that Israel is a new country...one cannot but be surprised to observe the prevailing conservatism....It looks as though there exists an inner conviction in every citizen of this country that this is a problem that will never affect him or other members of his family. It is a kind of natural insurance against such risks. He belongs to the honest and law-abiding part of the community, while "the others," the criminals, are depicted with such somber traits, that only punishment is what they deserve. Such being the case, it is no wonder that this country—that could have led the world in different aspects of criminology and penology—is limping behind the more advanced systems in these matters. (Drapkin, 1979, p. 136).

Another critic of the current Israeli form of criminal justice is Clemens Thoma. Unfortunately, says Thoma,

the current scholarly investigation of the rabbinic penal and legal norms is mostly not very accessible. Halakhic studies are today conducted mainly within orthodox Judaism, and published in Hebrew, and have adopted an approach based on internal Jewish systematics rather than a critical or historical one. (Thoma, 1979, p. 65)

What has occurred in both modern Israel and in the United States is that the type of *halakah* (legal material) which appeared in the Torah was gradually translated into the positive law of modern penal codes. Such codes are written in the same presumptive language as that of the Torah— if a prohibited act is committed, a prescribed penalty will be applied. The language of judgment and punishment are pervasive. Taken at face value, the language of *halakah* seems to support a theology of retribution. The material cannot be taken at face value, however, for several reasons.

First, the Judaic understanding of law is much broader and deeper than is that of any secular, positive legal system. The term is primarily theological, used to convey all of the dimensions of the relationship between God and the covenant people.

Secondly, the *halakic* material was only quasi-legal. Even when applied in tribunals, the context was more religious than civil. The Hebrew patriarchs were concerned for an orderly and peaceful society and were called upon to arbitrate disputes. But their primary concern was for the molding of a religious people who would adhere to God's law:

> Take heed to all that I have said to you; and make no mention of the names of other gods. (*Ex. 23:13*—RSV)

Thirdly, then, some of the language which appears most precisely legal was actually homiletic. The idiom of judgment and punishment described with-whom and about-what God became "angry." C.G. Montefiore suggests that, in both the Hebrew Bible and in rabbinic commentary, God's wrath and punishment were directed toward:

> (1) all who worship idols (i.e., upon very many non-Jews), (2) all enemies of Israel, (3) all heretics and sceptics and deniers of the Perfection, Immutability, and Divineness of the Law, (4) the high-handed and unrepentant wicked even among the Jews. (Montefiore & Loewe, 1974, p. xxxi)

The 23rd chapter of Exodus conveys this notion. For example:

> But if you hearken attentively to his voice [that of an angel] and do all that I say, then I will be an enemy to your enemies and an adversary to your adversaries. When my angel goes before you, and brings you in to the Amorites, and the Hittites, and the Perizzites, and the Canaanites, the Hivites, and the Jebusites, and I blot them out, you shall not bow down to their gods, nor serve them, nor do according to their works. . . (*Ex. 23:22-24*—RSV)

These homiletical exhortations and the range of the legal codes were intended to promote exemplary behavior and to build social cohesion. The codes of Leviticus were written "as if" the Israelites were living according to the Law of God. Deuteronomic law is especially idealistic. To a far greater extent this is true of the Talmudic material. The *Mishnah*, says Jacob Neusner, "is utopian. Self-evidently, it hardly requires carrying out, in concrete practice, the bulk of its laws, or even expects most of them to be kept (Neusner, 1979, p. 149).

Fourthly, some of the references to prohibitions and punishments are synoptic. For example, laws pertaining to acts of violence and the making of restitution which appear in chapter 22 of Exodus are paralleled in Leviticus 6 and in Numbers 5. Thus, references to stonings of offenders may be the same account of an actual event (Lev. 20:27 and Num. 15:36) or, more likely, the authors' repetitive and exaggerated approaches to deterring the Hebrews from wickedness.

Finally, it is probable that a ritualistic form of expiation or atonement in the temple, rather than an applied punishment, accomplished the redress of crimes or sins in the bulk of cases. Numbers 15 and Leviticus 4 describe the type of offerings to be brought and the atonement to be made by the priest if a person sinned "unwittingly." But even those who deceived and lied about their theft or oppression could be forgiven through ceremonies of atonement:

> The Lord said to Moses, "If any one sins and commits a breach of faith against the Lord by deceiving his neighbor in a matter of deposit or security, or through robbery, or if he has oppressed his neighbor or has found what was lost and lied about it, swearing falsely... he shall bring to the priest his guilt offering to the Lord, a ram without blemish out of the flock... and the priest shall make atonement for him before the Lord, and he shall be forgiven for any of the things which one may do and thereby become guilty." (Lev. 6:1-3, 6-7—RSV)

In summary, the *halakic* material of Judaism is significant because it represents the first sources to be given the status of Scripture, Christianity and Islam are influenced by it, Western laws have been influenced by it, and it represented a tempering of tribal codes. The *Encyclopedia Judaica* indicates that the interaction between law and religion in the written Torah represented norms different in a number of significant respects from any previous codes or religious understandings:

> First, the unity of morality and law in the Pentateuch created a new basis of authority for the behavioral precepts of Hebrew civilization,
>
> Second, individualistic morality gave way to nation morality which was addressed to the people of Israel as a corporate moral entity, and
>
> Third, despite the exclusivity of the covenantal relationship between God and the Jewish people, God's role in the enforcement of legal-moral norms is clearly pictured as universal. (Encyclopedia Judaica, 1971, p. 1480)

The non-legal material in Scripture and commentaries is *haggadah*, the stories, teachings, prayers, and sermons. Within this material is found the second legal strain—an overriding concern for ascertaining and adhering to God's law, but in an even broader framework of meaning and in the unique Jewish conception of justice.

These collections of writings were intended to impart to believers the difference between "life," union with God, and "death," rejection of God.

For the Jew, this distinction is communicated through the concept of Law, the essence of Judaism:

> The relation of the Law, or I had better say, of the Torah, to God (for the Torah is not limited to the Pentateuch) is very curious. . . . God loves Israel, because Israel possesses and accepts the Torah. God loves the Law even more than He loves Israel. Israel was offered the Law and accepted it, and God is grateful. . . . [The Law] was regarded, I suppose, as the necessary link between heaven and earth and between man and God. Man required it for his moral and religious well-being. (Montefiore & Loewe, 1974, p. xxxiii)

Haggadah is more literary in nature; its form was emergent, as was that of *halakah*. The authors told stories of creation, recited genealogies and, as a means of promoting identity and cohesion, described the making of a covenant with Yahweh. They recounted the miraculous way in which God had rescued the Hebrews in the Exodus from Egypt. Once the people understood the significance of Exodus, God was continuously portrayed as taking "saving and reconciling action" toward Israel.

The authors of Scripture used the Semitic tendency of anthropomorphism to convey certain of their notions about God. One ancient source narrated that Adam and Eve "heard the sound of the Lord God walking in the garden [of Eden] in the cool of the day" (Gen. 3:8). The same source also describes, in Exodus 4:24–26, a Yahweh of a very demonic sort who attacked Moses. The God in this pattern of thought became angry, just as humans become angry. On the one hand, early Hebrews thought it necessary to appease this angry God in the same way that cultic gods were appeased by sacrifices at the altar (Richardson, 1950, p. 91). On the other hand, they were struggling to move away from cultic patterns.

The sources for the Pentateuch were concerned about the problem of idolatry. Hence, they wrote about covenant. They were concerned about the temptations faced by their people, so they told the story of Adam and Eve's temptation to disobey God. They were concerned about interdependence and right relationships, so they expressed themselves in apodictic form: "You shall not kill" (Ex. 20:13) and "You shall love your neighbor" (Lev. 19:18).

Their concern about justice prompted the psalmists to compose hymns which conveyed the idea that all history begins and ends with justice:

> Righteousness and justice are the foundation of thy throne; mercy and truth go before thee. (*Psalm 89:14*)

> Righteousness and faithfulness now meet,
> Righteousness and Peace now embrace;
> Faithfulness reaches up from earth
> and Righteousness leans down from heaven (*Psalm 85:10–11*)

Within the spirit of the Jewish law, there was always an obligation to care for your neighbor:

> Is there a poor man among you, one of your brothers, in any town of yours in the land that Yahweh your God is giving you? Do not harden your heart or close your hand against that poor brother of yours, but be open-handed with him and lend him enough for his needs. (*Deut. 15:7-8—Jerusalem Bible*)

It is precisely this obligation which was expanded in the prophetic sections of the Torah. The prophets Isaiah, Jeremiah, Amos, and numerous others were concerned for economic and social justice. They found strict adherence to law, and to form, offensive when the "appeal to the law" was made at the same time that there was "uncharitableness toward one's neighbor (Amos 2:6, 8:4, Jer. 8:8) (Gutbrod, 1965, p. 35). The purpose of the prophets was quite different from telling their people what the Lord expects or prohibits. Their purpose was to call their people—individuals and the Hebrew nation—to a new understanding of the meaning of integrity. There are consequences to our actions, said the prophets. God will chastise individuals and the nation Israel for lack of integrity.

Gerald Austin McHugh contends that the purpose of the language of judgment and punishment was to

> turn the Israelites away from their sinfulness and back to the path of righteousnous, which led to life in communion (covenant) with Yahweh. Yahweh's judgment and punishment were never final, as they would have been had punishment essentially been retributive in nature. The healing nature of punishment was embodied in the covenant with David. . . . This notion is best summarized (although by no means wholly contained) in the prophet Ezekiel's later writing where it is written:
>
> "As I live, says the Lord God, I swear I take no pleasure in the death of the wicked man, but rather in the wicked man's conversion, that he may live. Turn, turn from your evil ways! Why should you die, O house of Israel?" (*Ezekiel 33:11*) (McHugh, 1978, pp. 91–92)

While we might view the choice of the language of judgment and punishment as unfortunate, we can find within it the deeper meanings—the descriptions of a dynamic relationship between a loving God and a Hebrew people attempting to conceptualize and live out the life of faithfulness. It is easier, perhaps, for us to identify with the saving and reconciling idiom when it is cast in terms of a "parent" finding it necessary to intervene with love and discipline when "children" have gone astray.

There is always a proactive element to the understanding of God in both the *haggadah* and the *halakah*. The theology of Judaism is substantive. God relates to the Hebrews in love and with integrity. God is concerned with the quality of human life and interaction. God "says" that human beings should not deliberately inflict pain upon one another but that they should be involved in "peacemaking."

The Judaic connotation of justice (*tsedeqah*) is one of that which "makes things right." Poetically, the prophet Isaiah expressed the meaning of justice as follows:

> In the wilderness justice will come to live
> > and integrity in the fertile land;
> integrity will bring peace,
> > justice give lasting security.
> My people will live in a peaceful home, in safe houses,
> > in safe dwellings. (*Isa. 32:16–18—Jerusalem Bible*)

Divine justice (*tsedeq*) is synonymous with holiness or rightcousness. Human justice (*tsedeqah*) is "rightness."

In their Scripture and tradition, Jews have urged caution in judgment, have shown reluctance to punish, and have exhibited the desire to make atonement, restitution, or reconciliation when conflicts have occurred. This is their interpretation of "making right," "making peace," or achieving *shalom*. The predominant theology is one of restoration.

"Jewish law," says Horowitz, "presents one of the most striking examples in human history of social evolution, of a development from the rude and savage to the refined and humane" (Horowitz, 1963, p. 1). The intent and spirit behind Jewish law can inform our interfaith dialogue on punishment and can provide an ameliorative influence on the punitiveness of our society. It was, after all, Israelitic-biblical thought which first was "permeated by the reality of a God who always creates the new" (Pannenberg, 1973, pp. 402–403).

B. The Scripture and Tradition of Christianity

> Yes, God loved the world so much that he gave his only Son, so that everyone who believes in him may not be lost but may have eternal life. (*John 3:16—Jerusalem Bible*)

The essence of Christianity is that God so loved humankind that God became human. This act of "loving justice" on God's part is consistent with but, in the Christian view, qualitatively and quantitatively different from the "saving justice" which Israel experienced in "the righteous God who sets his people free, not because they are mighty or worthy, but because he loves them and chooses them as his own" (Documents of Vatican II, quoted in Wren, 1977, p. 45).

While Christians share the Hebrew scriptural heritage, it is the New Testament message which distinguishes Christian from Jew. Judaism and Islam center on the revealed Word and grace through law; Christianity centers on Christ as "the Word" and on "the Word lived out."

The focus of the Word differed from the Law of the Torah. The religious context had changed. The concept of the monotheistic God had been firmly established within Judaism. Although there were many forms of apostasy exhibited, it was no longer necessary to place so much emphasis on the language of judgment and punishment in order to communicate the idea that Yahweh was a jealous God who would not tolerate idolatry. Only once does the New Testament indicate that Jesus spoke of wrath in the Old Testament vein:

> For great distress shall be upon the earth and wrath upon this people; they will fall by the edge of the sword, and be led captive among all nations; and Jerusalem will be downtrodden by the Gentiles, until the times of the Gentiles are fulfilled (*Luke 21:23b-24*—RSV)

There is a more pronounced eschatological[2] tone to God's "vengeance" in the New Testament. God's saving action is now centered in Christ and he frequently casts judgment in terms of eternal life—it is more closely associated with the possibility of heaven or hell. In the New Testament there is a shift from the nation Israel as the recipient of divine wrath to the individuals who reject God (John 3:36, Rom. 1:18, Eph. 5:6).

Anger does not give way entirely to love in the New Testament. Jesus exhibited anger against injustice. Also, in parables he attributed anger to the character representing God—"the master" or "the king." The anger of God was still, on occasion, described anthropomorphically and there was a definite continuation of the Jewish conviction that when there was grave injustice, the God of the Covenant was not neutral but took the side of the oppressed.

The political and social context had changed. Christianity emerged out of the Messianic strain of Judaism during the expansion of the Roman Empire, at a time when Judaism was living under subjugation and was beset by internal dissensions. It is doubtful that Christianity existed as a distinct religious movement before the destruction of the Second Jewish Temple in 70 A.D. Prior to that, says W.D. Davies, "Christianity was a movement within Judaism. Jesus was seen as the long-awaited Messiah and, in the Judaic tradition, as 'the New Covenant'" (Davies, 1978, p. 1466).

Davies explains that, after the fall of Jerusalem, the pharisaic leaders gathered to assess their situation. It was then that they began to realize

---

[2] The theology of ultimate of "last things," such as death, judgment, heaven and hell.

that the Christian claim to achieving grace through faith in Christ rather than through the law posed too great a threat for rabbinic Judaism:

> It was the desperate necessity for Jamnian Judaism to close its own ranks against dissidents and to elevate the *Torah* as interpreted by the Pharisees still more to be *the* way of Jewish life and the reaction to these among Christians and Jews that contributed most to the emergence of what we call Christianity as a distinct religion. (Davies, 1978, p. 1471)

The Word in the New Testament proclaimed that, although the nation of Israel no longer existed, God still loved the covenant people. God had become human in order to demonstrate that love. The primary purpose of Paul and other writers of the New Testament was to testify to the resurrection of Jesus Christ, to the nature of the new life "in Christ," and to the grace which they experienced from "knowing Christ."

Another purpose of the Word was to renew the prophetic call to justice and integrity. Paul's letters (the earliest c. 50 A.D.) were composed in the context of a dialog with Judaism:

> They are criticisms of the faith, law, institutions, and worship of Jews not from without but from within. Although probably more critical of Judaism than those churches founded by other apostles, the Pauline churches also existed on the threshold of the synagogue. (Davies, 1978, p. 1471)

This historically contextual understanding of the relationship between Christianity and the Torah best explains Paul's wrestling with the formation of his own view of law. The law was under criticism. Differences over interpretation and practice had contributed to the factionalism which kept Israel from overthrowing their Roman conquerors. The advent of Christ brought a new ethic, said Paul. He struggled to articulate that ethic.

For Paul, "grace involved not a rejection of the values of the Mosaic law but, on the contrary, an internalization of those values. 'The Mosaic law is in itself holy,' he stated, 'and the commandment is holy, just and good'" (Berman, 1974, p. 98). In Galatians, Paul recognized that the law had a "preparatory role." But it is, says Davies, a mistake to think that Paul's response to the law was monolithic or even one that evolved chronologically. Paul's style was polemic. He was addressing concrete disputes within congregations and he frequently made bold assertions in his letters to those congregations. In Romans, Paul "finally asserts in 10:4 that Christ is the end of the Law" (Davies, 1978, pp. 1479–1480) and indicates that justification comes only through faith.

It was the Gospel writers (Matthew, Aramaic version c. 50 A.D. and Greek version c. 70 A.D.; Mark c. 64 A.D.; and Luke c. 80 A.D.) who more explicitly recorded Jesus' own attitude toward the law. The break with Judaism was occurring and the style of these New Testament authors was both more apologetic[3] and more theological.

The best way to describe Jesus' attitude, as portrayed in the Gospels, is that he maintained a tension between acceptance and rejection, and between censure and acceptance of those who adhered to the letter but not to the spirit of the law.

The Sermon on the Mount in Matthew 5:1–7:29 is the most comprehensive treatise on the issue of law and illustrates Jesus' acceptance/rejection dichotomy. Jesus said that he had come not to abolish the law and the prophets, but to fulfill them (5:17). He chastised the efforts of the scribes and Pharisees to relax the law to fit their own purpose. The requirements of the Kingdom, Jesus said, meant living in the spirit rather than in the letter of the law, e.g., not only are you not to kill your brother, but neither to be angry (5:21–26); not only to refrain from adultery, but also from lust (5:27–30). Also, Jesus approached the laws on divorce, swearing, piety, almsgiving, prayer and fasting in this same manner (5:27–37). Adherence to the form of the law, Jesus admonished, does not in itself fulfill the goals of faithfulness, reverence, charity, and genuine worship.

The Christian ethic of forgiveness is spelled out in Matthew 5:38–48. The proportional ethic of "eye for eye, tooth for tooth" was to be supplanted by turning the other cheek, giving your cloak, and going the second mile. Not only are you to love your neighbor but, especially, are you to love your enemy and those who are unjust. The significance of this ethic is captured in this commentary by Howard Clark Kee:

> This act, because it is not the normal human reaction, is intended to challenge the aggressor by grace rather than by retaliation. . . . Again, the act of grace, which contradicts ordinary human reaction to harsh treatment, is intended to overcome the wrongdoer by love rather than by a greater show of force. (Kee, 1971, p. 616)

Judaic concern for humility and restraint was reiterated in Matthew 7:1–5: "Judge not, that you be not judged;" and "First take the log out of your own eye, and then you will see clearly to take the speck out of your brother's eye." The Golden Rule, "So whatever you wish that men would do to you, do so to them," (Matt. 7:12), takes cognizance of a principle oft stated in Judaism and other religions and cultures of the times.

Jesus demonstrated repeatedly that he did not assume the "sin" of human-kind to be an accepted, unalterable state of affairs. His deeds toward those who might have been called "criminal" are of great interest to us.

---

[3] Apologetics is the branch of theology which deals with the defense and proof of Christianity.

Jesus did not punish, nor did he recommend or tolerate punishment. As the Gospels recount Jesus' actions, he intervened in the lawbreaker's life with radical acceptance and unconditional love:

In Mark 2:2–12—he said to a paralytic, "Your sins are forgiven."

In John 8:1–11—he confronted the situation with straightforwardness, saying to the woman accused of adultery, "Go and sin no more."

In Luke 19:1–10—he afforded dignity to the wrongdoer and tried to evoke introspection about the person's own situation of alienation and estrangement, saying to Zacchaeus, the dishonest tax collector, "I must stay at your home today."

In many different situations recounted in the Gospels, Jesus challenged wrongdoers or ailing persons to a conversion—belief in God and belief in their own self-worth as children of God. Clearly, Jesus rejected the law as a necessary mediator between human beings and God. The nature of genuine obedience, Jesus said, grows out of faith and demonstrated love.

According to Christians, the forgiveness ethic of the New Testament was validated by the resurrection. The resurrection, Brian Wren concludes, "meant that God himself had raised Jesus from death into a new and transformed life, thereby saying 'yes' to all that Jesus had said and done in his name." Jesus represented a radical form of *saving justice* and demonstrated a radical form of *loving justice:*

This love accepts people as they are, reaching out to every human being on earth, offering forgiveness, fellowship and hope, endlessly and without distinction, as Christ seeks to draw all humanity to himself. (Wren, 1977, p. 50)

In Judaism, the intent and spirit of the law were implicit, but sometimes blurred by the intricacies and subtleties of the *halakic* or *haggadic* style. In the New Testament the spirit of the law is made more explicit, as exemplified by the following passage from Romans:

Bless those who persecute you; bless and do not curse them. Rejoice with those who rejoice, weep with those who weep. Live in harmony with one another; do not be haughty, but associate with the lowly; never be conceited. Repay no one evil for evil, but take thought for what is noble in the sight of all. If possible, so far as it depends upon you, live peaceably with all. Beloved, never avenge yourselves, but leave it to the wrath of God; for it is written, 'Vengeance is mine, I will repay, says the Lord.' No, 'if your enemy is hungry, feed him; if he is thirsty, give him drink; for by so doing you will heap burning coals upon his head.' Do not be overcome by evil, but overcome evil with good. (*Rom. 12:14–21—RSV*)

This passage is an elaboration of all in the Christian Scripture which supports a theology of restoration. God "says" that human beings should love and serve one another, reach out in reconciliation and forgive—forgive seventy times seven, if necessary (Matt. 18:21–22; Luke 17:4).

The claim which Christianity makes is not only that Christ is a reconciling agent but that each Christian also has a ministry of reconciliation to perform:

> All this is from God, who through Christ reconciled us to himself and gave us the ministry of reconciliation; that is, God was in Christ reconciling the world to himself, not counting their trespasses against them, and entrusting to us the message of reconcilation. (2 Cor. 5:18–19—RSV)

The codes of restitution and retribution are virtually eliminated in the New Testament. The forgiveness ethic is meant to be applied:

> So if you are offering your gift at the altar, and there remember that your brother has something against you, leave your gift there before the altar and go; first be reconciled to your brother, and then come and offer your gift. (Matt. 5:23–24—RSV)

The *tradition* of Christianity is less supportive of a theology of restoration than is the Scripture. The historical influence of Christianity on the development of positive law in the United States is more discernible than is that of Judaism and Islam. The influence has been both benign and malevolent. Only in recent years has critical analysis of the historical interaction of Christianity and criminal law been given much attention. Gerald Austin McHugh is a Roman Catholic who practices law in Philadelphia. He is quoted extensively in this section because of the critical overview he developed in a 1978 publication. Christians, says McHugh:

> have a special obligation to confront contemporary penal practices, because historically Christianity has greatly contributed to their evolution.... Such phenomena as the popular acceptance of criminal law as a moral code, belief in the absolute right of the state to punish, belief in the ultimate justness of punishment, and the practice of imprisonment itself, to name just a few, have derived no small measure of force and legitimacy from Christian thought and practice....
>
> Church leaders in America, until quite recently, have been all too willing to assume that the state's administration of criminal law and penology was compatible with fundamental precepts—that the torch of justice had been safely passed from Church to state. (McHugh, 1978, pp. 1–2)

McHugh points out that 20th century attitudes and legal practices cannot be directly compared with those of the time of the early church. He cautions that many present Christian justifications for punishment of criminals "are remnants of an age where Church and state were considered, if not identical, at least as working for the same goals" (McHugh, 1978, p. 7). Another caution is that "the earliest Christian communities most likely had no conception of crime in a legal or social sense." Crimes against God or the regent were prosecuted more frequently than those of citizen against citizen. A third difference is that early Christians were discouraged from or would not have thought of taking a dispute to court—particularly, to a Roman court. McHugh paraphrases Paul's letter to the Corinthians as verification of the third point:

> Paul berates the Christians for taking disputes to civil courts. "If one of you has a dispute with a brother, how dare he go before heathen judges, instead of allowing God's people to settle the matter? . . . surely there is at least one wise man among your fellowship who can settle a dispute between the brothers." (McHugh, 1978, p. 12)

Prior to Christianity, criminal codes were largely objective in nature; they focused upon the offense committed. While proof of intent was required in Judaism (and, subsequently, in Islam) for the conviction of an offender, there was "no refined conception of relative degrees of guilt or personal moral standing." It was Christianity which stressed the idea of personal morality and "its two foundations, free will and individual responsibility" (McHugh, 1978, p. 14). The overall effect of this stress on morality was to shift the attention from righting the offense to concern for the spiritual and moral being of the offender. While this concern for individual morality was not alien to Christian theology, two problems arose. First, the problems of the individual offender became divorced from their economic, physical, and social contexts. In the early church there was strong sentiment for the proposition that the second coming of Christ was imminent. Concern for salvation and achievement of eternal life tended to overpower concern for the righting of earthly wrongs.

Secondly, with the introduction of the church-state alliance through the conversion of Emperor Constantine (c. 306–307 A.D.), the church became identified with a repressive political order. McHugh contends that the "empire became fully committed to the advance of Christianity, by whatever means necessary, including employing legal sanctions against the so-called enemies of Christendom." So zealous were Roman converts that it soon became necessary for early church leaders such as Ambrose and Augustine "to intervene in civil matters in an attempt to inject (humane) Christian values into legal and political maters" (McHugh, 1978, pp. 15–18).

Religious persons were now associated with a secular system of positive law. Roman law was not directed toward crimes such as blasphemy. It was assumed that God or "the gods" could deal with such offenses. Roman law spelled out offenses against persons—specifically, those against the emperor (Beach, 1979, p. 5).

It is ironic that the noted religious figure St. Augustine is cited for setting forth a theory of deterrence (c. 400 A.D.). Despite the fact that the primary purview of the church was in matters of sin and grace, Augustine recommended that Roman and church authorities punish some offenders so that others would profit from the example. This formula was perhaps seen by Augustine as a strategy for limiting and controlling the forms of punishment. Augustine was "known to frequently intervene in civil matters. In one case, involving the murder of friends of his, Augustine wrote a letter to the judge which is one of the most remarkable witnesses to the Christian principle 'love of enemies' ever recorded" (McHugh, 1978, p. 18).

In 529 A.D. the Justinian Code was adopted. It spelled out measures of positive secular law which could be made and changed through legislation or through common usage (*tacito consensus populi*). It also made a distinction between *fas lex divina* (precepts of religion, morals, and ethics) and *ius lex humana* (binding law enforced by human agencies).

St. Thomas Aquinas (1225–1274) confirmed that there should be a distinction between divine and secular law for two reasons: first, to protect religious matters from undue interference, and second, to protect citizens from undue coercion. In *Summa Theologica*, Aquinas conceded that he found acceptable those absolute rulers who were guided by reason but that, since those rulers were rare, he found a regime of positive law to be preferable. (Riga, 1978, p. 1431) By this time, whatever its rationale, the church had put its imprimatur upon the forerunner of the present-day, punitive penal code.

The Middle Ages saw the development of a number of practices and attitudes which directly influenced criminal justice in the United States. First, the church accepted the "ordeal" as a means of determining the guilt or innocence of an offender: if the offender was defeated in a duel, for example, guilt had been verified. Anne Strick attributes the origin of the modern adversary trial system to the medieval "trial by ordeal" (Strick, 1977).

Another church practice (to which the American penitentiary was directly traceable) was that of building monastic retreats and isolation cells. Seventeenth century Benedictine monk Jean Mabillon wrote that they were more like workshops than prisons, but historical evidence indicates that they were often used as the worst kind of prisons, "grounded in a hell-fire and damnation theology" (McHugh, 1978, p. 20).

The developments which McHugh calls pivotal were the formalization of canon law by the monk Gratian around 1140; the canon's encoding of a section on criminal and disciplinary sanctions; and the church's prevailing upon secular government to prosecute and carry out prescribed sentences.

The result was a growing legalism and an "increasing acceptance of the law as an instrument of God's will" (McHugh, 1978, pp. 21–23).

By the end of this period the stage was set for a larger role for criminal justice because criminals were now seen as "wicked and depraved individuals, a threat to the common good." Theologically, contends McHugh, "the medieval period saw the deemphasis, if not the loss, of the loving, conciliatory spirit which marked earlier Christian teaching about offenses." He believes this shift was tied to the medieval goal of establishing a Christian kingdom on earth (McHugh, 1978, pp. 25–31).

Meanwhile, in Northern Europe, the Protestant Reformation contributed to the growing legalism. Both Martin Luther (1483–1546) and John Calvin (1509–1564) asserted that the law of God is the moral (natural) law and that human beings have a responsibility to obey it. However, because they thought humans so subject to sin, there was a need for positive secular law which could be administered by civil magistrates. They saw these magistrates as "servants of God." Luther and Calvin thought that the proper state of human affairs was one in which the church inculcated an obedient attitude toward civil authority and the state accepted the ethical wisdom of the church.

Luther and Calvin shared St. Paul's conviction (Romans 13) that civil authorities should be those who revered God and who desired to carry out the divine law. The unintended effect of their advocacy of the civil administration of justice, however, was to strengthen the position of those who believed in punishment and who gradually fashioned a theology of retribution to support their position.

When other Reformation figures and Christian jurists saw what was happening, they more consciously advocated the doctrine of natural law as a means of providing a restraining and civilizing influence on criminal law. Jeremy Taylor and Richard Hooker, leaders of the Anglican Reformation (c. 1650); Hugh Grotius (1583–1645), Dutch jurist and theologian; and Samuel Pufendorf (1632–1694), a Lutheran theologian, all acknowledged the necessity for natural law. In *De Officio*, Pufendorf wrote that positive law is never sufficient to implement the law of nature; without the primary motivation of religious faith, interpersonal relations inevitably become demoralized (Outler, 1955, pp. 5–17). William Blackstone (1732–1780), English jurist, went so far as to say that no human laws are of any validity if they are contrary to the will of God (Cohn, 1971, p. 41).

In the 17th and 18th centuries a secularization of the natural law concept was occasioned by the emergence of rationalist doctrines, legal concepts of natural rights, emphasis on national sovereignties, and the humanism of the French and American revolutions. It was in France at this time that Napoleon established the first police force and that "the State" first assumed the role of the injured party in the prosecution of criminal cases.

These strands of religion, deistic humanism, and pragmatism converged in the United States. In the colonization period, religious evangelicalism, pietism, millenialism, and utopianism were dominant. The Puritans of the reformed tradition sought to establish "the new Israel" in America. With a revival of "divine legislation," harsh punishments were devised as a means of keeping pure the people of the New Covenant.

Interestingly enough, it was Enlightenment thinking, the religious impetus of the Quakers, and the idealism of Protestant revivalists which led to the establishment of the major innovation of criminal justice in America, the penitentiary system (Madigan, 1980). There was a belief that if society was corrupt and corrupting, the removal of individuals from its temporary influence and their exposure to the benevolent influence of enlightened minds—those of Scripture, for example—would encourage, if not guarantee, their moral reformation.

Richard Symes describes the Quaker influence as follows:

> The distinctive and central doctrine of Quaker belief is that of the "inner light." It was in the well-ordered penitentiary, which provided both silence and solitude, that Quaker reformers saw the opportunity for the regeneration of the criminal. (Symes, 1978, pp. 95–99)

The Quakers formed prison societies and persuaded the Pennsylvania Legislature to designate the Walnut Street Jail in Philadelphia as a state prison.

Revivalism most influenced the further development of the penal system in Western New York State. Symes says that in the 1820s, precisely coincident with the development of the "Auburn" system, enthusiasm boiled over. During this time, four traditional Christian doctrines were elaborated in ways which were conducive to the work of prison reformers. These doctrines were: the millennium, the benevolent nature of God, the freedom of human will, and the cooperation of human beings in the attainment of salvation (Symes, 1978, p. 107). The concern for penitence was combined with the Puritan work ethic, and the prison industry was instituted in Auburn, New York.

Blake McKelvey described this period in *American Prisons: A History of Good Intentions:*

> When the Rev. Enoch Wines was made secretary of the New York Prison Association in 1862, he said: "Our work is mainly the work of humanity and benevolence. . . . It is a philanthropy akin to that divine benevolence that calls backsliders to repent."
>
> Among the people who were presuming to show the American public how to reform its criminals, very few considered it necessary to make a protracted study of the problem. They had the feeling that their natural spirit of Christi-

anity and common sense required only the baptism of experience to secure them good standing in the calling. They quoted the Bible to prove the reformability of criminals, but their faith more frequently came out of a warm feeling. Zebulon Brockway, who built the Rochester jail, did so after being converted in the Finney revival. (McKelvey, 1977, pp. 67, 10)

Historian David Rothman's comment in *The Discovery of the Asylum* serves as an appropriate summary on the effect of revivalism:

The prison would train the most notable victims of social disorder to discipline, teaching them to resist corruption. And success in this particular task would inspire a general reformation of manners and habits. The institution would become a laboratory for social improvement. By demonstrating how regularity and discipline transformed the most corrupt persons, it would reawaken the public to these virtues. (Rothman, 1971, p. 107)

The inauguration of the American Penitentiary, with the amplification of the criminology and theology associated with it, is yet another instance in which Christianity gave its blessing to the development of a monstrosity. The motivation of those concerned for the spiritual conversion and rehabilitation of offenders was based on what they considered to be a theology of restoration; the result supported the development of the most retributive penal system in the Western free world.

Gerald McHugh acknowledges that Christian thought and action have been responsible for positive strides in human rights, both in social and criminal justice. Yet he holds Christianity largely responsible for the repressive nature of criminal justice because of what he terms five "Failures of Witness":

First, divorcing the concepts of law, justice, and punishment from the Old Testament "Hebrews" self-understanding as a people of God." To "do so, in Emil Brunner's analogy, is 'as devastating in its effects as a transfusion of blood between different blood groups. Healthy blood so transfused is fatal'" (Brunner, quoted in McHugh, 1978, p. 91). In complete concurrence with this criticism is Herman Bianchi, head of the Criminological Institute of the Free University in Amsterdam. Dr. Bianchi asserts, "The application of biblical ideas of power and retribution, detached from *tsedeqah* (the Hebrew concept of justice-righteousness) is one of the most regrettable factors in the history not only of Christianity, but of our entire cultural system" (Bianchi, 1973, p. 309). The Greek and Roman ideas of justice and law which most influenced Christianity, argues Bianchi, are most concerned with form, while the Hebrew concepts are most concerned with substance and results. *Tsedeqah*, says Bianchi:

is a creative and energetic concept. It is valued, as is a fruit tree, by its results. The idea of *tsedeka* is not *intententional* but *sequential*. . . .

Martin Buber introduced the German word *"Bewahrung"* as a translation for *tsedeka*. The German verb, *bewahren*, can best be translated into English as "to stand the test." It has the meaning of a sequence of human actions whereby the actor proves to be a true and not a phony person, one who does not only make formal justice but substantial justice come true. . . .

On the one hand, therefore, *tsedeka* is an attitude, consisting of a care for the fellow-being, making things come true, commitment to role performance in legal action. If *tsedeka* were only this awareness it might quite easily develop into formality, like justice so often does. *Tsedeka* is also the contents of the result it has to achieve. Strange as it may sound to a Western ear, we can say that *tsedeka* has to result in an acquittal. (Bianchi, 1973, pp. 312–313).

A second "failure of witness" was the church's mistaken understanding of itself as the Kingdom on earth. Having all but abandoned a concept of the church as "the body of Christ" and the "servant community," the church assumed a conquering zeal, supporting its own hierarchy with coercive sanctions against all who would dissent (McHugh, 1978, p. 102). We have previously related how this self-understanding contributed to the development of positive criminal law.

A third "failure of witness" entails a "spiritual hedonism" in which Christianity became so intent upon personal salvation that love of God and belief in God became means rather than ends. The individual was exhorted "to forsake pleasure in this life in return for greater pleasure in the next one." This hedonism had not only spiritual but, also, social implications. When an excessive individualism exists, persons begin to "make decisions on the basis of what will bring them the most personal gain (McHugh, 1978, pp. 103–104). L. Harold De Wolf spells out some of our current manifestations of individualism in what has become a classic description of the paradox of "the two Americas:"

America A is generous, community-minded, benevolent, and humane. All three of our high ethical traditions have contributed to it. Christian teaching emphasizes loving-kindness, fellowship, active concern for the weak, and the sacred dignity of every human individual. . . .

Unfortunately, over against America A stands America B. America B is tight-fisted, individualistic, self-righteous, materialistic, aggressive, impatient, vindictive, and prone to violence. (DeWolf, 1975, pp. 123–124)

In addition to contributing to the climate of violence, excessive individualism has, as previously described, contributed to the tendency to divorce crimes from their causal contexts. Concern for the individual's fate in the next world diminishes concern for the interdependent community in this world.

A fourth "failure of witness" is a Christian theology which is "often dreadfully naive" and which lacks a sufficiently critical and historical consciousness. McHugh cites a painful example of the way in which Christians are naive about criminal justice:

> During the Attica uprising [in 1971], via television and the press, many Americans encountered prisoners as human beings for the first time. Simultaneously, when the truth about the riot became known, many Americans recognized that the truly criminal actions which took place were not committed by the prisoners, but by those who were sworn to uphold the law. Attica stands as a reminder to American Christians and non-Christians alike that naive assumptions about the depravity of the people we call criminals, and about the righteousness of the state in its exercise of power, are dangerously irresponsible. After Attica, to seriously consider a literal interpretation of Romans 13 as an acceptable foundation for Christian thinking on criminal justice would be gross self-deception, an unwillingness to see the truth as it stares us in the face. (McHugh, 1978, p. 141)

When Christians simplistically assume that the law could not be "used in perverse and truly criminal ways" or when they naively assume "that their well-intentioned reform measures will necessarily succeed in spite of the inherently destructive character of prisons," (McHugh, 1978, pp. 141–142) they are failing to respond to Christ's exhortation to "perceive and understand" (Matt. 13:10–17) the truth of the human and political situation.

This naive approach to theology, which does not take cognizance of its roots, distorts the original understanding of the relationship between God and the human family and the introduction of the language of judgment as a means of expressing God's active presence and concern.

The fifth "failure of witness" is related to "the broader failure of Christians to adequately identify with the socially outcast." Most Americans refrain from examining the economic basis of the so-called criminal activity which is prosecuted by our law enforcement system. McHugh warns that "failure to recognize the truth of prisoners' claims of oppression, that in a tragically real sense society is an enemy to them, will only lead us to persist in erroneously thinking that we can reasonably demand justice from individual lawbreakers while tolerating injustice on the part of the community as a whole" (McHugh, 1978, p. 149). Failure to identify with the socially outcast is to abandon the model of caring and service demonstrated by Jesus. This lack of exposure to pain in all of its dimensions eventuates in a distorted view of human nature and distorted social policies.

In retrospect, it seems that the evolution of a theology of retribution has been tied to the development of church-state relations in the countries in which Christianity has flourished. Christianity influenced, but could not contain, the excesses of power wielded by states—particularly when the excesses were associated with well-intentioned reforms initiated by the Christians themselves.

The United States and Christianity are at a critical juncture in regard to their positions on criminal law. It is time to reassess criminal law, claims that this is a Christian nation, that church-state interests are synonymous, and any claims which support a theology of retribution. It is time for the religious community to measure those claims against the explicit theology of restoration in the New Testament.

C. The Scripture and Tradition of Islam

We have set thee upon a Highway (Shari'a) of Command, do thou therefore follow it. (*Qur'an, Sura xlv*)

The believers indeed are brothers; so set things right between your two brothers, and fear God; haply so you will find mercy. (*Qur'an, Sura xlix*)

The part of the world in which Islam emerged is renowned for the oldest legal systems in recorded history. Classical Islam itself dates from the time when Islam saw itself as a "religio-legal system wholly rooted in a divine revelation" (Rosenthal, 1961, pp. 46–47). The Prophet Muhammad (570–632 A.D.) received from Allah the *lawh*, which had preceded society and is as eternal as God. The *lawh* is safely preserved in heaven on the *Sura* (Qur'an 85:22)[4] It contains the divine judgment about all that exists on earth.

As in Judaism, *lawh* is the heart of the Islamic religion. Whereas Judaism is said to be a theocracy—a society centered on God and one in which there is no distinction between the religious and the secular—Islam is sometimes said to be a nomocracy—a society which centers on the law of God. In that law, "the whole spirit of the faith may be said to be epitomized" (Khadduri, 1961, p. vii).

Islam was infused by the Judaic culture of religion and ethics and by the Greek (Hellenian) culture of science and philosophy and, in many respects, brought a unity to the two (Burton, 1977, p. 3). The Scripture of Islam acknowledges its roots in both Judaic and Christian religious tradition:

In the footsteps of the prophets We sent Jesus, son of Mary, to confirm the Torah,

---

[4] The import of this is that God's message is eternal. "The 'tablet' is not to be understood in a material sense, made of stone or metal. It is 'preserved' or guarded from corruption." From the *Qur'an*, translation and commentary by Abdullah Yusuf Ali, Vol. II (Cairo: Dar al-kitab al-Masri), p. 1717.

We gave him the Gospel, confirmation of Torah and a guidance and lesson to
those who would avoid the wrath of God.
Let, therefore, the people of the Gospel judge in accordance with what God
revealed.
Who so does not judge on the basis of what God has revealed is in sin.
(*Quran 5:46–47*)

There are numerous ways in which Islam brought a unity, also, to the two
faiths. Muslims unabashedly associate themselves with the Law and the
Prophets: 29 prophets are acknowledged; Jesus was one of them and Muhammad was "the last." Islam acknowledges the Scriptures: "the Books,"
the "Word" of Judaism and Christianity. Islam in no ways limits its membership to Arabic peoples. Anyone who surrenders to the law of Allah is a
Muslim.

However, the *lawh*, the Word, was revealed to Muhammad[5] in a differ
ent time and place, so the thrust of the Word in Islam was directed toward
the Arabic situation. The concept of monotheism was not firmly established in Arabia. Therefore, in its legislative sections, the Islamic Scripture
resembles the Judaic more closely than the Christian. Muhammad felt
called by Allah to bring the Law and the Gospel to the Arabic people. He
wanted his people to know Allah and to be led by Allah to give up their
barbarity, tribal rivalry, and idolatry. "It is not clear," says Haim Cohn,
"that Muhammad intended to establish a new religion.... The Qur'an is
an instance of a secondary revelation to a given people after that divine
law had already been revealed primarily to other peoples" (Cohn, 1971,
p. 10).

In Islam, the significance and focus of the Word is indicated by the very
name of the religion. Islam is the Arabic word "to surrender" (derived
from *salaam*, which translates to "the perfect peace that comes when one's
life is surrendered to God.") A Muslim, then, is one "who surrenders." The
primary purpose of the Qur'an is not to regulate the relationship of man to

---

[5] Muslims tend to say that the *lawh* was dictated or was recited to Muhammad by the
Angel Gabriel and tend not to say that the *lawh* was revealed. The intent of this distinction is
to emphasize that the law was pre-existent and that it was given to Muhammad as a corpus.
The conception is similar to the way in which the Jews say that the Law was given to Moses,
but different in that Muslims do not recognize the ongoing and dynamic process of revelation
through other partiarchical or prophetic figures, as do Jews.

The Qur'an was, however, collected in the same manner as were the Torah and the New
Testament. In *The Philosophy of Punishment in Islamic Law* (Doctoral dissertation, Claremont Graduate School. Ann Arbor, Mich.: University Microfilms, 1980, pp. 30–31), Mustafa
Kara says, "Because of the traditional oral culture of the Arabs, the writing of the Qur'an was
not contemplated during the Prophet's lifetime; only certain communications were written
down by secretaries.... The Qur'an was not collected from the hearts of men only, but also
from other fragmentary renditions of it which had been recorded during the Prophet's lifetime
on palm leaves, stones, leather skins, and shoulder bones."

his fellows but his relationship to his creator (Coulson, 1964, p. 12). "The Qur'an is not and does not profess to be a code of law or even a law book, nor was Muhammad a law-giver in any Western sense. The Qur'an is an eloquent appeal. . . to obey the law of God" (Vessey-Fitzgerald, quoted in Cohn, 1971, p. 9).

Nevertheless, Muhammad had, for the Islamic community (*umma*), the same sense of destiny under God as did the Israelites in their covenant with God. Muhammad reacted negatively to the unmitigated fatalism and to the moral inequity in pre-Islamic Arabic culture. He also faced the task of unifying numerous tribes which were without political, legal, or spiritual ties into a cohesive religion and society. When Muhammad turned to God, the message he received was one "of hope in the overriding power of Allah, the Compassionate, the Merciful, who guides people in the path and who is only too ready to turn to those who turn toward him" (Schact, 1969, p. 16).

While the focus of the Scripture and tradition of Islam is on Allah, and while there is a graphic description of the relationship to Allah in the afterlife, the mainstream of Islam does not have an "otherworldly" character. Fadlou Shehadi of Rutgers University maintains that, "In terms of ultimate religious responsibility, this is the life that counts. . . . Islam is encompassing. . . . Thus man's entire life becomes a religious enterprise." Shehadi goes on to explain, however, that this should not be construed to mean that one would consult a religious source for technical guidance on other matters. "The most distinctive feature of the encompassing character of Islam is that some injunctions are meant to be applied as state laws. This gives the encompassing character a specifically political form. . . . Islam unifies the life of many by its pervasive and over-arching religious duties. It does not, however, put all duties on the same level of importance. Some duties are fundamental (Shehadi, 1980, pp. 4–5).

The Qur'an explains why the *lawh* was revealed to Muhammed:

that you may warn Mecca, the Mother of Cities (*42:5*)

you have been sent the Truth (*35:25*)

O mankind, surely you are the ones who have need of God (*35:16*)

Let there be one Community among you, inviting men to good, bidding to honor, rejecting what is disapproved; such as those who prosper. And be not as those who divided and fell into disagreement after the clear signs had come to them; for them there is mighty punishment (*3:105*)

The language of obedience in the Qur'an is cast in terms of judgment and punishment. Although theoretically the *Sharī'a* is revealed, it incorporates both divine and human law, as did the Torah. The legislation of the common law, *urf*, was combined with the language of the Torah and the

New Testament and with revelation to formulate the *Shari'a*, the high-way, the way to be taken by the faithful. "The classical theory of *Shari'a*," asserts Mohammed Arkoun, "is the outcome of a complex historical pro-cess" (Arkoun, cited in Thoma, 1979, p. 75).

Further, says Mustafa Kara, "Islamic law is no more or less than the epitome and result of a particular stage in the history of evolution of Arab society. Crime was, then, defined not as the commission or omission of an act in violation of a law forbidding or commanding it, but rather the com-mission or omission of an act that is in violation of moral/universal laws" (Kara, 1980, p. ii). Comparatively few, approximately 80, of the 6,000 verses in the Qur'an have strict legal significance. (The entire Qur'anic legislation is not great in quantity; approximations range from 200 to 600 verses, depending on which of the matters of duty and morality are con-sidered legislative in nature, and the bulk of those are concerned with religious duties and rituals.)

From these 80 verses have come, however, a theory of deterrence, a complex set of prohibitions, and distinctions between levels of offenses. Criminal law, explains Kara, involved:

> transition from old tribal custom to divinely ordained norms and ethics which had a general tendency and aim that, in contrast, were more humanitarian. The new spirit of the law, although forbidding most customary acts, was nonetheless often conciliatory. The only exception was when the "right of God (*haqq al-Lah*)" became involved (Kara, 1980, p. 50)

The Prophetic legislation takes two forms. *Hadith* is the oral legislation of the Prophet as reported to his companions and later recorded in the Qur'an. *Sunna* is the applied Tradition (literally, the "trodden Path"). There are six books of Prophetic Sunna (collected c. 250–300 H; c. 850 A.D.).

The word *jarima* (crime) derives from a word meaning "an improper profit or gain." In the Qur'an it came to mean "any improper, immoral, il-legal, or irreligious act." Other connotations are "sinful," "any act de-tested," or "any deed contrary to right and justice" (Kara, 1980, pp. 41, 133–134).

In Islamic legislation there are three categories of crimes. *Hadd* are the crimes with punishments which are fixed and which are the prerogatives of God. These crimes are theft, adultery or fornication, the drinking of alcoholic beverages, slander or defamation, robbery, and apostasy. These crimes appear to be the most serious because they indicate that the offender committing them has not surrendered to Allah. Caution should be used in regard to terminology such as "more serious." Any disruption in the rela-tionship with Allah or inside the community was considered serious. The distinction of crimes which are the purview of God *(haqq al-lah)* is a more pragmatic one: these are under the jurisdiction of Allah and religious figures, whereas other injuries might be adjudicated by community members. In theory, since God's law is immutable, the penalties for *hadd* crimes are fixed and mandatory. The penalties are applied, however, by the Imam and can be mitigated according to the individual's circumstances (age, mental or physical capacity, status as free or slave) and according to the manner in which the offender confesses and repents.

Qasās (or *kisas*) are crimes of death or physical injury. While more serious in terms of consequences to the victims, they may not entail more severe sanctions. Here it appears that the Qur'an was attempting to temper the *lex talionis* of the *urf* and of the Torah:

> Surely we sent down the Torah, wherein is guidance and light. . . . And therein we prescribed for them [the Jews] "A life for a life, an eye for an eye, a nose for a nose, an ear for an ear, a tooth for a tooth, and for wounds retaliation"; but whosoever forgoes it as a freewill offering, that shall be for him an expiation. Whoso judges not according to what God has sent down—they are the evildoers. *(Qur'an 5:48–49)*

The amount of restitution (retaliation or blood money) may be fixed by a given community and carried out by the civil authorities or by the parties involved. The significant aspect of these verses is that they suggest the forgiveness ethic of the New Testament. The Prophet considered forgiveness in such situations a virtue, and some of the Schools of Law which emerged after the time of the Prophet concurred.

Ta'zir are lesser crimes such as usury, treason, and cursing. Not all of these offenses are spelled out in the Qur'an. The penalties attached to them by the community are meant to have a deterrent effect against social or political disruption.

The Qur'anic references to the *hadd* crimes (see Kara, 1976, pp. 151–177) are as follows:

> sexual offenses—Suras 4:15, 16, 25; 17:32; and 24:2, 30
> wine drinking—16:67; 2:219; 4:43; 5:93, 94
> robbery—5:41, 42
> slander—24:4, 5, 11–25; 25:23–25
> apostasy—16:106; 2:217; 4:89; 8:49; 9:68

The crime of theft is one which is interesting to consider in detail. First, because it is said to be a "clear, specific and strong *hadd*, with a *hadd* punishment":

The man or woman guilty of theft, cut off their hands to punish them for their crimes as deterrence, from God. He is mighty and wise. But whoever repents and amends his ways after committing evil shall be pardoned by Allah. Allah is forgiving and merciful (*Qur'an 5:41–42*)

Secondly, because it is the instance most frequently cited in the United States by those who advocate harsher, more certain punishments for the sake of more effective deterrents. Thirdly, because even though the punishment is said to be a "right of God" and "immutable," the applied punishment is subject to extensive variation.

In the Prophetic tradition, if the amount stolen exceeds the minimum prescribed, the right hand is cut off. A second conviction necessitates cutting off the left leg. Stealing for the third and fourth times may carry the penalty of cutting off the repeater's left hand and right leg, consecutively (Kara, 1980, p. 100).

But in the Sunan are also provisions for two alternative punishments— one *ta'zir* and the other compensatory—if the proven theft does not fit all of the elements of a *hadd* crime, including whether the property stolen: (1) is that of another individual who is not a relative (state properties and that of the masters of slaves is excluded but could be covered under another category); (2) was taken with the owner's knowledge and out of his sight (deceit, snatching and embezzling are excluded); (3) was secured inside a closed area (pastured animals, trees and certain borrowed goods are excluded); (4) was valued in excess of the price of a shield made of cast iron (one-quarter to one *dinar*); and (5) whether there is evidence which is absolutely clear (Kara, 1980, pp. 160–163). Finally, according to verse 42 of Sura 5, "whoever repents and amends his ways after commiting evil shall be pardoned by Allah."

This example alone, of the ways in which the supposedly immutable and static law of Islam could be tempered, is enough to cause us to question widely held Western assumptions that the Scripture of Islam demands a theology of retribution. It suggests that the theology of Islam is as complex as that of Judaism and Christianity and that only appreciation for the historical/cultural context, plus word and form study, can unlock the meaning of the "criminal legislation."

Some of the passages which indicate that the purpose of God's judgment is to "save and reconcile," in addition to Sura 49 and 5:41–49 previously cited, are these:

But God, in His infinite mercy and love,
Who forgives and guides individuals and nations,
And turns to good even what seems to us evil,

Never forsakes the struggling soul that turns to Him,
Nor the groups of men and women
Who join together to obey His Will and Law
And strengthen each other in unity and truth.
(*Commentary, Abdullah Yusuf Ali, C. 6*)

The law of equality is prescribed to you in cases of murder. . .But if any re-
mission is made. . .then grant any reasonable demand, and compensate him
with handsome gratitude. This is a concession and a Mercy from your Lord.
(*Sura 2:178*)

If any of your women are guilty of lewdness, take the evidence of four witnesses from amongst you; and if they testify, confine them to houses until
death do claim them, or God ordain for them some other way.

If two men among you are guilty of lewdness, punish them both. If they repent and amend leave them alone; For God is oft-returning, most merciful.
God accepts the repentance of those who do evil in repentance and repent
soon afterwards; to them will God turn in mercy: For God is full of knowledge and wisdom. (*Sura 4:15–17*)

The Islamic Scripture indicates that the individual also has a responsibility for forgiveness and reconciliation:

And if ye do catch them out, catch them out no worse than they catch you out:
But if ye show patience, that is indeed the best course for those who are patient. And do thou be patient, for thy patience is but from God; nor grieve
over them: and distress not thyself because of their plots. For God is with
those who restrain themselves, And those who do good. (*Sura 16:126–128*)

Repel evil with that which is fairer. (*Sura 23:93*)

O you who believe, look after yourself, he who goes astray will not harm you,
so long as you let yourselves be guided. (*Sura 5:104*)

It is a duty for the Muslim to build community, as well as to reconcile it.
Each Muslim is to greet another with, "Peace be upon you." To do so increases your good qualities, and "It increases the good of your household."
"When two Muslims meet and clasp hands, 70 pardons are distributed between them." "By Him in whose hand is my soul, you will not enter paradise until you believe, and you do not believe until you love one another."
The Prophet said, "Shall I tell you what is better than prayers, fasting, and
almsgiving?" The Companions said, "Of course!" And he said, "Reconciling
enmity. The evil of enmity is death." It is a duty to intercede on behalf of
those who have need. "There's no alms finer than an alms of the tongue."
It is a duty to be charitable, to avoid mixing with the rich and to seek
the company of the poor and do good to orphans. The Prophet said, "Beware of sitting with the dead!" Someone asked, "And who are the dead?"

The Prophet answered, "Those who do not have need." Abu Hamid al-Ghazali (d. A.H. 505/1111 A.D.), in *Revification of the Sciences of Religion*, wrote:

> Regard no one with an eye that sees his worldly estate as great, for this lower world is insignificant in the eye of God and all that it holds is little. No matter how much the people of this world may exalt you, they have exalted worldly matters, while you dwindled in the eye of God.... do not be submissive to them because of their affection and praise for you.... Or [on the other hand] if you receive evil from them, and something from them strikes you that may hurt you, then [remember that] their affairs are all under God, so seek refuge with Him from their evil and do not worry about requital, for that adds to the distress and wastes one's life. Never say to them "you have not known my place" for I believe that if you are worthy of it, God will prepare a place for you in their hearts, since it is God who inclines ears to love and to aversion. Be very attentive to the right and deaf to the wrong in what they say. (Williams, 1971, p. 27)

There is an undeniable social dimension within Islam. In most religions there is a strong sense of community. "Still, it is safe to say that only in Islam has the awareness of belonging to a unique, supranational community been so strongly developed. Islam is not a nation-state (it transcends national loyalties) but it is a community of believers bound together in a brotherhood more vital than that of blood" (Williams, 1971, p. 8).

Two analogies depict the strong pull of social solidarity: "The Faithful are to one another like the parts of a building—each part strengthening the others;" (Yamani, 1972, p. 60) and "Every individual is charged with the care of society. Life is like a ship at sea in which each member of the crew has a vital function" (Williams, 1971, p. 41).

The Scripture of Islam exhorts its adherents to faith and obedience, to exemplary life, to love of brothers and sisters, and to the building of community. The tenets of the Qur'an could be characterized as the foundation of a theology of restoration. What God "says" in the Qur'an about punishment is that those who wish to obey God's law will not engage in the *hadd* crimes or in any act which lacks integrity toward God or other human beings. If an offense is committed, restitution should be made. If an offender repents, the Imam can pardon and an act of expiation can be performed. If an offender does not repent, or if a victim does not forgive, penalties may be exacted. Forgiveness between human beings is considered a virtue. However, crimes against God should not be overlooked.

The criminal legislation of the Qur'an exhibits the same two legal strains found in the Torah. First, an encoding and a tempering of the common law: "The breaking of deeply imbedded and provocative tribal custom was the initial task of Qur'anic legislation" (Kara, 1980, p. 42). Secondly, the broader construction of God's concern for and the consequences of human actions molded into a highly idealistic law for spiritual and communal life, a law "revealed to effect a qualitative social change" (Kara, 1980, p. 48).

The tradition of Islam is highly complex. On the one hand, the tradition is more historically accurate than is that of Judaism and Christianity because the sources are more recent. On the other hand, it is extremely difficult for many reasons for Western minds to understand Islamic religion and culture. One of the major reasons is that the historic rivalry between Christianity and Islam has prejudiced Western sources on religion and law. There are few of them and they frequently are contradictory. Hence this is an area in which there is a critical need for extensive interfaith dialog.

The judicial actions of Muhammad (just as the actions of Moses, the judges of the Torah, and Jesus and New Testament figures) fall into the categories both of Scripture and Tradition. It was in Mecca that Muhammad first received the revelation. For the first 13 years of his Prophethood, he was messenger of God, interpreter, and spiritual leader. When he moved to Madina, where a group of followers were able to openly practice Islam, he became not only a spiritual but a political leader. By this time he was asked to rule on as well as to interpret the Qur'anic legislation. The reports of his actions are precedent-setting because the Islamic theory of jurisprudence rests on the Qur'an and Traditions of the Prophet. A theory of jurisprudence is made difficult because the Prophet's style was *ad hoc.* Joseph Schact postulates that Muhammad was a poet rather than a theologian; a prophet rather than a legislator. When confronted with concrete situations and pressed by his followers to make a judgment, he improvised (Schact, 1969, p. 10).

Conversely, Mustafa Kara says that Muhammad sometimes had himself appointed as a judge but indicates that the Prophet's decisions were indeed somewhat contradictory, because, first, he followed no method or detailed code and the tradition was oral; secondly, he dealt with the mitigating or aggravating circumstances; thirdly, because he was primarily concerned with the religious dimensions of the problem; and fourthly, he dealt with changing situations (Kara, 1980, pp. 55–72).

There was a pronounced hardening of attitude toward offenders between the Meccan and Madinan periods.

The legal rules. . . grew in stages from being merely advisory and limiting. . . to totally forbidding. . . . The penalty for. . . prescribed acts also developed in severity. In the case of adultery, it developed from a simple punishment of detention to a minimum of one hundred lashes and one year's banishment (for the Muslim single person), to death by stoning (lapidation) for the married. (Kara, 1980, pp. 179–180)

The more severe punishment in Sura 24 is believed to have been prescribed after the less severe in Sura 4[6] (Kara, 1980, p. 61; & Burton, 1977, pp. 72–78).

Muhammad Abdul-Rauf made a review of 30 terms pertaining to sin and concluded that there was a distinct difference in attitude between the Meccan and Madinan revelations:

> In the first place it can be easily observed that words with strong repugnant connotations bearing more on the attitude of sinners, such as *tughian, ijram, fujur, sharr* and *israf*, predominantly belong to Mecca. Likewise are words denoting absolute loss in the wrong direction like *dalal* and *ghayv*, and words denoting the motive of choosing disobedience and dislike of reflection such a *iba* and *utuww*. On the other hand, words which describe the act itself as being indecent, foul or disapproved, such as *fahishah munkar* and *rijs* are chiefly Madinan or are exclusively so. This is important because it reflects the shift of emphasis from the attitude of rebellion or disobedience which was the major meaning content of sin in the Meccan revelations, to the acts themselves which became the central attention during the Madinan age. (Abdul-Rauf, 1963, p. 116)

Mustafa Kara indicates that Islamic penal sanctions also developed from the general to the particular and from light penal sanctions to, ultimately, capital punishment. One of the reasons he attributes for this shift is that penal sanctions "became heavier only after the Muslim community and its government grew larger and stronger and, more importantly, only after it attained solidarity.... Mohammed and his new religion, while still in its infancy, could not then offend followers and prospective converts by insisting on changing their long-established habits and customs suddenly" (Kara, 1980, p. 182).

From the time of the Prophet's death, *ulūsi* (study of the law) became necessary because the Umma (community) began to split and fall into disagreement. Two major factions emerged. The *Shi'ites* (traditionalists) contend that the Qur'an is infallible and the Prophet is an infallible source of divine law. The Sunna can be transmitted only in a line of direct authority through the Imams, from Muhhad. According to this view, an Imam cannot be elected by the community. He is appointed by God and is infalli-

---

[6] The point may be academic, however, because both versus are followed by provisions for repentance and forgiveness. Another caution to keep in mind is that two sources warn about problems of glossing and inaccuracies in the Qur'an and Suna. Kara says, "It is nonetheless a fact that certain *Hadith* and *Sunna* were fabricated by those who aspired to render a certain number of their own doctrines and beliefs as though they were sanctioned by the Prophet" (ibid. 61). John Burton says, "It is questionable whether the reference to stoning appeared in the original Qur'an" (op. cit., pp. 72–81). In the process of form criticism, he found evidence of glossing, omission, and addition. He says, further, that severe penalties for adultery or theft were never widespread.

ble (*ma'sum*). The *Sunnites* (consensualists) contend that it is necessary for law to be interpreted and this occurs through the process of *ijmā* (consensus). An Imam can be selected by the people and is guided by Allah. The Sunnites are the majority group and call themselves "the people of the tradition and the collectivity" (Williams, 1971, p. 33). By the 8th century, these factions had organized into "schools of law" and later developed many branches, each of which stated their views in creedal statements.

In this respect, the development of Islamic law is not unlike that of the Judaic. In pre-Islamic Mecca there had been the rudiments of legal administration. Arbitrators (*hakam*) were often chosen and public officials were charged with the task of recovering compensation in cases of homicides or injuries. After Islam emerged, a system of courts emerged also. *Caliphs* (religious figures) succeeded the Prophet; *qadis* (judges) succeeded *caliphs*. When cases were tried, a rigid standard of proof was required. The testimony of two male witnesses was essential; the rules on the admissibility of evidence were rigid. But the victim had a choice between arbitration and the courts. Many chose arbitration and a *kahim* (priest) was frequently chosen as the arbitrator.

As times changed, there was no way to avoid law-making and interpretation. Gradually, the Consensualist perspectives were regularized. In the 9th century, in the *Risāla*, Ash-Shafi'i (b. 767) provided one of the most systematic formulations of the *ijtihad* (juristic reasoning) which he claimed was necessary to the application of law. Law, said Ash-Shafi'i, has four roots: the Qur'an, the Sunna, Ijmā (consensus) and Qiyās (reasoning by analogy) (Coulson, 1964, p. 133).

The activity of the adherents of the schools of law could be likened to the activities of the rabbis in Talmudic times. The roles of *ijtihad* and *ra'y* (personal opinion) were hotly contended. There was debate, also, as to whether theological speculation (*kalām*) involved an improper perspective on the validity of human reason. After a three-century period of intense activity, most sources indicate that the level of scholarly activity in religion and law tapered off and that there was no significant ferment until the present time.

Coulson describes the transition in this way:

> Eventually, the scholar-jurist recognized the legitimacy of the non-Shari'a tribunals under the broad doctrine of *siyasa*, the principle that the Ruler has the right, or more properly the duty, to provide for the effective administration of law in the public interest (*maslaha*) by organizing, where necessary, jurisdictions alternative to the Shari'a courts. The *siyasa* doctrine ultimately rests upon the text of the Qur'an itself: "Obey Allah, His prophet and those at the head of your affairs." (Coulson, 1978, 1447, 1449)

Until modern Islamic nations adopted Western civil and criminal codes, there was no positive law and little legal literature in the strict sense.

Mustafa Kara criticizes Islam, saying that, when faced with the alternatives of breathing new life into inherited doctrines and adapting them to current needs or seeking inspiration elsewhere, Islam has always chosen the second alternative. This has constituted an Islamic dilemma, since Islam has traditionally claimed full jurisdiction over questions of social morality without always providing practical answers.

Fazlur Rahman is critical on another front. He says that *kalām* (theology) does exist and that it is inevitably a higher science than *fiqh* (legal science) because it concerns propositions about God, Prophethood, and humanity. But its scope, according to Rahman, is too limited. It lacks a view of human nature and a social dimension:

> The theologians have been too much preoccupied with God and His nature; they have ignored the nature of man and his function. A science of Islamic morals can be made possible only when man is put in the center of interest, for the Word of God has come to man for the sake of man. (Rahman, quoted in von Grunebaum, pp. 94–97)

Within Islam, new nationalism and religious revivalism is currently lessening the influence of Western criminal procedures. In a number of countries, a unified system of national courts has been established, which includes a system of appeals courts (*muzalim*). But there remains a tension between religion and the development of substantive law:

> In 1927, King Ibn Saud conceived the project of having [divine] Islamic law codified. The Hanbali school of law prevails in Saudi Arabia; but the code was to be based not only on Hanbali doctrine.... Under the protest of the Hanbali *ulama* (religious scholars), however, he had to abandon the project.

> When King Amanullah of Afghanistan tried in 1924 to introduce a new penal code, the innovation of which amounted to nothing more than the introduction of monetary fines and the restriction of the discretion of the *kadi*,... by introducing a graded system of punishments, he was forced by the *ulama* to replace it by an amended version which amounted to its repeal. (Cohn, 1971, p. 47)

Another approach is that of Pakistan. In February 1979, on the occasion of the Prophet's birthday, a penal code designed to "make all laws in Pakistan conform to the tenets of Islam" was adopted. Included in the severe sanctions are flogging for drinkers of alcohol, amputation for thieves, and stoning for adulterers. However, when questioned by reporters, General Zia cast doubt on the likelihood of implementation of the sanctions:

> For example, he said, the Islamic rule that an adulterous act must be witnessed by four people for the penalty to be exacted makes a sentence of stoning to death "impossible."

He added that although two sentences of amputation of hands had been imposed under martial law, the penalty had not been carried out. The military courts reportedly were unable to find a surgeon willing to perform the operation. (Trumbull, 1979)

The intent of the laws appears to be aimed, primarily, at providing a unified religious tie among Muslims. General Zia extolled the orthodox Muslim morality as a superior "way of life" and announced the establishment of Shariat courts with judges versed in Qur'anic ethics. Reporter Trumbull commented:

Pakistan's move reflects an increasingly conservative religious trend among some Moslem nations. In Iran, conservative Islamic clergymen are trying to revive adherence to Islamic Law. Libya is led by Col. Muammar el-Qaddafi, who is considered a religious revivalist, and Saudi Arabia's leaders also are conservative on religion. Moslem fundamentalist movements also are strong enough to have an impact on governments in Malaysia, Indonesia, Afghanistan and Egypt. (Trumbull, 1979)

In the United States there are two major Islamic communities. First, there is the World Community of Al-Islam in the West (formerly the Black Muslims). Under recent leadership, they have been more open to dialog and ecumenical ties. The Nation of Islam tends to advocate punishment of offenders but is reluctant to turn that power over to state courts, because it is deemed their own responsibility to decide upon sanctions and to carry them out. Secondly, there are Islamic communities centered in diplomatic and academic circles. They have become more visible with current emphasis on the Mideast.

These two communities will need to provide insight on the issue of theologies of retribution or restoration. For the debate continues. Representative of a retributive perspective is a statement by Ayatollah Khomeini of Iran:

If the punitive laws of Islam were applied for only one year, all the devastating injustices would be uprooted. Misdeeds must be punished by the law of retaliation: cut off the hands of the thief; kill the murderer; flog the adulterous woman or man. Your concerns, your "humanitarian" scruples are more childish than reasonable. Under the terms of Koranic law, any judge fulfilling the seven requirements [that he have reached puberty, be a believer, know the Koranic laws perfectly, be just; and not be affected by amnesia, or be a bastard, or be of the female sex] is qualified to be a judge in any type of case. He can thus judge and dispose of twenty trials in a single day, whereas the Occidental justice might take years to argue them out. (Khomeini, 19xx)

Quite another view is that represented by Mohammed Arkoun. In an analysis of Islamic attitudes toward the death penalty, he summarizes the theological and legal dilemma faced by Islam:

The Quran represents in every case an attempt to mitigate the harsh collective attitudes imposed by a sociological apparatus without any form of political control. The overall direction of its teaching is towards a respect, even an exaltation of the human person(*al-insan*), who is created by God and responsible to him for grave sins (*kaba'ir*), one of which is murder (*qatl*). . . .

The Quran, then, protects human life, introduces distinctions and confirms the norms and attitudes that had been in force for a long time in the common law or '*urf*. . . . These rules regarding punishment are in fact an expression of a system of protections for the emerging Muslim community that was threatened by the existing tribal society with its clan solidarities. It is worth noting, however, that the new community made use of the same methods for the formation of alliances and oppositions in order to establish itself. To do this, contingent and secular norms and practices were raised in the Quran to a transcendental level (the price of blood, stoning, the emancipation of slaves and so on). The Islamic doctors and lawyers continued to take the historical and social circumstances surrounding the Quranic interventions (*ashah al-nuzul*) into account, but they at the same time neglected to study the theological difficulties raised by the legal verses. (Arkoun, cited in Thoma, 1979, pp. 76–77)

In his dissertation, Mustafa Kara thoughtfully raises both theological and legal issues. In answering his own question about whether or not there are any justifications for punishment, Kara suggests that penal sanctions were misused in Islam in two ways. First, they were misused in Islam, as they were in Christianity, for the purpose of expanding the faith. Secondly, they were made excessive and employed to retributive rather than to utilitarian ends in protecting the community. The original legal strain within the Qur'an represented a tempering of the existing common law. But the welding of religious and civil authority had a detrimental effect in the long run.

Islamic law tended to develop at the same pace as secular morality and ethics, in an essentially retributive vein. Penal sanctions evolved without continued infusion of the theological substance of the Qur'an. The broader theological strain—the theology of consequence, of confession and forgiveness, of reformation and reconciliation—was dissipated. The theology of restoration, in which Islam blends the Judaic Spirit of the Law with the Christian conception of grace, needs further articulation.

II. COMPARATIVE THEOLOGIES

There is a high degree of consensus among Judaism, Christianity, and Islam on the most fundamental theological concepts. The Law, or the Word, revealed to each of the three faiths came from the same God. The purpose of the Law was to describe the ideal relationship between God and human beings. The language of judgment and punishment in the Scriptures was an idiom used to portray God's "considered opinion," "will," or "plan" for human conduct.

Those who adhere to a *theology of restoration* find their grounding both in communal and ultimate values common to the three faiths. Here are some of those values, some of "the facts," shared by Judaism, Christianity, and Islam:

1. Belief that there is one God, our creator, who is loving, just, and faithful to human beings.
2. This monotheistic God is a living, acting, sustaining, and saving God. God's saving action is depicted frequently in the Scriptures in anthropomorphic terminology, in theophanies (divine appearances), or in dramas of liberation such as those involving the Israelites' escape from Egypt.
3. This monotheistic God directed revelation to specific persons and to specific nations or situations. All three faiths share the Hebrew scriptural tradition. Islam recognizes both the Old and the New Testament:

   In the footsteps of the prophets We sent Jesus, son of Mary, to confirm the Torah.
   We gave him the Gospel, confirmation of Torah and a guidance and lesson to those who would avoid the wrath of God.
   Let, therefore, the people of the Gospel judge in accordance with what God revealed.
   Who so does not judge on the basis of what God has revealed is in sin.
   (*Qur'an 5:46–47*)

4. Human beings are created in God's image. This is expressly stated in all three Scriptures. Therefore, human nature must be inherently good. It is also clear, however, that because of their freedom, human beings can "sin"—stray from God's will.
5. The model which God sets forth for dealing with "sinners" is one in which God's actions depict the consequences—not the punishments—experienced by individuals and nations who fail to discern and act on God's purpose. It has been said that God's moral law is as inevitable as the law of gravity. If this is true, then the seeds of consequence are implanted within human beings and are inherent in their deeds.
6. God's justice is a reconciling justice. It is synonymous with holiness or righteousness, with God's unitary Being and concern for the unity of all creation. It is significant that the Hebrew word *shalom*, the Greek word *eirēnē*, and the Arabic word *salaam* all have the fundamental connotation of "organic unity." Doing justice, for God, aims at restoring unity or wholeness.

7. In all three Scriptures, human beings are to employ God's models of intervention and of saving justice. It then becomes a human responsibility to "judge fairly," to "set things right," and to achieve a form of "acquittal" and "reconciliation," in the same kind of loving/saving action which God demonstrates.

The adherents of a theology of restoration contend that these "facts" are at the heart of their Scripture and tradition. They respond negatively to the questions, "Does God punish?" and "Does God intend that human beings punish one another?"

There are, of course, discreet differences among the faiths. It might be said that Judaism is exceptional for its sense of unity with God and for its anthropology; that Islam is exceptional for its sense of religious unity and social solidarity; and that Christianity is exceptional for its ethic of forgiveness and reconciliation.

There are differences among the faiths in regard to their understanding of law and in their view of the relationship between religion and civil authorities. Some of these are inherent distinctions, but most are developmental differences which can be attributed to historical and contextual factors, to misunderstandings, to deliberate misinterpretation by zealots, to varying interpretations by orthodox, non-orthodox, or mystic strains within each faith, or to the glossing and alteration of Scriptures by translators or exegetes (see Kara, 1980, p. 61; & Burton, 1977, pp. 72–78).

On the question of punishment, the opposing theologies found within each faith are of far greater significance than are the differences among the faiths. The division into theologies of restoration or retribution within each faith depend upon how the adherents of the religions—be they Jew or Christian or Muslim—think about God and about the nature of human beings. Rationales for a theology of retribution have been adopted within each of the three faiths by adopting one or more of the following courses:

1. Interpreting Scripture literally. When God is described anthropomorphically as being angry or as being a judge, the ensuing consequences of God's "wrath" are seen as punishment. Those who interpret Scripture literally also consider God's "words" to be inviolate.
2. Interpreting literally the "law" codes found in the Pentateuch; the legal material of the Qur'an; or selected verses such as Romans 13:1–7 in the New Testament which indicate that all persons should submit themselves to governing authorities.
3. Defining justice as a literal *lex talionis*, a "tit for tat," and failing to appreciate the theological or ethical implications of returning an "evil for an evil," also forgetting that the code of *lex talionis* set limits upon extraction of restitution or retribution.

4. Adopting a negative view of human nature. The account of "the Fall" in Genesis is frequently cited as the basis for such a view. Some of the ramifications of that view are an emphasis on sin; a belief that free-willing persons having moral capacity are totally responsible for their actions; and a belief that, when free-willing persons choose a wrong course, it is incumbent upon God's agent(s) to inflict punishment in order to dignify their humanity.
5. Advocating that the type of expiation or atonement once accomplished through religious rituals as a means of providing a catharsis for communities outraged by crimes, should now be accomplished through public guiltfindings and penal sanctions.

The adherents of a theology of retribution respond positively to the questions, "Does God punish?" and "Does God intend that human beings punish one another?" We have arrived in the 20th century, at a point where this theology is used to justify a punitively oriented "just deserts" concept of criminal law.

III. SUMMARY OF THE INFLUENCE OF RELIGION ON THE DEVELOPMENT OF WESTERN VIEWS OF PUNISHMENT

The way in which criminal law evolved was influenced by the degree of political power exercised by each of the three faiths. Judaism emerged as a theocracy but experienced so many periods of captivity and dispersion that it administered very few criminal laws. Islam emerged within Arabic nations with full political power but suffered prolonged periods of subjugation. Christianity emerged among a subjugated people and, even when in the course of history its power was aligned with crowns and empires, it for the most part preferred that secular authorities take the responsibility for administration of criminal penalties.

Originally there was no distinction between sin and crime. Of the two, for peoples attempting to become monotheistic, sins against God were considered the more severe. Gradually, certain acts became known as crimes, and while both sins and crimes were forbidden in God's law, the administration of sanctions for crimes took on a more secular orientation. Haim Cohn, a modern Israeli jurist, asserts that this change occurred when societies realized that perfection in the administration of God's law was unattainable (Cited in Cohn, 1971, pp. 7–12).[7]

---

[7] Cohn has written an extremely useful treatise on the anthropology of law. He says that there are two processes which have occurred in most societies. First, human law has been "divinized" in order to give it authority and to remove it from the realm of human frailities so that it may have a greater deterrent effect. This so-called "divine" law serves other purposes, as well. In answer to the perplexing questions of early religionists about why sinners often appeared to be "blessed with success" and about the difference in reward between "those who

Throughout history, more and more of the religious law which pertained to "sins" or "crimes" came under secular jurisdiction. Justifications of expiation, in combination with justifications of retaliation, restitution, retribution, and deterrence, were mixed into a cauldron of punishment. The original desire for atonement within a religious setting changed into a hard-and-fast conviction that it is necessary for the state to take strong action against deviant or violent behavior. We have seen how religious influences have transferred to the state the authority and the power to take such action.

The notion of "criminal" intent was present in Judaic and Islamic law: a person could not be adjudged guilty unless they had proceeded on their reckless course despite warnings. The notion of intent was much more highly developed, however, by the Roman church. Here, it is useful to recall Gerald Austin McHugh's contentions about the Christian influence: (1) prior to Christianity, criminal codes were largely objective in nature, focusing on the offense and the penalty rather than on the person. Christianity stressed the idea of personal morality; (2) the pagan "ordeal" was adopted as a means of determining guilt or innocence and it evolved into our adversarial trial method; (3) monastic prisons were developed; and (4) in the medieval period there was a marked decline in the Christian tradition of forebearance with offenders (McHugh, 1978, pp. 18–20).

Attitudes and penal codes become frozen at essentially the medieval level. We have not only adopted but have intensified the notion that lawbreakers are not members of the community who made a wrong decision, but that they are "wicked and depraved individuals, a threat to the common good." This attitude was, of course, the forerunner of the oft-noted Puritanical influence on criminal law and practices.

The medieval attitude has changed only to the extent that (1) religiously based theories of human rights and due process—particularly those developed in English common law—have ameliorated it; (2) forms of punishment have changed from sacral expiation, to bodily punishment, to monastic penitence, back to corporal punishment and then, with the advent of the Industrial Revolution, to the substitution of "doing time" for corporal punishment; and (3) religious or humanitarian reforms have from time to time been able to cause shifts in emphasis in penal codes and practices.

One of the major reasons behind our failure to modify our retributive notions is that we have mistakenly believed that the nature and extent of

---

actively comply with the law and those who only abstain from violating it," it was useful to be able to speak of inherited guilt and of deferred punishment by God.

The second process of secularization occurs both by default and by design. Secularization by default occurs, inevitably, when human frailties and dissension emerge as implementation and adaptation of law proceed. Secularization by design occurs when religiously based societies realize that divine law is impossible to administer perfectly and decide to transfer responsibility to authorities other than those who have divine status (kings) or ordained succession (*Jewish Law in Ancient and Modern Israel*, op. cit., pp. 7–12).

crime as we know it, and that the nature of penal practices, are directly comparable to biblical and medieval times. To refute that belief, we need to remember that the legal material and practices in Judaism, Christianity, and Islam were far more significant as religious exhortations than as criminal law. Punishments were the exception rather than the rule; great caution was urged in judging; forgiveness was viewed as a virtue; and strict procedures resulted in few sanctions. Further, the research of persons such as Bianchi, Cohn, Foucault, McHugh, and Rothman indicate that the historical situation was quite different from ours. Until the time of the Industrial Revolution, the crimes most often punished were those against God, the religious institution, or the king. Most of the acts which we now call crimes were handled through tribal councils, community arbitration, or civil courts.

Another little-understood influence of religious significance is the fact that we have lost the original meaning of many of the key words of our faiths. In so doing, we have lost their religious depth and their symbolic significance for the restoration which needs to occur when a community has been shaken by a crime. This survey has touched on form criticism— the context and genre in which Scriptures were written—but has barely dealt with textual criticism. In order to appreciate the richness, complexity, and subtleties of theology in the Hebrew Scripture, the New Testament, and in the Qur'an, it is necessary to engage in the study of key words. Word study is also a necessary and painstaking portion of building the case for a theology of restoration.

When traced in their original Hebrew, Aramaic, Greek, or Arabic, key words such as justice, peace, mercy, and even vengeance or wrath take on shadings and meanings which are different from their current English connotations. When that occurs, a picture of God's "enduring patience" and "will to save" replaces the picture of a capricious and vindictive God.

As an example, let us return to the notion found at the beginning of the Torah, the notion that God becomes angry. Obviously this is key to the question about whether God punishes. By using scriptural concordances and commentaries, we find that the Hebrew root words, (aph, anaph, naqam) frequently associated with "wrath," "anger," or "vengeance" are those implying "snorting" or "deep breathing." The writers of Scripture were story tellers who embellished their stories for the purpose of making their point. They wanted their readers to ask, "When did God become angry?," "What was God angry about?," and "What did God do?" The answer, according to the story tellers, was that God "breathed so forcibly" that human beings became aware of it. Thus, God had communicated the cause of the anger and the need to have the offending individuals or nations change behavior.

It is interesting, next, to look at the meaning of "avenging." One root word is *yasha*, "to give ease, safety"; another is *naqam*, "to breathe out."

Thus, God intervened and took saving action in order to ease the situation and once more to be able to "breathe easily."

What if God found that the offensive behavior was not ceased and that it became necessary to intervene? English translations frequently indicate that God punished offenders. There are several Hebrew root words for punishment and each is of great interest: *chasah* means to "keep back, restrain"; *yasar*, "to chasten, instruct, teach"; *amash*, "to fine"; *paqad*, "to inspect, look after"; and *naqam*, "to be punished," has the meaning of "to be avenged" which is cited in the previous paragraph. Punishment was associated with *chet*, "sin"; *challath*, "erring"; *avon*, "perversity"; and *tokechah*, the need for "reproof."

When this type of word study is undertaken, it unravels the seeming contradictions between what has been assumed to be language of judgment and punishment with a passage such as "God is slow to anger and abundant in lovingkindness" (Ex. 34:6, Num. 14:18).

An examination of Scriptures and traditions makes it obvious that the religious community in the United States has an urgent need to understand the nature of its influence on criminal law, and to understand and to interpret both the beneficial and the detrimental factors it has brought to bear. The religious community also has an urgent need to understand and to interpret for today the meaning of our religious language and symbols—to clarify when it is that we speak eschatologically, when we speak literally, when we use metaphor, and when we use overstatement as a homiletic device. Only through such understanding and interpretation will a theology of retribution be invalidated and a theology of restoration be given credibility.

IV. THE PROBLEM WITH PUNISHMENT

If anyone destroys a man it will be reckoned to him as if he had destroyed a whole world. And if anyone preserves a man's life, it will be reckoned to him as if he had preserved a whole world. (*Mishnah Sanhedrin 4:5*)

No one man, and no human community, has sway over the human conscience or the right to judge it. Punishment is more than the exercise of control and authority of one man over another; it is an attempt to invade the human conscience, to exercise judgment upon personality, and, in virtue of this judgment of a man's conscience, to dispose of his life and liberty. In this sense man has no judge but God. So the ecclesiastical law holds. (Saleilles, 1913, p. 38)

The right to punish for God alone is meant. We dare not punish, only future woe prevent. (Haracourt, quoted in Saleilles, 1913, p. 38)

The deliberate infliction of a painful consequence raises serious question for a religious community which is motivated by love and trust. The validity of punishment as a means of achieving positive behavioral change is challenged, then, by the very definition of punishment.

Even though the legal basis for a decision to punish is "presumably an expression of the good or just decision (cited in Flew, 1979), the motivation of the punisher is immediately brought into question. How is it possible to impose pain for someone's benefit? Is it not apparent that "the idea of retribution and respect for life are in contradiction?" (Honecker, cited in Bockle & Pohier, 1979, p. 60). If we assume that the infliction of pain is indeed contrary to the interests of the offender, then does it not follow that punishment is administered for the sake of meeting vicarious or ulterior motives of the punishers?

The vicarious or ulterior aspect of punishment can take the form of the sheer exercise of power. It can use the individual offender as a means of accomplishing the end of keeping the rest of society lawful or moral. It can take the form of retribution, in which case the offender is punished as a means of expressing the outrage and alleviating the anger of the victim or the community. In any case, it is necessary to question whether this is healthy for anyone—for the victim, the offender, or the community. An insight by Gabriel Marcel pertains to this point:

[B]efore human beings can bring themselves to participate in, or approve of, destructive actions against others, it is first necessary for them to lose sight in their own minds of the very humanity of the people who will suffer as a consequence. (Cited in McHugh, 1978, p. 151)

When human beings lose sight of the humanity of other persons and inflict pain upon them, then the "sin" or the "crime" is compounded. Powerful arguments have been and need to be made against punishment and retribution. Mustafa Kara argues that "the willing of an evil to correct another evil. . . is no justification at all." Further, he says:

To punish them for the sake of deterring others—besides being immoral—is a fallacy according to existing reality which can be proven empirically. The retributive position, since it does not rest upon any principles of crime prevention but is based upon vague notions of blameworthiness, morality, and responsibility, ought to be rejected as a principle of justification.[8] (cited in Kara, 1980, pp. 210, 237)

The U.S. Catholic Conference made a similar argument in a 1973 statement, saying, "It is necessary in any case to raise serious moral objection to

---

[8] Kara, op. cit., pp. 210, 237. It should be noted that Kara acknowledges the justification of specific deterrence, sanctions designed to elicit the offender's confession of error, reformation, and behavior change.

tormenting one man unjustly in order to instruct or caution another" (U.S. Catholic Conference, 1978, p. 33).

Gerald Austin McHugh finds retribution theory problematic because, in the final analysis, it is built upon "the concept of desert." "Unless," says McHugh, "it is valid to think in terms of rewarding or punishing human beings on the basis of what they deserve, retribution theory is baseless" (Cited in McHugh, 1978, p. 101).

From a religious perspective, one immediate fallacy of "desert" is that if the "bad" (the "others") deserve punishment, then the opposite side of that equation would indicate that the "good" (the "we") deserve only the best. That sort of reasoning violates our most fundamental notions about God and creation. Scripture tells us that God provides out of love, not out of a duty to reward or punish. It tells us also that the greatest human failing is *hubris* (pride), a puffing up of our own virtues in comparison to the frailities of others. The concept of desert violates the concern for community and interdependence spelled out in Judaism, Christianity, and Islam. It is explicitly rejected in the New Testament in the parable of the laborers in the vineyard (Matt. 20:1-16) and in Jesus' chastising of those who would seek reward for their actions (Matt. 5:46).

Thus the notion of desert is challenged on the basis of its excessive individualism. "The idea of desert," McHugh says, "flourishes in a society where individuals are considered separate entities in competition with one another." He also criticizes the concept of desert for its flawed psychology. When desert is used to the end of deterrence, it "posits no requirements that any personality change or transformation of character occur"; it is ultimately "based on a pleasure/pain model of human behavior"; and it is a theory which "holds that human beings respond best to coercive means" (McHugh, 1978, pp. 104–109).

The use of coercion can perpetuate the cycle of violence. It can reinforce withdrawn or suicidal behavior, perpetuating the offender's self-image of being worthless or of being a "proverbial victim of circumstances." It can escalate feelings of alienation or rage and result in further lawbreaking or lashing out at society or individuals. From the standpoint of our knowledge about human behavior, punishment can be challenged because it does not model the behavior it wishes to induce.

In the arena of criminal law, we are beginning to understand the extent to which we reap what we sow in our approaches to human behavior. The revelations of J. Gordon Liddy, a major Watergate figure, are an example. "My first memory is of absolute, overwhelming fear," reported Liddy. The fear he described was occasioned by the figure of his paternal grandmother standing over him, beating him and saying, "Bad, Bad!" The fear did not subside for Liddy during his childhood. The source of fear was transferred from family figures to monstrous fabrications of childhood terror and was finally projected outward into behavior so stunted and cynical that a guard in the prison where Liddy was held once exclaimed, "It's true what they say. You are a fascist" (*Time Magazine*, 1980).

We are becoming aware, also, of the high correlation between child abuse and later imprisonment of the victims of that abuse for crimes of violence; of the punitive family and juvenile justice backgrounds of some of the most highly publicized crime figures of our nation, including Charles Manson, Richard Speck, and Gary Gilmore. When these correlations are understood, it suggests that punishment is counterproductive as well as morally questionable and inhumane.

Psychological insights tell us that, while outward compliance and control may be attained by punishment, the ability to trust will be damaged or destroyed. Individuals can learn from widely varying stimuli—negative as well as positive—but the negatives which are internalized will inevitably manifest themselves in some form of problematic future behavior.

Punishment can be challenged on extremely pragmatic terms. It is expensive in both human and fiscal terms. The approximate annual cost of operating our criminal justice system is currently 30 billion. Imprisonment is an astronomically expensive form of punishment. Punishment represents poor stewardship of our nation's resources when more effective, more humane, and less costly alternatives exist or could be created.

Even if punishment were justified as a deterrent, it is problematic because of its inherently escalatory nature. "If a mild punishment does not achieve the desired results, the temptation is powerful to go on to a harsher punishment," contend the authors of *Instead of Prisons*. A quote from Richard Korn reinforces their point: "In order to remain effective, punishment must continually become more severe" (Knopp et al., 1976, pp. 51, 58). A question then arises about when "to stop turning the screw." Capital punishment is, of course, the final "turn of the screw" and one which our nation is again utilizing in its "war against crime." The practice of execution must be questioned on religious and moral grounds, and also in terms of its potential for error in taking the life of an innocent person and its potential for escalating the climate of violence when it imposes death.

The case against punishment is a compelling one. Yet we continue to rely on it as a cornerstone of our criminal justice policies. On the one hand, we do so out of inertia, out of fear, and out of the frustration of not knowing of or believing in a "better way." On the other hand, the history of the interaction of religion and law suggests that we rely on punishment because too many people mistakenly believe that God "says" that we should punish.

The first, and the final, challenges to punishment should be on religious grounds. The rationale we build in the case against punishment and in the case for restoration and reconciliation will come only out of the prayerful probing by the people of faith—prayerful probing into their Scripture, their tradition, their personal intuitions and convictions and, last but not least, the guidance of the Spirit. Our "facts" must fit together consistently.

We can begin with the understanding that the Scriptures of Judaism, Christianity, and Islam say that love, forgiveness, and reconciliation are greater needs than are punishment and retribution. As human beings, we can affirm that we are physical/psychic/social/spiritual entities; that we have a deep need to forgive and to be forgiven when conflict occurs; and that atonement cannot occur at only one level. A wholistic response is called for as an alternative to the pain-inducing, alienating dynamic of punishment.

The theology of a people invariably influences the structures which emerge to cope with situations of conflict. Too often, the shapers of theology are unaware of that influence and, hence, of their own responsibility. Under such conditions, their silence lends theological justification to prevailing practices. We must now raise to a conscious level the discrepancies which exist between our tenets of faith—including love, inclusivity, interdependence, and forgiveness—and the systems of punishment which have developed and are being expanded in the United States.

V. TOWARDS A NEW PARADIGM:
A THEOLOGY OF RESTORATION

This study of punishment has been undertaken because of deep dissatisfaction with our current situation. Because of the complicity of the religious community in the emergence of "the American way of punishment," it is time to make a call for repentance—a "turning around"—and a challenge to work for a new paradigm of restoration.

Conflicting religious claims have so complicated the issue of justice, and so intimidated both believers and non-believers, that it is incumbent upon the religious community to reinterpret scriptural values for a world grown tired of the cycle of violence and vengeance. Mohammed Arkoun of the Sorbonne argues that abolition of the death penalty and torture depend on the good will of leaders. "If they have the necessary intellectual development, the right religious convictions, and good political aims," he says, then humanitarian reforms can occur. (Arkoun, cited in Thomas, 1979, p. 81). This represents a challenge to the people of faith to infuse our nation's leadership with "the right religious convictions." But it first challenges those people of faith to construct a clear theology and to build alternatives to the punishment paradigm.

Developing an emerging "orthopraxy"—which involves a dialectic between doctrine, faith, and action—could show the religious community those paths which have the greatest likelihood of resolving disputes, preventing victimization, restoring offenders, and building faithful communities and nations. "Orthopraxy," suggests Clemens Thoma of the Lucerne Theological Faculty, "has a higher status than orthodoxy (Thoma, cited in Bockle & Pohier, 1979, p. 70). The law, if we define it as God's will and purpose, is *to be done.*

There are four platforms which could be constructed through a process of interfaith dialog and action to form the foundation for a theology of restoration:

1. A shared theology. Each of our three faiths affirms that God is good. What does that affirmation mean for us? In Matthew, Jesus indicated that God is ultimately dependable and worthy of trust:

> Ask, and it will be given to you; search, and you will find; knock, and the door will be opened to you. For the one who asks always receives; the one who searches always finds; the one who knocks will always have the door opened to him. Is there a man among you who would hand his son a stone when he asked for bread? Or would hand him a snake when he asked for a fish? If you, then, who are evil, know how to give your children what is good, how much more will your Father in heaven give good things to those who ask him!
>
> So always treat others as you would like them to treat you; that is the meaning of the Law and the Prophets. (*Matt 7:7-12—Jerusalem Bible*)

Frederick Douglass was acting on such an affirmation when he decided that "God is good and that God knows what is best for everyone (see p. 149). The founders of Judaism, of Christianity, and of Islam were acting on such affirmations.

Some bold reaffirmations on the part of the religious community might restore a sense of congruence between God's law and modern legal practices.

2. A shared theological anthropology. The term "theological anthropology" is recommended as an alternative to the traditional term "doctrine of humanity" for two reasons. First, it is meant to convey that all human beings come from and should be oriented toward God, and secondly, it is intended to encompass all of the psychological and sociological dimensions of human existence.

Each of our faiths proclaims that human beings are created in the image of God, and each of our Scriptures contains anthropocentric ideals and concerns. Wolfhart Pannenberg, a German theologian, advocates what he terms a general anthropology of law:

> Through the quest for the meaning of man's humanity, law—as the existing form of human society—is connected to the idea of God.

... What man is has never been decided in the sense of a fixed concept of his nature.... He has to produce himself. (Cited in Pannenberg, 1973, p. 408)

Thus, for law to be relevant, it cannot be deduced from fundamental principles; rather, it must emerge from a coherent view of human nature and from shared experience—a sort of orthopraxy. If human beings are convinced of their own dignity and worth, then they will try to "produce themselves" as non-violent, nurturing persons who do not harm others. When crime or violence does occur, they will find ways to support victims. They will find ways to both confront and support offenders. They will act as forgiving beings who see even the wrongdoer as a brother or sister. They will refuse to permit some humans to become instruments of the state for purposes of general deterrence against crime. They will refuse to selectively punish persons in order to maintain the social and economic inequities of the status quo. They will call forth and develop their instincts for loving/ saving action, attempting to model the biblical conception of justice— making right, building peace, and achieving *shalom*.

3. A shared definition of ethical natural consequence, of individual and societal responsibilities, and of mutual dependence within community. Perhaps the most helpful way to extricate ourselves from the traditional thicket of "sin" language is to adopt a term used by David Funk of the Law and Religion Section of the Association of American Law Schools. His term, "ethical natural consequence," (Funk, 1979, p. 16) recalls to mind the cycle of estrangement and consequence (the cycle of sin and judgment) depicted in each of our Scriptures. In the course of our interfaith dialog, we can transfer the implications of that cycle to crime—a particular form of estrangement—and to the modern experience of consequence.

Most Americans do not have a strong sense of consequence. They do not view the problem of crime in its social context, nor do they examine the socio-economic genesis of most so-called criminal activity. McHugh's warning bears repeating here:

Failure to recognize the truth of prisoners' claims of oppression, that, in a tragically real sense society is an enemy to them, will only lead us to persist in erroneously thinking that we can reasonably demand justice from individual lawbreakers while tolerating injustice on the part of the community as a whole. (see p. 149)

Only as we set aside notions of desert, as we are fully cognizant of our corporate responsibilities, and as we respond to problems in their total context, will we demonstrate that we understand the meaning of ethical natural consequence, of individual responsibility, and of mutual dependence within community. Far more important than what God "says" about punishment, after all, is what God "says" about *justice*—in its individual and social/economic manifestations, and its preventive and reconciling aspects.

4. A shared methodology of restoration. Punishment is unacceptable, we have said, because it is retroactively applied, it is inherently escalatory, and it deliberately inflicts pain upon a human being.

As an alternative to punishment, we are looking for a restorative methodology which actively involves and engages the will and value system of the individual offender. The reason that *hadd* crimes are left to God's jurisdiction, says Kara, is that genuine reform occurs only when the errant individual has voluntarily confessed and decided to make a change in behavior (cited in Kara, 1980, p. 216). The models of Judaic and Islamic arbitration and of Jesus' intervention worked toward the same end.

Except where healing or pure restraint in the interests of personal safety are required, integration of self and resocialization should be the goals of actions taken toward offenders. These goals need not be cast in the language of "salvation" or in any religious terminology. The psychological/behavioral and religious ends are the same. We are looking for a restorative approach which helps us break out of the so-called "doing good" dilemma—the present mindset which understands our only alternatives as those of punishment or treatment.

John Hogarth, who participated in a 1973 Canadian Law Reform Commission, described as an alternative a socio/educative model which is characterized by the widest possible participation and by openness of communication and trust between the persons participating in conflict resolution (Hogarth, 1974, p. 78).

Herman Bianchi, of Holland, incorporates the methodology of dispute resolution into what he calls "the *assensus* model." He maintains that it is the responsibility of the community to "equalize the overwhelming imbalance of litigating parties and overcome the negative effects of professionalism" so that disputing parties can define a contract to which they can assent. Bianchi elaborates:

> Crime control has to be "communitized." Most crimes are problems between an actor and a victim within their community. Most crimes of aggression are committed between persons living in the same community. It is, therefore, a problem that has to be coped with by all the members involved and not by profesionals who are in fact outsiders. (Cited in Bianchi, 1973, p. 4)

Even in the case of severe injury or homicide, Bianchi believes that it is the responsibility of the community to help victims and their families to realize both the futility and the counterproductiveness of retribution. It is a special responsibility of the religious community, he contends. It is his hope that every mosque, temple, and church will open their doors to offenders and provide sanctuary during the time that the offender negotiates with his or her own victim, and with the community, about the terms under which he or she could be integrated back into community life (Bianchi, 1978).

Harold DeWolf formulates these concerns into what he calls "social defense:"

> Criminal justice ought to be designed to protect a community of persons freely seeking fulfillment of their compatible interests against disruption by its own members, and after disruptions nevertheless occur, to restore such community with special concern for the persons most deeply affected. (Cited in DeWolf, 1975, pp. 172–173)

This deep conviction about the nature and spirit of justice has been shared recently by two bereaved persons. The first expression is from an article written by Rabbi Judea B. Miller after a beloved aunt had been murdered:

> If gentle old people like Tanta Yetta are ever to be safe, we must all somehow learn the more to cherish life, as she did. We must learn and teach the preciousness and beauty of a human life to a humanity that has forgotten.
>
> If we use the atrocity of Tanta Yetta's murder to persuade society once again to execute criminals—this would be to give her pious life the ultimate indignity (Miller, 1980).

The second, which was written by the son of a murder victim, appeared on a poster entitled "Killing Him Would Not Be Right:"

> If my father taught me anything about life, it is that God gives life and only He has the right to take it away. The God that I came to know, through my father, was one of love and mercy. . . not one of vengeance. We suffered as a family when he died. But we have found it in ourselves to feel compassion for this young man and we ask you to do the same. Killing him, to us, simply would not be right. (Riley quoted on a Fellowship of Reconciliation Poster, 1979)

These anguished statements bring us full circle to Frederick Douglass' conviction that "God is good and that God knows what is best for everybody." It brings the religious community full circle to accept the challenge to evolve a theology of restoration for today. Harmony, justice, and peace cannot be imposed. They can exist only when there is integrity in the individual relationships and structural dimensions of our communities and nation.

APPENDIX A. REPRESENTATIVE POLICY STATEMENTS ON CRIMINAL JUSTICE

1. Judaism

The 45th Biennial General Assembly of the Union of American Hebrew Congregations in their resolution on capital punishment in 1959 stated:

> We believe it to be the task of the Jew to bring our great spiritual and ethical heritage to bear upon the moral problems of contemporary society. One such problem, which challenges all who seek to apply God's will in the affairs of men, is the practice of capital punishment. We believe that in the light of modern scientific knowledge and concepts of humanity, the resort to or continuation of capital punishment either by a state or by the national government is no longer morally justifiable.

> We believe there is no crime for which the taking of human life by society is justified, and that it is the obligation of society to evolve other methods in dealing with crime. We pledge ourselves to join with like-minded Americans in trying to prevent crimes by removal of their causes and to foster modern methods of rehabilitation of the wrongdoer in the spirit of the Jewish tradition of *tshuva* (repentance).

> We believe, further, that the practice of capital punishment serves no practical purpose. Experience in several states and nations had demonstrated that capital punishment is not effective as a deterrent to crime. Moreover, we believe that this practice debases our entire penal system and brutalizes the human spirit.

> We appeal to our congregants and to our co-religionists, and to all who cherish God's mercy and love, to join in efforts to eliminate this practice which lies as a stain upon civilization and our religious conscience.

The Board of Trustees of the Union of American Hebrew Congregations adopted a statement on crime in 1968 which opted for alternatives to prison and reform of the criminal justice system. It was based on the philosophy described here:

> Crime must be brought under control within the framework of a free and moral society, operating under the rule of law. We reaffirm the biblical concept that the criminal is a human being, capable of reshaping his life. "I have no pleasure in the death of the wicked, but that the wicked turn from his way and live." (Ezek. 33:11) Rather than inflicting increasingly harsh punishment and curtailing civil liberties we should treat the causes of crime and disorder

and reject proposals which ignore those causes by emphasis upon vengeful or unconstitutional means.

2. *Christianity*

In recent years a number of denominations have issued statements on criminal justice. The following survey does not purport to be exhaustive but highlights pronouncements of readily available policy statements.

Roman Catholic.   The New York State Catholic Conference "Statement on Criminal Justice" in 1975 discussed proper Christian response to crime, saying that the Gospels clearly teach we should forgive injuries and seek reconciliation (Matt. 18:21–22 and Matt. 5:38–44). They further elaborated that:

> Within the realm of the virtue of justice, where an offender can repay or restore what has been wrongfully taken from another, there is an obligation of so doing. Where there is no proper source of restoration, there exists no authority or justification for the taking of in-kind retribution in terms of wrong for wrong, hurt for hurt. When the administration of criminal justice becomes a system solely of retaliation, there is no longer true Christian justice. The administration of criminal justice in our society should be characterized by forgiveness, reconciliation, rehabilitation and renewal.

> The word "punishment" admits of a variety of concepts. Its real meaning becomes apparent when we look at (1) the motive for "punishing" and (2) what it hopes to effect. If the motive is solely retaliation or self-satisfaction for something suffered, it is non-Christian. The purpose of punishment is to correct, to expiate, to educate, to restore, to reconcile and to renew. Its validity becomes dependent upon the effectiveness of the mode chosen. At times it also becomes necessary to restrain the offender because of evident danger of harm to self or others. It is again the mode and the proposed effectiveness which shall determine whether it is just or unjust.

These views were expressed nationally by the U.S. Catholic Conference in their statements, "The Reform of Correctional Institutions in the 1970's" (1973) and "Community and Crime (1978). From the 1973 statement:

> Christian belief in the potential goodness of man and recognition of every human being's dignity as a child of God redeemed by Jesus Christ cause us to recoil from any form of punishment which is degrading or otherwise corrodes the human personality. Abuses cannot be justified on the basis of their effectiveness as deterrents to crime. It is necessary to raise serious moral objection to tormenting one man unjustly in order to instruct or caution another.

From the 1978 statement:

We should seek to express to the offender disapproval of his or her criminal behavior together with a strong willingness to accept that individual's reintegration into society as a contributing member. Having communicated our disapproval of criminal behavior, it behooves us to be willing to greet this ex-offender in the spirit of reconciliation and forgiveness of our Lord.

We do not challenge society's right to punish the serious and violent offender. We have to seek methods of dealing with violent crimes which are more consistent with the Gospel's vision of respect for life and Christ's message of God's healing love. Correction of the offender has to take preference over punishment, for the Lord came to save and not to condemn.

In efforts to reduce and prevent crimes, believers have to strive to exemplify the attitudes of Christ our Lord, who loved His enemies, who forgave those who persecuted and executed Him and who taught that love and forgiveness are the only forces that can overcome evil and hatred.

The factors that contribute to crime are intensified where family and community life are weakened and personal responsibility lessened. These factors include: economic and social deprivation, toleration of injustice and discrimination, false values of materialism and greed, lack of respect for one another, loss of personal responsibility for one's actions and moral choices, failing to love one's neighbors, and toleration and condoning of organized and white collar crime by some officials and citizens. Any effective response to crime ought to focus on improving our community life, on strengthening our families and neighborhoods, on rooting out economic deprivation and social injustice, and on teaching basic values of personal responsibility, human dignity and decency.

As Christians, we have a particular responsibility to see that the message communicated to the offender and to the community reflects Christian principles, including the rights to life and human dignity, responsibility to protect the right of all persons; mercy and compassion for those less fortunate; forgiveness of those who offend and harm us; and the openness of a loving and healing community.

Quaker (Society of Friends). In 1976 in New York, a revision of the section on response to crime in *Faith and Practice* was adopted by the Yearly Meeting. The revision advocated abolition of prisons, acknowledging the necessity of restraining the dangerous few in an humane environment:

Friends are becoming increasingly clear that prisons are a destructive and expensive failure as a response to crime. The prison system is both the cause and result of violence and social injustice, and serves the powerful as an instrument of social controls of the powerless. We are increasingly clear that the caging of human beings, like their enslavement, is inherently immoral and is as destructive to the cagers as to the caged. Friends are therefore turning from concern for reforming prisons, to a concern for their virtual abolition, and for their replacement with new, non-punitive and humanly creative responses to crime.

The great challenge that lies before us is to find and develop these new alternatives, based on economic and social justice, on empowerment of the human spirit, and on fulfillment of the human needs of all the people.

Friends need to foster awareness about the true issues of criminal justice. There is a need to expose the roots of violence and injustice in our society; to trace the social connections between the uses of power and the persistence of exploitation, racism, sexism, war and prisons; to heal the social and personal traumas inflicted by these conditions, and to build a nurturing, caring community that will take away the occasion for crime.

In *Struggle for Justice*, a book written in 1971 by a working party of Quakers, law and punishment were examined.

Law should deal only with a narrow aspect of the individual, that is, his criminal act or acts. The law should be applied uniformly to all offenders. Criminal sanctions should be imposed only when other remedies have proved inadequate. Alternatives and adjuncts to penal sanctions should be truly voluntary and available to all.

The imposition of punishment is superior to doing nothing when either there is strong reason to believe that the behavior in question is capable of being deterred or when the norm is one where non-compliance is generally felt to be so serious that doing nothing will be unacceptable to individuals or groups in society.

Lutheran. The Board of Social Ministry of the Lutheran Church in America prepared a study guide, "Reform of the Criminal Justice Systems in the United States and Canada," in 1972. They advocated distinguishing between "sin" and "crime" by decriminalizing victimless acts. Believing perversion of justice to be the most profound threat to the entire system of law and government, the study asked that the church support all attempts to see that the rights of the weak, the poor, the widow, and the fatherless were not trampled by the forces of law and order. They described the function of the criminal system:

For Christians, criminal justice systems are one manifestation of God's law in its political function contributing to the preservation of human life and liberty in spite of the destructive and enslaving effects of sin. Such a system must: (1) identify and apprehend those who are accused of violating laws duly enacted by the body politic's chosen representatives according to a rational and equitable system of justice based on the rights of all men to life, liberty and the pursuit of happiness; (2) prosecute on behalf of the state and guarantee of adequate defense for those charged with criminal activities; (3) implement sanctions against convicted criminals, such as fines, suspended sentences, compensation to victims, probation, imprisonment and parole.

Because of their responsibility for the weak and defenseless given to them by the Lord, Christians must take special interest in the protection and rehabilitation of alleged and convicted offenders. The Christian Church and each individual Christian should make every effort to maintain the bonds of common humanity with alleged and convicted offenders.

Believing in a Lord who has ruled out vengeance as a proper human motive for action, Christians will use their influence to restrict the objectives of the criminal justice system to the protection of "all members of society from seriously harmful and dangerous conduct."

We punish to correct. If certain types of punishment do not correct, they ought to be abandoned.

Victims of crimes against property should be reimbursed up to a reasonable maximum as an expression of interdependence of all citizens. This New Testament exhortation to share one another's burdens should be applied by distributing the real cost of crime more equitably among all citizens.

The Sixth Biennial Convention of the Lutheran Church in America in 1972 adopted a social statement entitled "In Pursuit of Justice and Dignity: Society, the Offender and the Systems of Correction." While decrying the growing incidence of lawlessness and unchecked criminal behavior, the statement also discusses the counterproductiveness and unfairness of the criminal justice system. Following are some excerpts from the statement:

The popular assumption that confinement is normally the most appropriate penalty for criminal behavior has proven itself fallacious. The socially destructive results of "warehousing" offenders are compounded by the fact that a disproportionate number of persons so confined are young, poor and members of minority groups. Thus, in addition to reinforcing alienation and lawlessless in individual inmates, confinement facilities contribute to the widening of dangerous cleavages within the general society.

For society to seek increased security and order by means of a larger and more efficient prison system is for it to sow the seeds of its own destruction.

It needs to be clearly said that in North American society it is the poor who bear the brunt of society's ire toward the lawless. Organized and "white collar" crime have the poor as their chief victims. Yet the persons who commit such crimes often escape the hardship borne by the poor offender.

Distinctions among persons are relative, provisional, and subject to divine judgment. Distinctions between groups should be made only for purposes of social utility and well-being. Particularly demonic is the inclination of societies to treat those whom it has defined as criminals as altogether alien to the human community and deserving, therefore, of total separation from normal social life.

A social system which defines crime is itself capable of criminality. A society may be as much in need of correction as the individuals who deviate from its norms.

The task of civil institutions which relate to criminal justice is to facilitate the socialization of offenders in such a way as to preserve their dignity and the safety of the general community as well.

Presbyterian.   Abolition of prisons as they now exist was the stated goal of the 184th General Assembly (1972) of the United Presbyterian Church U.S.A. in its statement, "Justice and the Imprisoned." This calls for a shift from "philosophies [of correction] that espouse custodial or rehabilitation systems. . . concerned principally with personality change and the reform of the individual offender, to a nonpunitive philosophy that recognizes social responsibility both on the part of society and the offender and which is oriented toward cooperative efforts with prisoners and ex-prisoners to remove barriers to full participation in community." The theological reasons are presented:

Jesus came so that all persons might have life and have it more abundantly. God acts to make human life more human and this includes those which society calls deviates and criminals. Rehabilitation, then, is God's goal for all life. Criminals and non-criminals stand in need of renewal and fulfillment.

Respect for the dignity of this human personality must become a major consideration for all persons in the society. Dignity proceeds not alone from respect given by others but more importantly from the right of determination of the self, engagement in creative labor and wholesome interaction with others. Recreation and rehabilitation require, for the criminal and non-criminal, life in a community that is both democratic and free. For the captive this means that rehabilitation should take place outside the walls of prison.

"Vengeance is mine, says the Lord." Human wrongs, therefore, should not be treated in a manner that further dehumanizes society or individuals. Persons must be held accountable for their acts, but acts productive of harm should not be followed by more harmful acts. The Christian must seek always to overcome evil with love. The reintegration of persons into community takes precedence over the deterring of persons from evil; the persuasion of persons to do good is prior to making them pay for the injury done to others; this law of love is the criterion for justice and not the fears and prejudices of anxious persons.

The Policy Committee of the Synod of the Northeast (Presbyterian) passed a resolution in February 1980 that resolved among other things to:

1. seriously address the societal conditions that send young people of racial and ethnic origin to prison in record numbers far exceeding their share of the total population and
2. recognize our call from God to encourage the building of safe, restorative, caring communities in which victim, victimizer, and community members may learn the power of forgiveness, healing and oneness in God.

In "The Church Speaks: Capital Punishment," published by the Presbyterian Church U.S., the following question-answer was given:

Q. Isn't rehabilitation opposed to justice? Isn't it dangerous and unrealistic?
A. Opposed to retributive justice, yes, but redemptive justice, no. And it is about as dangerous and unrealistic as forgiveness. Rehabilitation in the Christian sense is the detailed process in human life of God's redemption. It is based on the premise that no person is totally incorrigible or irredeemable.

Baptist.   The 1971 American Baptist Convention Resolutions on Penology listed areas needing reform and recommended actions based on the biblical perspective given below.

The Old and New Testaments perceive that love and justice are deeply intertwined. Love becomes a God-initiated motivation to care for every other person—relative, friend, neighbor, stranger, enemy. Social justice is love working to institutionalize or structure relations where, in conflict situations, everyone can be treated as equitably as possible in light of his needs and abilities.

The present criminal justice system focuses upon punishment rather than rehabilitation. In both detention and correction/punishment/rehabilitation the emphasis is upon separating the prisoner from the rest of the community. Then at the end of the period of detention or imprisonment, there is a problem of reintegrating the person into the community, a problem which has in large measure been created by the very way in which society has chosen to view and treat him. The only just purpose of pretrial detention and the primary purpose for confinement in a penal institution is the holding of those persons who are a danger to themselves or others.

Episcopal[9].   The Episcopal Church in the 1969 General Convention urged the elimination of inhuman prison conditions and the replacement of the attitude of punishment with that of rehabilitation. They also urged use of all available resources of influence and manpower to bring about drastic revision and reform of Federal, state and local penal systems. Reform, not alternatives, was the focus.

---

[9] It should be noted that both the Baptist and Episcopal resolutions were passed before the 1971 tragedy at Attica focused the nations's attention on the destructiveness of prisons.

Union Methodist. The resolution, "Ministries in Crime Prevention, Criminal Justice and Conflict Resolution" adopted by the United Methodist Church in 1976 recommended alternatives to prison. It gave these reasons:

> The Church, especially, with its mandate to love and its commission to share redemption, must point to those just changes that must be made in the society and individuals and which would serve in the real prevention of crime.

> Since incarceration is by its very nature dehumanizing and destructive, The United Methodist Church states its belief that every responsible means should be used to reduce the present jail population and to use methods such as release on recognizance, bail, diversion, fines, restitution, social service sentences and probation to keep people out of jail.

Unitarian. The General Assembly of the Unitarian Universalist Association in 1974, noting that the present court and penal systems damaged personalities and wholesome human values, and that the Assembly "affirms, defends and promotes the supreme worth of every human personality," and "wishes to give every individual a chance for fulfillment," resolved that jail and prison populations be reduced through provisions for community-based correctional programs and other alternatives to incarceration. They also recommended a moratorium on prison construction and decriminalization of victimless crimes.

Mennonite. In establishing the Offenders Ministries Program, the Mennonite Central Committee also recommended a new response to crime.

> We must encourage alternative responses to crime which heal rather than those such as prisons which repeatedly have been demonstrated to be ineffective in preventing crime and to be damaging to persons. And we must also recognize that the problem of crime is closely connected to injustice within society as a whole.

> In the biblical view, crime involves ruptured relationships between persons and this requires reparation and reconciliation. The Bible stresses a nonjudgmental attitude and unconditional love—acceptance replaces rejection, forgiveness is substituted for vengeance and reconciliation takes the place of condemnation.

Mormon. Joseph Smith, founder of the Mormons, in his "Views of the Powers and Policy of the Government of the United States" (1844) advocated restitution in the form of community service:

> Petition your State Legislatures to pardon every convict in their several penitentiaries, blessing them as they go, and saying to them, in the name of the Lord, "Go thy way and sin no more."

Advise your legislators, when they make laws for larceny, burglary or any felony, to make the penalty applicable to work upon roads, public works or any place where the culprit can be taught more wisdom and more virtue and become more enlightened. Rigor and seclusion will never do as much to reform the propensities of men as reason and friendship. Murder only can claim confinement or death. Let the penitentiaries be turned into seminaries of learning, where intelligence, like the angels of heaven, will banish such fragments of barbarism. *Amor vincit omnia.*

National Council of Churches.   Statements of the National Council of Churches of Christ include a Human Rights resolution of 1963 which maintained that:

Christians believe that man is made in the image of God, that every person is of intrinsic worth before God, and that every individual has a right to the fullest possible opportunities for the development of life abundant and eternal. Denial of rights and freedoms that inhere in man's worth before God are not simply a crime against humanity, they are a sin against God.

A 1967 resolution on "Crime Control and Public Morality" dealt mainly with seeing that the poor and oppressed were given all the rights afforded the affluent. Churches were urged to aid in offender rehabilitation by establishment of halfway houses and by acceptance of offenders into the Christian community.

The 1972 resolution on "Jails, Prisons and Courts" cited many miscarriages of justice and urged:

Member churches and local congregations to support the development of a wholly different philosophy and policy in court and correctional procedures: one that would have as its goal rehabilitation rather than punishment; and one that would eliminate or reduce the time of incarceration from large numbers of offenders through the institution of a variety of community-based treatment programs.

The NCCC Governing Board adopted its first policy statement on criminal justice, "Challenges to the Injustice of the Criminal Justice System: A Christian Call to Responsibility" in late 1979. It specifically addressed the needs of people subjected to the criminal justice system. It outlined the task of redirecting them back into community life with the least amount of harm done to them, their families, and society itself.

The statement reflected on the meaning of justice and concluded that biblically, justice/righteousness is the structural norm in the convenant of love that creates community. It is the substance of a community which finds its proper human shape in the biblical *shalom*, energizing and harmonious peace. It then follows that:

The laws of any society—the requirements it defines for the behavior of its members—must reflect its commitment to justice among all its members. In short, the function of law is to promote and protect the condition of *shalom*. To the extent that it does not do so, but instead reflects the interests and privileges of the powerful, law itself is unjust and the "criminal justice system" is poisoned at its source.

This understanding of justice is also a key to a theological understanding of the social categories of "crime," "offender," and "punishment." All human societies have to deal with the behavior of individuals and institutions that violate the just laws of the community. Such behavior in the theological context noted tears the fabric of justice; that is, it disturbs the *condition* of justice/righteousness intended to characterize life. When this occurs, action must be taken. Theologically understood, the motive and purpose of such action is *not* "punishment of the offender" but the *repair* of the damage done to the fabric of justice/righteousness and the *restoration* of the condition of shalom.

Christians believe justice is achieved through restitution and not retribution.

Greek Orthodox. The Greek Orthodox Church issued in 1976 a paper on Contemporary Issues by "Extastes," Stanley S. Harakas. It enumerates differing perspectives within the Orthodox Church on the issues of jails, punishment, prison reform, and capital punishment. Harakas acknowledges that a first perspective favors "swift, predictable punishment for every offender; a second sees reform of the criminal as the task of the penal system," and each finds support for their position within the Christian faith.

Harakas holds that "crime must be punished, if only to maintain public order and to restrain criminal activity. But it also clearly seeks the return of the criminal to a good, law-abiding life; he maintains that the criminal justice system is in need of extensive reform, and that while "the Greek Orthodox archdiocese was correct in joining with other Christians to urge the abolishment of capital punishment," the archdiocese and all Christians should couple that act with "strong efforts in the direction of prison reform."

APPENDIX B. RESPONSES TO THE PAPER

1. Rabbi Allen I. Freehling
(University Synagogue, Los Angeles, California)

In advance of this consultation, a few of us were given an opportunity to read Virginia Mackey's paper. She has researched her subject with great skill, written her thesis with precision, and shared with us a compassionate message of both hope and challenge. As I read and then reread her paper, I found myself totally engrossed with the essential thesis. Initially, it seems to be so idealistic. Quite frankly, it appears to be very impractical. But her ideas force themselves upon us, permeating a superficial layer of skepticism to rest at a deeper level of understanding. Finally, agreeing with her that contemporary society's ways of handling those who perpetrate misdeeds do not work, I began to consider her proposal within a particular context. It is underscored by this question: "If we have failed thus far to deal adequately with wrongdoing, and since the writer has caused us to approach this matter from a new starting point, wouldn't we be foolish not to accept her doctrine as a viable alternative and attempt to expand upon her basic premise?"

It was at this point that I began to liken Rev. Mackey's message to statements rendered by our venerable biblical prophets. As she has done, they, too, ignored public consensus and well-established community patterns. Unafraid to be radicals in the company of reactionaries, they spoke up with courage and conviction. The writer trods a well-worn path our scriptural sages first cleared.

In all too many instances, our prophets functioned at a time when their contemporaries had eyes, but they closed them to reality. They had ears, but they refused to listen. Surrounding them were men and women who had mouths, but they refused to speak out. Hopefully, this paper will cause many men and women to respond by joining the writer in her quest for a new approach to solving today's problems of communal injustice.

As she insists throughout her work, retribution has never worked as a permanent deterrent. It has not stopped wrongdoing. Therefore, restoration must be tried for no other reason than to determine its effectiveness in a world gone mad in chaos and confusion, in a time when we daily experience gross evidence of man's inhumanity to man.

I wholeheartedly endorse Rev. Mackey's compelling proposal. I have chosen to venture forth beyond that which is in the paper, to mandate with which it closes, calling upon us to develop a "theology of restoration." Because of my own characteristics and traits, and imbued by the teachings of our prophets, I am inclined to insert an additional word in her call, and to articulate a *"practical theology of restoration."*

The leadership of Reform Judaism in America is in agreement with the paper's thesis. When the Board of Trustees who govern the Union of American Hebrew Congregations convened in May 1968, they said, "Crime must be brought under control within the framework of a free and moral society, operating under the rule of law. We reaffirm the biblical concept that the criminal is a human being, capable of reshaping his life." ["I have no pleasure in the death of the wicked, but that the wicked turn from his way and live." (Ezek. 33:11)] *"Rather than inflicting increasingly harsh punishment and curtailing civil liberties, we should treat the causes of*

crime and disorder and reject proposals which ignore those causes by em-
phasis upon vengeful or unconstitutional means."

The Central Conference of American Rabbis has also spoken out on the
side of a "theology of restoration." Reform's rabbinic body has declared,
"The right of society to protect itself against those who constitute social
menaces implies also the solemn obligation to do everything possible to
remove the causes which tend to make men criminals and to make punish-
ment corrective in spirit rather than retributional."

Thus, the full force of America's Reform Jewish community, in statements articulated by its lay and rabbinic leadership, acknowledges that
just as God does not punish, the Lord does not intend that human beings
should punish each other.

This is not to ignore the fact that we are suffering the pain of extensive
crime in the United States. Ours is a violent society in which murders are
committed each year at rates that far surpass any other nation on earth.
Added to these cruel acts, which violently rob victims of their very lives,
are massive numbers of assaults, forcible rapes, incalculable robberies and
thefts. As a result, American's communities have taken unto themselves a
siege mentality. Homes have become armed camps. Security systems have
become popular devices. Men, women, and children have learned to defend themselves in self-imposed ghettoes. Social intercourse between
peoples of different racial, religious, and social groupings are all but non-
existent. Bi- and multi-racial and religious social justice projects and programs have fallen upon hard times. We are a nation which is besieged by
crime and awash in fear!

Under these circumstances, the vast majority of our citizenry champions
the cause of law and order. They obviously opt for a "theology of retribution." Their anger and anxiety compel them to meet brutality with force—
for them "an eye for an eye" is not enough; they call for "a life for an eye"
as they choose to ignore the limits imposed upon us by Exodus 21. Thus
both the presence of crime and our society's reaction to it generate a moral
crisis that needs to be confronted and surmounted.

To break the cycle of crime-punishment-crime, we must labor in two
vineyards concurrently. On the one hand, it is obvious that our judicial
and penal systems need to be reshaped. Also, it is necessary that we amend
laws which prohibit former convicts from taking their responsible place
within society. If we continue to deny them civil rights and job opportunities, then we are forcing them to perpetuate their criminal ways. And we
are obligated to do battle with those who wish to reinstitute capital punishment. It simply does not deter crime. Finally, we must be among those
who demand gun control so as to eliminate the manufacture, importation,
transportation, advertising, sale, transfer, and possession of handguns except for use by the military, police, security personnel, and licensed-regu-

lated pistol clubs. We can hardly reduce crime and punishment if guns are in the hands of people ill-equipped emotionally to curtail their use.

The other area of labor that demands our attention is the attitude of people and the nature of the society which we are building. If we are to avoid being adherents of a theology of retribution and if we are to accept a theology of restoration, then we have no choice but to echo and live by the words of Deuteronomy: *"Tzedek, tzedek tirdof*—zealously pursue justice!" This means that, like the prophets of old, we have to be concerned about the plight of all peoples, struggling with them to guarantee each person's human and civil rights, all groups' economic justice. On this subject, the U.A.H.C. has declared:

> We reaffirm our commitment to the concept of human dignity. Poverty and discrimination are inextricably related. Racial justice is inseparable from economic justice. What is at stake in the struggle to achieve equality of treatment for the individual are the spiritual values of our civilization, the economic well-being of our nation, and the moral leadership of America in a multi-racial world. . . .
>
> This national commitment must recognize that the fight against poverty and discrimination requires a truly comprehensive, coordinated approach of all segments of society, public and private, and the extensive investment of much more financial resources. We take cognizance of various proposals calling for some form of minimum income maintenance and we urge immediate study of various proposals to arrive at an effective, equitable method of providing for all Americans an annual minimum income with dignity.
>
> As Jews, we strive to perpetuate a tradition which recognizes that help to fellow human beings is a matter of right, not a matter of charity. We, therefore, welcome and support public programs designed to develop human and material resources to which all citizens are entitled in an enlightened society as a fulfillment of communal responsibility.

The importance of Rev. Mackey's paper is that it forces us to think in terms other than what appear to be today's societal norms. It reasserts religion's major contribution to the advancement of humankind, calling for love and justice as the only viable alternative to hate and injustice.

In the spirit of restoration, let every person feel that his own deeds determine the fate of mankind, recalling the teachings of the Talmud: "He who does one good deed may tip the scale on the side of merit for himself and for all mankind." Were all of us to renounce retribution and reach out to one another with love, concern and compassion, then we would live with a sense of greater responsibility. And the world would be a far better place in which to live.

As we have been taught, it is a loving God who promises in Deuteronomy:

See, I set before you this day life and prosperity, death and adversity. For I command you this day, to love the Lord your God, to walk in His ways, and to keep His commandments, His laws, and His norms, that you may thrive and increase. I have put before you life and death, blessing and curse. Choose life—if you and your offspring would live—by loving the Lord your God, heeding His commands, and holding fast to Him.

Just as we worship a God who wishes to restore the evildoer to a seat of glory, once there has been atonement for misdeeds, so must we—servants of the Lord—turn away from retribution and consider ways of restoring all peoples to their rightful place within the kingdom of God.

2. Dr. Rolf Knierim[10] (Professor of Old Testament, School of Theology at Claremont and Claremont Graduate School)

First of all, I would like to express my appreciation for the paper. It is a formidable paper, particularly with regard to the variety of aspects that Ms. Mackey addresses: from the Old Testament, the New Testament, Islamic and other traditions, through Church history or the history of the European civilizations and right up to the sociological analysis of our modern problems. As for my own field, I could begin to list some points in which we are beyond the state in which you present Old Testament scholarship. We make different sorts of distinctions. But I grant you that it is virtually impossible for anybody who undertakes such a study to be everywhere accurate and up to date.

Let me underwrite or affirm one thing that seems to pervade all statements, including those made by the members of the panel, that our traditions from which we have come are just as much part of the problem as they are part of the solution to the problem. I solidly support this assumption which points to one side of our discussion. Also, I fully underwrite the basic assumption in Ms. Mackey's paper that the entire question of criminal law and criminal procedures should in the religious traditions be dictated by the intentionality of reconciliation rather than punishment. As a matter of fact, Ms. Mackey, I believe that this affirmation can be substantiated, e.g. in my own field, in an even more fundamental way than your paper has done. Nevertheless, you have masterfully and correctly attested to the civil and criminal procedures in the biblical tradition. Their intentionality is quite clear. It is also quite clear that our own interpretive tradi-

---

[10] Prof. Knierim is coeditor of *The Forms of the Old Testament Literature*, a 24 volume commentary published by Eerdmans. As coauthor, he is responsible for the interaction of the legal texts in Exodus, Leviticus, Numbers, and for the interpretation of the legal institutions in ancient Israel.

tions are phrased primarily in terms of God's anger and of punishment. Interestingly, the ancient Hebew language has no word that would be the etymological equivalent to our word "punishment." And the texts show indeed that God's anger, even God's judgment, are with very few exceptions dictated by the intentionality of reconciliation.

Now, however, I would like to highlight four questions that seem to me to be emerging, and that seem to have to stand in the center of any kind of discovery or rediscovery of the foundational assumptions in our religious heritages, and that have to be conceptualized if we as religious communities today are to make a contribution to the problem of criminal law in the society at large.

First question: What is the relationship between law and justice? We hear the word "law" on the one hand, and the word "justice" on the other. Let me say outright that in the Old Testament tradition and in its Ancient Near Eastern background, these words expressed essentially different notions and were not interchangeable. Ten years ago, when in this nation the slogan "law and order" had high visibility, the words became for many, dirty words. I believe that we still suffer today from the negative connotations, from the dirtification of the words "law" and "order." At that time, I said in public lectures and sermons—mostly to the delight of those who liked what I said, but also to the distress and anger of those who didn't like what I was saying—a society without justice and righteousness will have a lot of problems with law and order, and with criminality; and it will tend to become totalitarian through law and order regardlesss of justice. But a society that is established on justice and righteousness will have much less problem with law and order. It will be less of a police-state. Today I have to emphasize that we must no longer leave the categories of law and order in a negative sphere, and that we must not speak of justice and righteousness only at the expense of law and order. Our own accentuations in the recent past when programmatically adopted for today are well intended for religious people, but they are quite unrealistic and not good enough substantively.

The understanding of justice and righteousness is deeply related to the understanding of world-order, of a cosmic and natural order that is created for, but in no way created by, us humans. Justice and righteousness are the balance of the life of this world. We do not create justice and righteousness. We recognize, acknowledge, and adhere to it—or not. If we throw the law and order of the justice and righteousness of the world away, the only real alternative is chaos. And I want to see anybody who is making a legitimate case for chaos in this world. I think this conference, when discussing criminal justice from the vantage point of religious communities, will have to consider fundamentally the relationship between justice and righteousness on the one hand, and law and order on the other;

and it will have to take seriously the legitimacy of each of these two realities.

Second point: I think it is necessary that we clarify semantically and substantively the meaning of reconciliation or restoration on the one hand, and of restitution on the other, and the relationship of both. Ms. Mackey's paper points this need out already. I presume that a society, even at its best, would have a few evildoers in its midst. Are we, because we are religious, to suggest that the process toward reconciliation for somebody who has committed a crime, a murder, a theft, who has done damage, involves nothing but forgiveness? How would you assume that in a trial, a judiciary procedure, such a person is outright forgiven by a jury or a judge, and not sentenced for punishment or retribution? Or are we to say that in the process of reconciliation some sort of restitution is necessary and required? It seems to me that any kind of religious or interreligious discussion that wants to make a solid and realistic contribution to the whole sphere and systems of criminal law in our societies has to address this problem, i.e. the problem of the legitimacy of imposed retribution at least for damage done.

The Old Testament clearly speaks about restitution. If a thief steals his neighbor's ox (and provided he is caught), he has to return the ox or to replace it and to pay a fine. He has to make "restitution." The Hebrew term used in this connection, *shillem,* which is related to *shalom,* means literally to make the (original) situation full, to restore it. Thus, reconciliation involves an act of restoration which requires restitution by the evildoer and sometimes even a fine. It involves the evildoer's share in the process of reconciliation, and not only the forgiving acceptance of him by the damaged party or community, so that the original situation of wholeness = peace can be restored.

Third question: What is the applicability of religious rules to a system of public justice that is not theocratically structured, embraced by, or based on one religion and its ethos only? You pointed out that the Christian community understands itself as the new humanity. Good: so far as we Christians are among ourselves, we can forgive ourselves—which of course is a fiction. Even in the best of the Christian traditions there was never only forgiveness and not also punishment both in theory and in practice. The idea of the hell-fire was an intensification of the idea of punishment that comes right out of the New Testament. To be punished were both the body and especially the soul. Have we figured out, in the updated theologies of our own ecclesiastic traditions, how forgiveness to the sinner and accountability of the sinner are to be related within our own religious bodies? If not, how should we be capable of suggesting to the public at large in a secular society that the principles of our ethos are translatable and transferrable into a system of public judiciary?

It seems that unless we address this question we say nothing of relevance to the public. We conduct an interreligious dialog which is nice but very removed from the question before us, namely, how to legitimately and rationally influence the public legislatures and judiciaries.

Fourth question: What is the relationship between justice and righteousness themselves and grace in our respective religious traditions?

I think of a story in Hosea 11 where the Lord is angry about Israel because in the course of more than four centuries she has failed to understand the meaning of her historical vocation. On the basis of legal evidence he administers justice and condemns Israel to death. Implication: a God who in the face of such overwhelming proof fails to pronounce such a sentence is not just. He does not represent the just order of the world, of his own creation. However, when God is confronted with the execution of his judgment, he breaks down and cannot do it, so the story continues. He decides not to execute His just judgment, a decision to which He is entitled on one ground: I am God and not human. What is pointed out in this story is that there is an enormous struggle, a struggle that affects God's very own identity. It is the struggle between the right, the legality, and the necessity of judgment, the *justice of judgment*, and between the right, the legality, and the necessity, the *justice of grace*. It is the question which of the two is the greater and the better justice, but also how the justice of grace can replace the justice of deserved punishment without the order of this world being thrown into chaos.

It is quite clear that those who tell such a story must know that, when realizing that they are alive, also realize that they owe their continued existence to such a struggle and such a precarious decision in the very depth, in the heart of the meaning of this world, a daring implementation of justice and rghteousness in the face of two seemingly irreconcilable principles on which this world exists either as order or as chaos.

What I mean with this story is the following: If a society or community, especially a religious community, looses the deep existential touch in its self-awareness that we all are first of all convicted sinners, we are bound finally to see the criminals in fundamental opposition to us, to tell ourselves that they are different, and that we are better and good. And that's what our culture has told us and our trivialized semi-theology recently: that we are nothing but good, that humanity is intrinsically good and not to be judged; that we all are okay and everything is okay: you are okay, I am okay, everybody is okay. And "god" has become a symbol for justifying our okayness. Thus when somebody is nevertheless found sitting in the pits, it is unavoidable that we have to disassociate ourselves from that criminal, that judgment is the only option of justice, and that we ourselves must judge. Where we have lost the knowledge that we continue to live despite the fact that we are convicted sinners, we are on no common ground whatsoever with the criminal. There is no need for grace for him. In fact, grace for him is no option of justice, and we would be unjust when being gracious. I wonder what kind of societal psychology might emerge if the Christian or religious communities would be capable of highlighting a sort of theology, ontology, and anthropology in which it becomes clear that first of all, the fact that we all exist and continue to exist reveals a justice in which the judgment of grace protects us from the judgment of punishment. Could it mean that we have to discover the belonging-together of all of us in the very foundations of our existence as the human species, in order to become capable of humanizing the profile and the policies of our systems of criminal justice?

And perhaps a final word: Ms. Mackey, you suggest, as a model for the whole problem-situation, a theology of reconciliation. I personally believe that your model is too narrow. I believe it must be replaced by a theology of justice because it can be argued that reconciliation is, and has to be, part of the process of justice. Justice is not exclusive of mercy. It includes mercy in its process, and always has in the history of human judiciary institutions as, e.g., the institutions of pardon and clemency demonstrate. Mercy or grace, however, have to be legitimate. And the criterion for the legitimacy of grace is whether it fulfills rather than destroys justice. The whole problem of reconciliation has to address the problem and to be dealt with in the realm of justice. In this sense, it has to bind the problem of criminality and the reaction to it into a holistic perception of reality—ontologically, sociologically, psychologically—in which reality and the human community are perceived to be established and guided by justice and righteousness.

If justice and righteousness are the basis, I think we will have a new perspective on the relationship between punishment and reconciliation in our perception and administration of law. Law can be deeply unjust and unrighteous. What kind of society will we have to have in order to have just law, also just criminal law? Or more just law and more just criminal law? In order to have justice in law, in its punishing and reconciling functions, we will have to look more intensively at our social system of justice, because, whatever our legal systems are, they reflect first of all the justice or injustice, or the combination of both, of the society and everything in it.

3. Esther Heffernan, O.P. (Professor of Sociology, Edgewood College, Madison, Wisconsin)

The following quotation is a contemporary Roman Catholic response to "violence and crime," the reports of which fill our mass media and provide the occasion for our coming together. It is an expression of Christian reflection on "living under God's law," taken from Bishop Dozier's Pastoral

Letter for Christmas 1972, addressed "to the people of the Diocese of Memphis." and appropriately entitled "Justice: God's Vision—Man's Discipleship."

> God is calling us to live in a community of harmony, the harmony of justice and peace. The harmony was called a covenant by God, and by Jesus a "new covenant." Justice is so much a part of God's covenant that to worship God is to act justly towards others (1 John 4:20). The reason that love of God and love of neighbor have meshed is that each of us is a redeemed person. God lives in us and we in God. Sin against our neighbor violates the reconciliation Jesus won for us. . . . True justice helps preserve the rights of people to live and move and have their being in the dignity that is rightfully theirs as Children of God, members of his Household.
>
> We easily recognize and abhor direct, "hot" violence, such as terrorist attacks, bombings of buildings, murders and rapes. It is harder for most of us to get upset about indirect or "cold" violence, which does not seem as spine-chilling, but is so real that from day to day it chips away at our rights. Conscious decisions perpetuating inferior education in poverty areas are cold violence, landlords, who while collecting rents, do nothing about filth and rot in their slum holdings, commit cold violence; discrimination against women, and abandoning the elderly are forms of cold violence. Violence is done in the manipulation of minds, in wasteful misuse of the world's goods, in inadequate wages, in placing private interests over the common good. Cold violence frequently drives men into acts of direct hot violence. Whose sin is it then?
>
> Sadly we speak too often to one another in the language of violence, not in the language of love. . . . Justice denied through violence to any one of us, is justice denied to us all. We are all brothers. . . . There are many tensions in our community which do violence to our rights. Injustices such as unequal taxation and exhorbitant interest rates and exploitation of the consumer hurt us. Following the advice of Jesus to cast the beam out of our own eyes, we must sadly acknowledge that the first tension, however, arises between what we say and what we in fact do. We say we believe in God and yet this belief does not always enter our day-to-day lives. God calls us to love our neighbor. The Church in Memphis has frequently forgotten this. This Church has reflected the temper of our society.

This quotation touches the themes of this conference—a broad vision of justice; a deep sense of our redemption, dignity, responsibility, and sinfulness; and our sharing as a church—a community of believers—in sin and injustice.

The title of my written response to Virginia Mackey's excellent paper is formidable: "The Religious Community's Response to Violence and Crime in America—Dangerous, Dependent and Depraved: Relationships between Theologies, Political Power and Alternate Structures of Criminal Justice."

But the response is offered in the hope that a socio-historical approach within the American context will contribute to the continuing discourse on the relationship between politico-economic and religious motivation in the "legitimation" of the use of the coercive power of the state—the themes analyzed in Virginia Mackey's broad overview and reflected in Bishop Dozier's epistle.

What are some of the underlying meaning/motivations/structures for:

(a) the presence of "criminal codes" through which, by legislation, any behavior may be defined in such a way that a person becomes subject to the coercive power of the state; (b) that for such behavior persons become liable to "deprivation of liberty," historically associated with the commission of capital offenses, and provided for in our Constitution by the status of involuntary servitude or slavery "in the custody of the state"; and (c) the process of justification of the differential enforcement of the criminal laws and the use of this sanction of imprisonment?

The present-day controversies regarding social-class-linked definitions of crime; the perceptions of the "criminal"; and the function and range of criminal sanctions cannot be examined apart from an historical consideration of the religious, social, and political structures involved in defining the criminal law. The usefulness of an historical approach is well stated by Foucault (1979:51) in his challenging study of the development of the prison in France:

> Simply because I am interested in the past? No, if one means by that writing history of the past in terms of the present. Yes, if one means writing the history of the present.

However powerful the analysis of Foucault and others within the European context, the presence of the federal structure in the United States in the "administration of justice" appears to lessen the validity of using the church-sect, nation-state, Church-State, and class-status models derived from the European context for religious, social, or political analysis of "American society"; the religious foundations for the legitimacy of the state; and the development of the criminal laws and the prison. The presence of a multiplicity of state and federal criminal codes; local, state, and federal law enforcement agencies, court proceedings and sanctions; and a range of local, state, and federal, public, private, and religious "penal institutions"; makes possible the accommodation of divergent and possibly conflicting theological/philosophical positions regarding the person and the nation-state and the differentiation of the relationships between religion, morality, and law.

The "universe of discourse" within which the Declaration of Independence derived its meaning and also within which the Constitution and the

Bill of Rights were debated and shaped, and from which the various state constitutions, courts, and criminal laws and sanctions emerged, assumed the presence of "Natural and Divine Law." In order to explore the implications of the presence of divergent "orderings" of the natural and divine within the "reality" of the United States, we need to think of a schema in which divine law is revealed to humans by two paths: that of creation/ nature and that of word.

Central to the natural law tradition was the "self-evident" acceptance of the proposition that every human person was a social animal with a rational soul. This assumed the presence of an intellect and will to "seek the truth" and "pursue the good," capable of intellectual and moral judgments within human limitations.

While aware that the degree of "liberty" and rationality for any given act varied, the self-evident presence of a "soul" within oneself was the basis for assuming the *equal* presence of a rational soul in others. The issue of the theological debates within the Christian tradition of the time was not the presence of a soul, but of its *natural* religious state and the "freedom of the will' in regard to God. Was it *evil, wounded,* or "naturally good" in its ability to properly order its relationships with the divine, and with other humans—the moral order, in such a way as to "merit" or achieve salvation—to be "transformed in Christ" or to "seek and find God"?

Closely related to this central position was the distinction between the characteristics of a human as natural by *creation*—the nature of the species—and those *human* institutions which flowed naturally from those characteristics of a person as a rational social animal who needed the support of others, namely, the family, economy and community/city/nation.

The government's or state's natural function, in turn, was to ensure an ordering and security of the common or "good" life. The government, by its very *nature*, rested on the consent of those whose common life it ensured. Its particular form, whether monarchy, aristocracy, or democracy, or a combination of all, would be a function of circumstances, customs, and deliberate decision. The laws of this government—positive law—were applicable only to those within the jurisdiction of the government and when duly promulgated by legitimate authorities. They were "binding in conscience" only insofar as they were for the common good, although for public order they should be obeyed. But if they were in conflict with common or customary law—morality—or against the "law of God," they should not be obeyed.

While particular governments or states changed, the network of human customs and contracts (within and between families, economic combinations for production and trade, groupings for purposes within the local community, and gathered communities for the worship of the deity) which constituted *the moral order* remained. The mutual obligations—the contracts—which supported these institutions flowed from the *necessity* of the support of others for every person, a fundamental *dependency* of all persons.

The withdrawal from, or the breaking of, a contact required "naturally" a *restoration* of the relationship or a *restitution* for the harm done. This could include being "bound" to another for service/slavery, if this punishment was accepted under the positive law.

The critical questions of "dependency" were at the heart of many of the political struggles. If persons were "dependent" by status, then independence or "freedom" was always possible by human political actions, either through legislative and legal action or through changes in contractual or customary relationships within the moral order. If one was dependent "by nature," one was never capable of independence or liberty.

This question directly touched the critical issue of servitude/slavery. Should it be viewed as a status of a person either voluntarily assumed for some purpose, or assigned by positive law as a punishment for some crime? If this were the case, then a person would be bound to *work* for another, while remaining *equal* in all things natural to the person, including the right to worship, to an education, to marriage, and to "all things that pertain to the needs of the body." (Aquinas. 1948, pp. 2747–2751) Or was the slavery/servitude *natural*, flowing from the absence or limited possession of humanness?

However, in the argumentation regarding servitude/slavery, dependency may also be legitimated as a *providential* status rather than as a *human* status, and in that sense, not subject to human political action. In this context, servitude/slavery as a status in human society could be accepted or rejected by a "revealed word."

That position, of course, raises some of the most crucial historical questions—the presence or absence of a "word" side in the schema. What is the relationship of the human intellect and the Divine intellect? Does the human also contain the Divine? Is the "law" of "Nature's God" revealed in ways beyond that *natural* to the human person and achievable by human reason? Is there a knowledge beyond the wisdom of natural religion? Has God "spoken" through a "scripture" and/or in the "living tradition" of a "people" or a "church"? And does the "Word" judge human law and place "the church" or "the people" apart from or above the customary moral law or the positive law of the state? Does God "speak directly" to the human person to be a "prophet" of God's Word, or provide "graces above nature" to *assist* human actions"? And does this Word "destroy," or place a prophet "above," "merely human law"—either moral or legal? Does the "happiness" of "the people" or the "good life" include the state's responsibility for "salvation" in addition to supporting the natural rewards of a virtuous life?

An examination of the Declaration of Independence in the context of the schema reveals that it felicitously side-steps all of these questions. By relying on the "natural/creation" side of the schema, without denying the presence of the "word" side, this document had the potential either of reconciling or of concealing profound differences in response to the question of who had "membership status" in the "people of the United States," as well as who could participate in the governing as voter and officeholder; and who might be a "dependent," an "alien," or an "outcaste," was explicitly debated in the early years of the founding of the republic/democracy. What was the status of slaves, laborers, paupers, criminals, immigrants, blacks, Indians, non-conformists, Jews, Roman Catholics, Deists, Free-Masons, and infidels, as well as women and children? At least four deeply divergent responses to the relationship of church to nation-state were linked with these debates:

1. A vision of a new American people from many backgrounds developing an American common law, with a limited government and free churches or "gathered communities of believers" *in* America.
2. A "Church of America"—a church-nation taking its place among other developing church-nations—England, France, Spain, Prussia, and Russia among others—as a "Christian Commonwealth." The church would be supported, and membership in church and people determined, by the state legislatures as representatives of the Sovereign-people. Laws of the Sovereign are "absolute and without control" and to violate the law is to offend the Sovereign as the defender of the people and the faith.
3. America as the New Jerusalem—a chosen nation-people. The laws become "divine laws," the laws of a "covenanted nation," an expression of the "Divine Will." Their violation then becomes a "sin against God," deserving of death but open to His mercy, expressed through His agent, the magistrate.
4. America as the "new order," where the "enlightened" may "establish" "rational religion" and morality based on the "natural laws" of the "new sciences." Through the "experimental" use, by the virtuous members of the Republic, of the "benevolent" coercive powers of the state, the "unreasonable," the "ignorant" and the "ill-willed' may be "reformed."

Equally critical and controversial were (and are) three different understandings of servitude/slavery. They are critical both for the translation and understanding of "God's Word" in the Koran, the Torah, and the New Testament, and in our relationships with each other. For these differing meanings of servitude/slavery permeate our understanding of the meaning of "in the custody of the state":

1. The "bondage" of working for another to "pay off one's debts"—the traditional form of restitution available to the poor.
2. The slavery of an "enemy" or a "wicked person," who deserves death, but lives because of and at the *mercy* of another, at their disposal as an *instrument* of their will.
3. The "natural slavery" of the less-than-human—the "beasts," "savages," or "child-like"—the "lower orders" who need the control of the "enlightened." This, of course, was the ultimate justification of American domestic slavery as well as colonialism throughout the world. Then slavery becomes a "benevolent institution" justifying one nation or people controlling or civilizing another.

In the midst of the political struggles of this critical period in American nation-building over "membership" in the "commonwealth," the source of the law, and the presence of slavery/servitude, we also had a tax revolt. This reality might provide some solace to citizens, legislators, and administrators that their present-day dilemmas are not unique. Many of the new criminal codes abolished the death penalty (which Parliament and the American colonial legislatures had been demanding for an increasing number of property and protest offenses) as insufficiently "terror-provoking" because seldom carried out. In their place new state prisons were to be constructed for these condemned—civilly and socially dead slaves of the state. (*Ruffin v. The Commonwealth*, 21 Grattan [Virginia, 794–799, 1871]). These new buildings, often the first major construction of the "sovereign states," involved such high costs that in typical frugal fashion, five institutions—the almshouse, the house of corrections or workhouse, the local gaol, the "binding out" for service of those in debt or dependent on the local community, and the state prison—which were clearly distinguished in both law and social status, were merged in differing combinations. This mixed heritage has continued to the present day. Our prisons and jails are viewed as institutions of "terror" and "reformation," a place to "do one's time" and "pay off one's debts," centers of "social services," a place to house detainees before trial.

Paradoxically, taxes led to a revolution whose legitimacy was justified by an affirmation of a Bill of Rights ensuring equal justice under law. Property and taxes have deeply shaped the nature of that justice. We may question whether it reflects God's vision or our response in a discipleship of justice and reconciliation.

4. The Rev. Dr. Richard A. Symes (Pastor, First Presbyterian Church, Palo Alto, California; Member of the Criminal Justice Consulting Committee, Presbyterian Church, U.S.A.)

We were asked to respond to Virginia Mackey's paper by focusing on two questions. The first is, "What does it mean according to your tradition to live under God's law?" And the second is, "What does the perspective of your faith have to say about concepts of conciliation and reconciliation?

To live under God's law according to Christian faith means always to be ready for the possibility of resisting and opposing human authority, even highly sanctioned authority. Jesus, as we know, on some occasions broke with the religious laws and customs of his culture; on other occasions he affirmed and even radicalized them. However difficult it may be to discover exactly the circumstances surrounding his death, his unswerving obedience to God's law made him a criminal in the eyes of Roman law under which he was executed.

Early Christians frequently found themselves at odds with the laws of the Roman Empire, and repeatedly expressed their obligation to obey divine rather than human authority, but even the earliest record of Christianity does not endorse total opposition to secular rule.

The Christian community wavered between support and denunciation of the Roman Empire. Contrast, for example, Romans 13 ("Let everyone be subject to the governing authorities, for they are ordained by God") with Revelation 13, which scholars agree depicts the state as inimical to the purposes of God. Christians eventually made peace with the Roman Empire and helped shape Western civilization. But the peace was rarely an easy one and the identification of Christianity with the state always a troubled one. It was in the name of Christ that theocratic governments themselves were challenged and opposed. In 1945, Protestant theologian Dietrich Bonhoeffer was hanged in Flossenburg Prison for proclaiming that the will of God was in opposition to the laws of the Christian nation of which he was then a citizen.

I cannot remember attending a General Assembly of my own denomination, the Presbyterian Church, in which Christian pastors and lay folk somewhere in the world were not being prayed for because they were in prison for opposing in the name of Christ the laws and policies of their governments; sometimes it was our own government. American Christians, nonetheless, constantly have to be reminded, and usually it's by ethnic minorities of this nation, that God's law and the American way of life are not identical; that faiths, values and societal norms are as much in conflict as they are in congruence. For Christians to live under God's law means, then, to judge all human law in the light of what God specifically commands.

Moreover, to live under God's law is to live in the paradox of freedom and restraint, grace and judgment, forgiveness and social responsibility. God's love is free and unconditioned, unmerited by our works, by our attitudes, and even by our orthodoxies. That seems to me to strike out forever any ultimate distinction between the "we" and the "they" in our society; between the "good guys" and the "bad guys." Such distinctions, however they may need to be made provisionally for the sake of social order, and even for the sake of justice, are never final. Just because the law is not a means of salvation, just because the keeping or not keeping of it cannot coerce God into favor or disfavor, does not mean that it has to be abrogated or is useless.

What colleagues in the other faiths affirm is also evident to Christians, that the end of the law is neither order nor punishment, but justice. Obedience to the law is not for self-justification, but to express love to neighbor. Finally, to live under God's law means to gain a new appreciation for its positive reality. All three faiths seem to share that appreciation, at least in a theoretical way.

But our society by and large does not share a very positive view of law. It has I think frequently been noted that the poor and members of ethnic minorities in this country regard the law and its apparatus as hostile and inimical to their interests. Even among those groups of people who presumably have little to fear and much to gain from the law, negative feelings predominate. Perhaps the religious community can do more than reaffirm a theology of restoration. Perhaps it can redeem the notion of God's law and God's judgment as creative forces for the human community, and begin to insist that human law and human justice partake of some of that creativity.

Respecting the second question, which has to do with conciliation and reconciliation, the claim of Christian faith is that Jesus came to create not so much a new structure of belief as a new kind of human community. The fact that the Christian Church from time to time in its history has resisted the formation of that community does not validate the claim. Jesus began his ministry by calling into relationship with himself and one another people of diverse political perspectives, people of diverse races and classes, and perhaps most important, people who because of their age or their sex, their physical disability, their disease, their occupation and their moral behavior were considered beyond the reach of God's favor. Women and children, prostitutes and tax collectors, outcasts and renegades belong in the kingdom of God, according to Jesus. In his last hour, he extended the kingdom even to the crucified thief who was getting what society had decided were his just deserts. Only those who excluded themselves were outside the kingdom.

As this new community of Jesus moved into the wider and more pluralistic world, its universalism both waxed and waned. On the one hand, the community of Jesus included both Jew and Greek, both rich and poor, male and female, barbarian and Scythian, slave and free. These were not merely diverse elements of a very cosmopolitan society, they were frequently representatives of traditionally antagonistic and hostile people. What happened in the new community was that diverse hostility was broken down by their new identity as followers of Jesus and participants in a new age. On the other hand, as the new community more and more identified itself in terms of what it believed about Jesus, the state was set for the splintering and antagonisms which have characterized the Christian Church for much of its history.

I take the time to cite this historical example of a reconciled and reconciling community rather than just talking about ideas because I think it illustrates that Christianity had more than a good idea for a reconciled and universal community. It actually managed, however temporally and imperfectly, to incarnate such a society. Moreover, the partially realized dream of a reconciled and nonhierarchical community has continued throughout history to challenge and inspire human communities like our own that are threatened by homogeneity, violence, injustice, and disintegration. Christianity assumes, as do some other religions, that a universal community is not merely the child of human aspiration and hope, but a reality in the mind and purpose of a sovereign God.

The universal community into which God is in fact calling all people is to be marked off from all utopian visions by virtue of the fact that it takes alienation and hostility with complete seriousness. We are not talking about a fellowship of like-minded individuals who have some minor and interesting differences from one another. To underestimate the depth and the power, the savagery and the tenacity of alienation and hostility in our society is to deserve all the scorn and ridicule the right wing has heaped upon the "bleeding hearts." The perspective of Christian faith is that God did not underestimate the power and intensity of hostility directed against Him and His children, our sisters and brothers. The perspective of Christian faith is that God, by experiencing in His very nature something that we can only call death, paid the cost and absorbed and overcame and transformed that alienation and that hostility.

So, what I want to suggest in response to the paper is that we also will have to pay a price for a reconciled community in which the Shalom of God is reigning, and the price that we will have to pay is the price of justice and responsibility.

Let me make that less abstract. *If the human community is to be at peace with itself,* then all of us at this conference, among others, are going to have to do with less: less power, less wealth, less comfort, and less freedom, or there will be no justice. *If the human community is to be at peace with itself,* then all of us at this conference, among others, are going to have to recite the painful liturgies that these are, in fact, *our* prisons, *our* unjust laws, *our* corrupt system, *our* fear of violence, and *our* love of punishment. We are going to have to recite them until we gain the courage to alter our behavior and our institutions. *If the human community is to be at peace with itself,* we are going to have to deal not only with those around us who believe in a theology of punishment, but with our own internal ambivalence and misgivings.

As most of you know, the nineteenth century, particularly in America, was the age of the asylum; it was a time of fearing and therefore hating deviant behavior and abnormal conditions. In response to our fear and hatred, we had to cut loose from our communities those who we believed couldn't be reconciled into it: the orphans, the debtors, the jobless, the poor, the insane, and the criminal. We were under the illusion that by isolating certain types of people in satellite communities of their own kind, we would both protect the larger society from contamination, and transform those deviants into recognizable human beings who could at some future unspecified date be readmitted into the larger community. We did not discern, at least consciously, that we were causing those people a great deal of pain—that we were, despite our good intentions, punishing them simply because they did not fit in. Today we have begun to see the folly of our experiment. Most of our asylums have crumbled, although we still isolate from our communities, in other ways, those who don't fit in. It no longer seems such a formidable task to reconcile the orphans, or the vagrants, or the mentally ill, because for the most part they seem harmless. We would not punish them knowingly. But the last asylum still stands. The people for whom we want to throw away the key are those who have inflicted pain on others as well as on themselves, and we in turn have inflicted pain on them, and they have inflicted pain on us; and thus the tragic and endless cycle continues. The imprisoned, including the avaricious and the violent in our increasingly avaricious and violent society, the imprisoned, whom we have pushed to the boundary of their humanity, are surely the least reconcilable from a human standpoint. Most of the imprisoned, as we know, return eventually to our communities. We absorb them, absorb them without reconciling them, indeed without even recognizing them.

To reconcile the imprisoned to us according to Christian perspective would be to accept the necessity of reshaping and revaluing the communities in which we ourselves have become so comfortable. And the question with which I leave you is whether we are willing to pay the high emotional cost for that transformation?

5. Dr. Ala'Eddin Kharofa (Director, Muslim World League Office to the United Nations and North America)

My assignment is to comment on the paper of Rev. Virginia Mackey. Let me first congratulate her for this presentation which shows her grasp of the subject and erudition. However, there are some statements in her presentation with which one may not agree, and I will call your attention to them. Mostly these seem to relate to her sources, not about her statements.

1. The phrase "classical Islam" gives the impression that there is a modern Islam as against classical Islam. Actually, there is only one

Islam which was revealed to Prophet Mohammed fourteen centuries ago—and the same Islam is followed even today, without any change whatsoever.

2. The paper states that Islam acknowledged the Judaic and Christian scriptures. In fact, Islam does acknowledge the scriptures, but only in their original form. Islam has told us that some Judaic and Christian scholars and saints have changed their holy books.

3. The paper says rightly that Islam in no way restricted its membership to other people. You know that Islam is universal in its appeal, and considers mankind one vast family.

4. The paper is quoted as saying, "It is not clear that Muhammad intended to establish a new religion." Establishing or rather re-establishing Islam was Muhammad's primary aim. All other aims, whatever they might have been, were secondary to it. I also disagree with the statement that the primary purpose of our Koran, our holy book, is not to regulate the relationship of man to his fellows, but of the relationship to his Creator. In Islam, both relationships are equally important, and there is equal emphasis on each of them.

5. The paper says that legislation of the common law, *urf*, was combined with the language of the Torah and the New Testament and with revelation to formulate the Sharia, the way to be followed by the faithful. In fact, Islam has nothing to do with the Torah, nor with the Bible or (and this is very important) the customs of certain Arab people.

6. The paper quotes Mustafa Kara as saying that "Islamic Law is no more or less than the epitome and the result of a particular stage in the history of evolution of the Arab society." In fact, Islamic Law was founded by God and by Prophet Muhammad, and did not come into being through the evolution of the Arab society.

7. Rev. Mackey said rightly, "It is a duty for the Muslims to build community as well as to reconcile it." Each Muslim greets another with "Peace be upon you."

8. Rev. Mackey said, "The tradition of Islam is highly complex," and she explained this statement by saying, "It is extremely difficult for western minds to understand Islamic religion and culture." My comment on this is that the tradition of Islamic religion is very simple and straightforward and can be understood and followed by everyone who is willing to pratice it everywhere.

9. Rev. Mackey said,

A theory of jurisprudence is made difficult because the Prophet's style was *ad hoc*. Joseph Schact postulates that Muhammad was a poet rather than a theologian; a prophet rather than a legislator. When confronted with concrete situations and pressed by his followers to make a judgment, he improvised. Conversely, Mustafa Kara says that Muhammad sometimes had himself appointed as a judge but indicates that the Prophet's decisions were somewhat contradictory, because, first, he followed no method or detailed code and the tradition was oral; secondly, he dealt with the mitigating or aggravating circumstances; thirdly, because he was primarily concerned with the religious dimension of the problems; and fourthly, he dealt with changing situations.

In my opinion, Joseph Schact has made a great mistake, because the fact is that Prophet Muhammad, peace be upon him, was not a poet; he did not have the opportunity to learn how to read or to write. Moreover, Prophet Muhammad was a prophet and a religious leader, and when he was confronted with religious questions, he was waiting for relevation from God; then he was giving the decision. But if the question related to a worldly problem, he gave his opinion. Mustafa Kara's opinion that the Prophet's decisions were somewhat contradictory is wrong because we believe that Muhammad was infallible, as every Prophet and Messenger was. And he did not judge a specific case by two different decisions.

10. In another instance, Mustafa Kara criticised Islam because Islam always is not providing practical answers. In my opinion, this is a wrong statement since Islam has practical answers to every problem. Unfortunately, time does not allow me to go into this in any detail right now.

11. The paper says Fazlur Rahman is critical on another front. He says that *Kalam* (theology) does exist and that it is invariably a higher science that *fiqh* (legal science) because it concerns propositions about God, prophethood, and humanity. But its scope, according to Rahman, is too limited; it lacks a view of human nature and social dimension.

    The Koran is the primary source of Islamic jurisprudence. It has the answer to legal questions. Besides the pillars of Islam, jurisprudence discusses civil law, criminal law, merchant law, internatinal law, etc. Therefore, there is no contradiction between jurisprudence and theology, and some Muslin jurists were scholars in both jurisprudence and theology.

12. The paper after that discusses the problem of punishment in Islam very briefly, and I cannot go into it in detail. However, I would like to say very briefly that we are very proud of the system of criminal law and punishment laid down by Islam. It has to be noted that the incidence of crime in Islamic countries is much lower than it is in the West, and that is to a degree because of the Islamic penal system.

My friends, you are the leaders of this society. On your shoulders lies the responsibility to lead this country to the correct path. God will ask us, "What did you do for this society?" We are with you and Islam is with you completely in your aim to help this society to live in peace, and to be safe and secure. But Islam has different attitudes with the murderers and with the criminals. You always say that God is love. Well, if we love God, we have to follow His teachings also. We have to obey Him. He knows better than us. He commanded to punish the murderer in order that the society may live in peace and security. He didn't ask everyone to be punished. God does not have any hostility toward us. We believe as you believe that God is One and He has created us and He knows what is good for us. So He imposed certain punishment for the criminals so that the society could live in peace. For instance, you have to punish the one who is entering your house during the night or during the day, breaking your door or stealing your money. However, a small sin can be forgiven.

Do not think that Islam is a religion of harsh punishment. Do not think that Islam is a religion of hostility. Islam is the religion of brotherhood, mercy, cooperation, love. But when God asked us to punish the one who is committing adultery, He wanted to protect the whole society. When God asked us to punish a person who committed murder, He wanted the society to live in peace. After all, we are responsible to implement the laws of God, and these are the laws of God. You know, for example, the spate of crimes taking place in New York City. Why? Only because the criminals know that the law, and the police, and the power of the government are ineffective. Therefore, they freely indulge in crimes. This is the nature of human beings, and God, Who has created the human being, is All-Wise and All-Knowing, and He knows what is good and what is bad for the human being.

I wish to thank Rev. Mackey for the effort she has made in preparing her paper. May God bless her, and we shall look forward to hearing her lectures on Islam in the future. And I hope they will be in even greater detail and based on authentic and undisputable sources. May God bless you all, and I wish to thank you for your interest in Islam. I hope this interest will grow in the future.

REFERENCES

Abdul-Rauf, M. (1963). *The Quar'anic terminology of sin.* Unpublished doctoral dissertation, London University.

Alper, B., & Nichols, L. (1981). *Beyond the courtroom.* Lexington, MA: Lexington Books.

American Heritage Dictionary. (1971). New York: American Heritage Publishing.

Aquinas, T. (1948). *Summa theologica.* 3 vols. Trans., English Dominican Province. New York: Benziger Bros.

Beach, G.K. (1979). *By what right do some persons punish other persons?* Sermon, Unitarian Church of Arlington, VA.

Berman, H. (1974). *The interaction of law and religion.* Nashville, TN: Abingdon Press.

Bianchi, H. (1973). *Tsedeka* justice. *Review for philosophy and theology.* Nijmegen, the Netherlands: Central Printing Company.

Bianchi, H. (1978). *Returning conflict to the community: Alternative of privatization.* U.S. Lecture Series.

Bockle, F., & Pohier, J. (Eds.). (1979). *The death penalty and torture.* New York: Seabury Press.

Brunner, E. (1945). *Justice and the social order.* New York: Harper & Row.

Burton, J. (1977). *The collection of the Qur'an.* Cambridge: Cambridge University Press.

Cohn, H.H. (1971). *Jewish law in ancient and modern Israel.* Hoboken, NJ: KTAV Publishing House.

Coulson, N.J. (1964). *A history of Islamic law.* Edinburgh: University Press.

Coulson, N.J. (1978). Law and religion in contemporary Islam. *Hastings Law Journal, 29* (6), 1447, 1449.

Dale, F. (1980, April). *The need for religious America to examine how our nation approaches punishment.* Address to the National Religious Council of the National Council on Crime and Delinquency, Lexington Hotel, New York City, New York.

Davies, W.D. (1978). Paul and the law: Reflections on pitfalls in interpretation. *Hastings Law Journal, 29* (6), 1466–1480.

DeWolf, L.H. (1975). *Crime and justice in America: A paradox of conscience.* New York: Harper & Row.

Dozier, C.T. (1972). *Justice: God's Vision, Our Discipleship.* Pastoral Letter to the People of the Diocese of Memphis.

Encyclopedia Judaica, Vol. X. (1971). Jerusalem, Israel: Keter Publishing.

Foucault, M. (1979). *Discipline and Punish: The Birth of the Prison.* Trans. A. Sheridan, New York: Random House.

Funk, D. (1979). Religion ethical natural consequentialism, and the science of justice. *Capital University Law Review, 8,* (3), 16.

Goldin, J. (1957). *The Living Talmud.* Chicago: University of Chicago Press.

Gutbrod, W. (1964). *"Law" in Kittel's Bible key words, Vol. IV.* New York: Harper & Row.

Hallie, P. (1969). *The paradox of cruelty.* Middleton, CT: Wesleyan University Press.

Harding, A.L. (1955). *Natural law and natural rights.* Dallas: Southern Methodist University.

Hogarth, J. (1974). *Studies on sentencing.* Ottawa, Canada: Law Reform Commission of Canada.

Horowitz, G. (1963). *The spirit of Jewish law.* New York: Central Book Company.

Hovav Meir & Amir, Menachem. (1979). *Police studies.* New York: "Israel Police: history and analysis" Vol. 2, No. 2.

Ibn, J. (1978). In *The effect of Islamic legislation on crime prevention in Saudi Arabia.* Saudi Arabia: Ministry of Interior.

Jaffe, J. (1972). *So sue me!* New York: Saturday Review Press.

Kadduri, M. (1961) *Islamic jurisprudence.* Baltimore: John Hopkins.

Kara, M.A. (1977). *The philosophy of punishment in Islamic law.* Dissertation project, Claremont Graduate School, Ann Arbor, MI: Xerox University Microfilms.

Khomeini, the Ayatollah. *Sayings of the Ayatollah Khomeini.* New York: Bantam Books.

Kee, H.C. (1971). *Interpreter's one-volume commentary on the Bible.* Laymon, C.M. (Ed.). Nashville, TN: Abingdon Press.

Kittle, G. (1964). *Bible key words, Vol. IV.* New York: Harper & Row.

Knopp, F.H. et al. (1976). *Instead of prisons.* Syracuse, NY: Safer Society Press.

Madigan, K. (1980). *Religion, ideology and prisons: The impact of belief on reform movements.* Class presentation, Colgate Rochester/Bexley/Crozer Seminary.

McHugh, G.A. (1978). *Christian faith and criminal justice.* New York: Paulist Press.

McKelvey, B. (1977). *American prisons: A history of good intentions.* Montclair, NJ: Patterson Smith.

Miller, J.B. (1980). *Democrat and Chronical article.* Rochester, NY: Gannett Newspapers.

Montefiore & Loewe. (1974). *A Rabbinic anthology.* New York: Schocken Books.

Neusner, J. (1979). *Method and meaning in ancient Judaism.* Missoula, MN: Scholars Press.

Pannenberg, W. (1973). Toward a theology of law. (D.O. Lasky, trans.). *American Theological Review, LV* (4), 402–408.

Richardson, A. (1950). *A theological word book of the Bible.* New York: Macmillan.

Riga, P.J. (1978). Marsiglio of Padova. *Hastings Law Journal, 29* (6), 1431.

Rodkinson, M.L. (Ed.). (1918). *The Babylonian Talmud.* Boston: Talmud Society.

Rosenthal, E.I.J. (1961). *Judaism and Islam.* New York: Thomas Yossloff.

Rothman, D.J. (1971). *The discovery of the asylum.* Boston: Little Brown.

Rowley, H.H., & Black, M. (1962). *Peake's commentary on the Bible.* London: Nelson.

Saleilles, R. (1913). *The individualization of punishment.* Boston: Little Brown.

Shehadi, F. (1980). Islam as a philosophy/religion. *Arab Perspectives, 1* (6), 4–5.

Strick, A. (1977). *Injustice for all.* New York: Putnams.

Symes, R.A. (1978). *No mandate for a new order.* Doctoral dissertation, San Francisco Theological Seminary.

Time Magazine (1980, April 21, Vol. 115, No. 16). Special Section: Watergate's sphinx speaks. excerpted from *Will: The Autobiography of G. Gordon Liddy.*

Trumbull, R. (1979, Feb. 12). Pakistan adopting Islamic laws with their severe punishments. *New York Times,* pp. 1, 7.

Universal Jewish Encyclopedia, Vol. 6. (1942). New York: Universal Jewish Encyclopedia, Inc.

U.S. Catholic Conference. (1978). *Community and crime.* Washington, DC: author.

Wahrhaftig, P. (Ed.). *The citizen dispute resolution organizers handbook.* Pittsburgh, PA: Conflict Resolution Center.

Wickes, R.J., & Cooper, H.H.A. (Ed.). (1979). *International corrections.* Lexington, MA: Lexington Books.

Williams, J.A. (Ed.). (1971). *Themes of Islamic civilization.* Berkeley: University of California Press.

Williams, J.A. (Ed.). (1962). *Islam.* New York: George Braziller.

Wren, B. (1977). *Education for justice: Pedagogical principles.* Maryknoll, NY: Orbis Books.

Yamani, A. (1972). Islamic law and contemporary issues. C. Malik (Ed.), *God and man in contemporary Islamic thought.* Beirut, Lebanon: American University.

Chapter 3

Religion and Deviance: A New Look

Rodney Stark
University of Washington

The proposition that religion undergirds the moral order must be one of the most ancient notions in social thought—it is plausible that even the rude Neanderthalers knew of it (cf. Parrinder, 1983). Yet, in the 20th century it has fallen on hard times. One reason for this is that social scientists have rather hoped that nothing good could be said of religion (Stark & Bainbridge, 1985). But, perhaps even more important, efforts to demonstrate the empirical impact of religion on conformity often have turned up inconsistent and inconclusive results.

Indeed, my inability to discover consistent and robust empirical support for the proposition that religion sustains conformity to the normative order led me to abandon the sociology of religion at the end of the 1960s— I returned to it only several years ago. The fact was that for a long time about the only religious effects I could find were correlations between orthodoxy and opposition to drinking, dancing, and gambling among American Protestants. Whenever I searched for religious effects on behavior or attitudes more remote from religiousness per se, I found little or nothing.

My purpose in this essay is to reassert an ancient truth: religion does indeed have truly potent effects on deviance—it does greatly inhibit crime, delinquency, suicide, even the spread of syphilis. But these effects are elusive and unpredictable *unless they are approached in a truly sociological, not psychological, fashion.* The best way to explain this point is to recapitulate the journey by which I came to understand things that ought always to have been obvious.

HELLFIRE AND DELINQUENCY

In 1968 Travis Hirschi and I decided to test a self-evident hypothesis: that religious commitment is negatively related to delinquent behavior. To this

111

day I'm not sure why we bothered, and had the data not been readily at hand I assure you we would not have done so. In any event, the results confounded both conventional social science and common sense. Kids who attended church or Sunday school were no less likely to be delinquent than kids who did not attend. Kids who believed that hell awaited sinners were not less likely to steal from stores than were kids who lacked such beliefs. Nor did parental religious activity influence kid's delinquency.

Once our findings appeared in print (Hirschi & Stark, 1969), they were accepted uncritically. It was almost as if sociologists couldn't wait to assure the world that religion is unable to guide boys and girls along the straight and narrow, and this "fact" soon was enshrined in standard undergraduate textbooks. In contrast, decades of failures to find a correlation between family income and delinquency did not lead sociologists to accept that as fact (cf. Tittle, Villemez, & Smith, 1977; Hindelang, Hirschi, & Weis, 1981). Which simply reflects that most sociologists have faith in social class, but none in religion.

In any event, the fact was that Hirschi and I had failed to find the slightest trace of a religious effect on conformity, despite having a very large sample, a variety of apparently good measures of religious beliefs and behavior, and despite considerable statistical manipulation to remove possible suppressor effects. Moreover, within several years came a replication study. Based on data from several cities in the Pacific Northwest it too failed to find religious effects on delinquency (Burkett & White, 1974).

Almost a decade later, two new studies appeared. One was based on Atlanta teenagers (Higgins & Albrecht, 1977) and the other based on six wards (parishes) of the Mormon Church (Albrecht, Chadwick, & Alcorn, 1977). Both of these studies found what Hirschi and I had taken for granted that we would find—a strong negative relationship between church attendance and delinquency. At that point a fifth study that had gone unnoticed came to light. Based on a large Nashville sample it too found a strong negative religion effect, despite the fact that its authors said the effect was only minor (Rhodes & Reiss, 1970). So there it was. Two studies showed no effect; three studies showed a strong negative effect. Well, which should we accept?

Returning to the hunt, I soon discovered that so long as religion is conceived of as an individual trait, as a set of personal beliefs and practices, we can never know when and where religion will influence conformity, for research will continue to produce contradictory findings. But, if we move from a psychological to a sociological conception of religion, clarity leaps from the chaos. I am prepared to argue theoretically and to demonstrate empirically that religion affects conformity, not through producing guilt or fear of hellfire in the individual, but that religion gains its power to shape the individual only as an aspect of groups. Let me put it this way. It is not whether an individual kid goes to church or believes in hell that influences his or her delinquency. What is critical is whether the *majority* of the kid's *friends* are religious. In communities where most young people do not attend church, religion will not inhibit the behavior even of those teenagers who personally are religious. However, in communities where most kids are religious, then those who are will be less delinquent than those who aren't.

Life is social. It is through day-to-day interaction with our friends that we become implicated in conformity. If most of our friends are not religious, then religious considerations rarely enter into the process by which norms are adopted or justified. Even if we are religious, even if we do bring up religious concerns, these do not strike a responsive chord in most of our associates. In this way the effect of individual religious commitment is smothered by group irreligiousness and tends to become a very compartmentalized component of the lives of its adherents. This is facilitated by the fact that available data suggest very little tendency for people having conventional religious commitments to give these weight in selecting friends. That is, with the exception of kids from deviant religious backgrounds, religion plays little or no role in shaping attachments and therefore in relatively unchurched communities the religious kids will tend to have mainly unchurched associates (Bainbridge & Stark, 1981a; 1981b). Of course, the opposite occurs in communities where most people are religious. When most young people in a friendship network are religious, religious concerns will be amplified and made a valid part of everyday interaction. In such communities, individual variations in religiousness come into play simply because *individual commitment is energized by the group.*

Based on this line of theorizing I then set about demonstrating that I could predict where individual level correlations would and would not turn up in research. First, I computed the church-membership rates for the cities in which the published studies had been conducted. These conformed to the predicted pattern, the studies finding no religious effects having been conducted in communities where the majority are unchurched. I then obtained individual level data on religious commitment and delinquency for two communities differing immensely in their religious composition. For Provo, Utah, the city with the highest church-membership rate in the nation (96.6%), I predicted the correlation would be found. It was. For Seattle, a city with nearly the lowest church-membership rate in the nation (28%), I predicted no correlation between individual religiousness and delinquency. There was none. Finally, working with data for a national sample of 87 high schools I was able to make the individual level correlation appear and disappear by manipulating the religious composition of the setting (Stark, Kent, & Doyle, 1982).

So, where are we? Does religion limit delinquency? If we stick to the psychological level of analysis, we can only say, "Sometimes yes, sometimes no." If we move to the sociological level of analysis we can say, "Yes."

That is, if we conceive of religion as a group property, then we can say that in ecological settings where the majority are religious, religious people will be less prone to delinquency than irreligious people. But, where the group tends to irreligion, no individual effects will be found.

Interestingly enough, the same is true for the effects of sports participation on delinquency. In settings where high school sports are the focus of substantial community attention and admiration, boys who take part become substantially less delinquent over time. But no such effect obtains in communities where high school sports lack visibility (Stark, Kent, & Finke, 1987).

These findings suggest two things. First, we need sociological theories; to explain the moral order we must consider the properties of groups, not just of individuals. Second, sociological theories require that we base our research on sociological *units of analysis*. We cannot assess propositions about groups by examining traits of individuals. And, we cannot assess the impact of religion on conformity unless we examine variations among groups. Put another way, to rediscover religious effects we must rediscover the *moral community*—the neighborhood, the city, even the society.

THE MORAL COMMUNITY REVISITED

It was Durkheim (1897) who first gave effective statement to propositions linking individual deviance or conformity to variations in the social structure. People conform only if they are restrained by social bonds—humans are moral only to the extent that they are social. To explain what he regarded as the impending moral breakdown of modern societies, Durkheim contrasted life in modern urban societies with that of traditional rural villages, characterizing the latter as "moral communities." The moral community is based on two elements. The first is *social integration*, the density and intimacy of attachments among group members. The second is *moral integration*, the collective conception of the norms, and especially of religious beliefs that legitimate the norms. As we shall wee, Durkheim often considered moral intergration to be wholly derivative of social integration, although at other times he seemed to regard them as analytically distinct. In any event, Durkheim's major thesis was that conditions of modern life disrupt both social and moral integration. People became isolated social atoms and, as religious dissent leads to pluralism, society lacks the moral integration necessary to ensure conformity to the norms.

There are many defects in Durkheim's work. But his essential point that conformity is social seems well-taken. And, in fact, his thesis about moral communities once dominated research and writing in urban sociology, especially the form described as human ecology. Thus, Clifford R. Shaw and Henry D. McKay, in a series of studies beginning in 1929, found delinquency was much higher in urban neighborhoods having high rates of population turnover. Such neighborhoods would, necessarily, be low in social integration (Shaw & McKay, 1929, 1931, 1942). And, in a series of highly influential papers, Robert C. Angell (1942, 1947, 1949, 1974) found that cities higher in "moral integration" had lower rates of crime and suicide.

In recent years, however, these studies have been ignored and even sociologists of religion, who may have the largest stake in the moral integration thesis, have ignored the topic. There may have been many reasons for this. But an important one has been the seemingly grave practical limits on such research. It is hard enough to get sufficient funding to gather data from an adequate sample of individuals. It has seemed prohibitive to attempt to get funding to assess levels of religious commitment in a number of cities, for example. Even if we settled for sample bases of 500 respondents per city, it would require 10,000 respondents to characterize only 20 cities (and that would still only give us 20 cases for analysis). Indeed, data limits often were cited in the old moral community studies. The authors had to make use of available data and Angell, therefore, used published data on charitable fund-raising to operationalize "moral integration." Moreover, problems of limited data often lead to circularity in the moral community research. That is, various official deviance rates (crime, mental illness, suicide, etc.) were used to infer the lack of social and moral integration thus making it tautological to attribute conformity to integration.

The great irony is that while the moral community thesis seems to have dwindled into obscurity for lack of data, the necessary data were there all along! I cannot comprehend why they were not put to use. Some of you will have seen various recent essays in which I make use of the superb data on religion in America provided by special censuses of religious bodies conducted by the US Census Bureau from 1890 through 1936. I still blush to admit that I was a very active empirical sociologist of religion for 20 years before discovering these data existed. I rationalize that William Peterson, an outstanding demographer, published a long essay in the second-ever issue of the *Journal for the Scientific Study of Religion* (Peterson, 1962), regretting the failure of the US Census to ask religion, and condemning the Bureau's suppression of a national survey of religion it conducted in 1957, without ever mentioning these massive data sets. Still, every competant sociologist of religion ought of have known of these data, and they should have been *used* long ago. I find it utterly mysterious that the human ecologists concerned with the moral community thesis failed to know about or use these data, since they were trained to use census data and worked at the time when these religious statistics were still being collected and published. In any event, adequate data exist to compute church-membership rates for all states, counties, and larger cities for 1890, 1906, 1916, 1926, and 1936. Then, by applying correction procedures to the fine Glenmary data for 1971 and 1980 (Johnson, Douglas, Picard, & Quinn, 1974; Quinn, Bernard, Anderson, Bradley, Goetting, & Shriver, 1983) comparable contemporary church-membership rates can be obtained. In a series of recent studies with various collaborators, I have reopened the moral community thesis and have tried to demonstrate the meaning and impact of areal church-membership rates.

RELIGION AND SUICIDE

Since the fundamental thesis about community and conformity was developed in Durkheim's *Suicide* (1897), let us begin with that subject. Although it is commonly believed that Durkheim argued that religion played a major role in preventing suicide, in fact, Durkheim dismissed religious effects per se and regarded Protestant-Catholic comparisons as but an indirect measure of social integration. Catholic communities, in his judgment, sustained higher levels of interpersonal attachments. They also sustained a firmer normative consensus because they were not plagued with religious disagreement. These matters aside, Durkheim denied any role for religious faith in preventing anomie or limiting suicide. One of my first undertakings, once I had access to good contemporary data on religious membership, was to reopen Durkheim's analysis. The results were clear and reassuring.

First, Durkheim was right to suggest the importance of social integration. Assuming that cities will have lower average levels of attachments to the extent that their populations turnover rapidly, a very robust correlation between social integration and suicide rates exists.

However, Durkheim was wrong to reduce religious effects to those of social integration. Potent negative correlations between church-membership and suicide obtain when social integration is controlled. Furthermore, there is no "Catholic effect" in American data, not today, not at the turn of the century. Church membership reduces suicide, but the proportion Catholic among church members is irrelevant. What these findings suggest is that the religious impact on suicide is positive rather than negative. That is, it is not religious prohibitions on suicide that matter, for then clearly there ought to be Catholic effects. Rather, it is the comfort to be found in religion that sustains people against suicide. These comforts seem trans-denominational. This view is encouraged not only by our findings for the United States, but by the recent revelations that Durkheim did not actually find Catholic-Protestant differences in suicide rates in 19th Century Europe. That is, these long-celebrated "facts" can most charitably be described as arithmetic errors (Pope, 1976).

The important point is that truly potent religious effects on suicide now have been found in data for American cities and states for four different decades from 1906 through 1971 (Stark, Doyle, & Rushing, 1983; Bainbridge & Stark, 1981c). Indeed, the impact of church-membership rates on suicide dwarf the effects of most variables taken seriously in ecological studies of suicide. For 80 years sociologists have paid lip service to the importance of religion in preventing suicide. From now on it will be necessary for them actually to include religion in their theories and research.

RELIGION AND CRIME

The acid test of the moral integration thesis rests on demonstrating that religion prevents acts of criminal non-conformity. Thus I thought it very encouraging when I was able to show there are large negative correlations between church membership rates and official crime rates, based on 1971 data for American SMSAs (Stark, Doyle, & Kent, 1980). Thus, in the unchurched trench along the shores of the Pacific Ocean, where church membership is only half what it is in most of the rest of the nation, crime rates run far above those for the rest of the country. Once again, using data for early in the century, the findings were replicated (Stark, Bainbridge, Crutchfield, Doyle, & Finke, 1983). In the Roaring Twenties, as today, crime rates were lower to the extent that church membership rates were higher. Moreover, non-criminal deviance rates also responded to church-membership. For example, mental hospital admission rates for advanced syphilis were very strongly negatively correlated with church-membership rates in the 1920s. Controls for other important variables, including population turnover, did not weaken the results.

However, before we simply celebrate the resurrection of the moral community thesis in behalf of religious effects, it will be important to see the limits to these effects. The fact is that in none of our studies did church-membership display substantial correlations with *all* crime rates. Moreover, the exceptions were identical today and in the 1920s, and when social integration as well as church membership is examined. That is, while the total crime rate is strongly related to church membership and to population turnover, some of the categories of crime making up the total rate do not display these relationships. Burglary, larceny, and rape respond strongly to moral and social integration. But, homicide and assault do not. These patterns led Robert Crutchfield and me to suggest a reconceptualization of the phenomenon of deviance (Stark & Crutchfield, in press; Stark, Bainbridge, Crutchfield, Doyle, & Finke, 1983).

RATIONAL AND IMPULSIVE DEVIANCE

Some deviance reflects conscious exit from the moral order. A burglar consciously and intentionally breaks the law in pursuit of gain. Moreover, burglary tends to reflect a pattern of deviance having significant duration. People rarely commit one burglary and then stop. Instead, they repeat the offense—often until they are caught. Thus it is fair to say that burglars act in a rational, albeit illegal, fashion. But this is not true in many other epi-sodes of deviance. Often people seem to act without calculation of risk or gain, indeed, without stopping to think at all. They act on sudden impulse without consciously abandoning the moral order. Indeed, such people often feel intense remorse and guilt afterwards.

The available data suggest that the majority of homicides and assaults making up official rates of reported offenses are acts of momentary im-pulse. This explains why these rates are not correlated with social and moral integration—no stakes in conformity can restrain the behavior of those who act without stopping to think, whose behavior reflects irrational impulse. Indeed, acts of impulsive deviance lie outside the scope of *any* current *sociological* theories of deviance. All sociological theories of devi-ance assume a self-aware actor who chooses to deviate or to conform, and who displays patterns of deviance having some duration. Sociological theories have virtually nothing to say about brief moments of uncontrolled, irrational, impulse. Indeed, it is here that a fruitful division of labor with psychology would seem to be indicated.

In any event, the data show a consistent pattern. Not only today, but in the Roaring Twenties as well, the moral community influences only those crime rates that mainly reflect rational deviance. It has little or no impact on crime rates dominated by impulsive episodes. It is important that we recognize that impulsive deviance lies beyond the scope of sociological theories.

The distinction between rational and impulsive deviance, and the dif-ferential impact of the moral community on these two modes of non-con-formity, also challenges the image that faith results in conformity because it fosters mindless obedience. Social science writing on the role of religion in sustaining conformity usually stresses the lack of personal autonomy in-volved—the unreflective, ritualistic way in which the religious adhere to the normative order. The data suggest the opposite, that religion produces conformity to the norms only to the extent that people consciously weigh alternatives. As we have seen, fear of hellfire, in and of itself, does not pre-vent delinquency. Moreover, the religious climate of communities seems unable to stay the hand of the enraged lover, but does seem to deter many a burglar and forger. Thus religious effects on conformity lie primarily in the realm of the rational, not the irrational—not in blind superstition, as generations of social scientists have suggested, but in calculations of gain and loss.

CONCLUSION

In ads for *American Piety* (Stark & Glock, 1968), the University of Cali-fornia Press promoted another book that Glock and I had planned to write on the consequences of religious commitment. The book never appeared because we were unable to reliably isolate such consequences. At the time I concluded that if religion has no capacity to inhibit even behavior such as crime and delinquency, there is little reason to pursue the sociology of religion—and I promptly jumped ship.

As it turns out the swim did me good. Eventually I rediscovered sociology and learned to stop treating religion as an individual trait. When we treat religion as a group property, its effects are revealed in all their power.

REFERENCES

Albrecht, S.L., Chadwick, B.A., & Alcorn, D.S. (1977). Religiosity and deviance. *Journal for the Scientific Study of Religion*, 16, 263–274.

Angell, R.C. (1942). The social integration of american cities, *American Journal of Sociology*, 47, 575–592.

Angell, R.C. (1947). The social integration of cities of more than 100,000 population, *American Sociological Review*, 12, 335–342.

Angell, R.C. (1949). Moral integration and interpersonal integration in american cities. *American Sociological Review*, 14, 245–251.

Angell, R.C. (1974). The moral integration of american cities. II. *American Journal of Sociology*, 80, 607–629.

Bainbridge, W.S., & Stark, R. (1981a). The consciousness reformation reconsidered. *Journal of the Scientific Study of Religion*, 20, 1–16.

Bainbridge, W.S., & Stark, R. (1981b). Friendship, religion, and the occult. *Review of Religious research*, 22, 313–327.

Bainbridge, W.S., & Stark, R. (1981c). Suicide, homicide, and religion: Durkheim reassessed. *Annual Review of the Social Sciences of Religion*, 5, 33–56.

Burkett, S.R., & White, M. (1974). Hellfire and delinquency: Another look. *Journal for the Scientific Study of Religion*, 13, 455–462.

Durkheim, E. (1951). *Suicide*. New York: The Free Press (originally published 1897).

Higgins, P.C., & Albrecht, G.L. (1977). Hellfire and Delinquency Revisited. *Social Forces*, 55, 952–958.

Hindelang, M., Hirschi, T., & Weis, J.G. (1981). *Measuring delinquency*. Beverly Hills: Sage.

Hirschi, T., & Stark, R. (1969). Hellfire and delinquency. *Social Problems*, 17, 202–213.

Johnson, D.W., Picard, P.R., & Quinn, B. (1974). *Churches and church membership in the United States*. Washington, DC: Glenmary.

Parrinder, G. (1983). *World religions: From ancient history to the present*. New York: Facts on File Publications.

Peterson, W. (1962). Religious statistics in the United States. *Journal for the Scientific Study of Religion*, 1, 165–178.

Pope, W. (1976). *Durkheim's suicide: A classic analyzed*. Chicago: University of Chicago Press.

Quinn, B., Anderson, H., Bradly, M., Goetting, P., & Shriver, P. (1982). *Churches and church membership in the United States 1980*. Atlanta: Glenmary.

Rhodes, A.L., & Reiss, A.L., Jr. (1970). The religious factor and delinquent behavior. *Journal of Research in Crime and Delinquency*, 7, 83–98.

Shaw, C.R., & McKay, H.D. (1929). *Delinquency areas*. Chicago: University of Chicago Press.

Shaw, C.R., & McKay, H.D. (1931). *Report on the Causes of Crime, 12,* 13, Washington, DC: National Commission on Law Observance and Enforcement.

Shaw, C.R., & McKay, H.D. (1942). *Juvenile delinquency in urban areas.* Chicago: University of Chicago Press.

Stark, R., & Bainbridge, W.S. (1985). *The future of religion: Secularization, revival, and cult formation.* Berkeley: University of California Press.

Stark, R., Bainbridge, W.S., Crutchfield, R., Doyle, D.P., & Finke, R. (1983). Crime and delinquency in the roaring twenties. *Journal of Research in Crime and Delinquency, 20,* 4–21.

Stark, R., & Crutchfield, R. (in press). Intentional and impulsive deviance: A reconceptualization. *Criminology.*

Stark, R., Doyle, D.P., & Rushing, J.L. (1983). Beyond durkheim: Religion and suicide. *Journal for the Scientific Study of Religion, 22,* 120–131.

Stark, R., Doyle, D.P., & Kent, L. (1980). Rediscovering moral communities: Church membership and crime. In T. Hirschi & M. Gottfredson, (Eds.), *Understanding crime.* Beverly Hills: Sage.

Stark, R., & Glock, C.Y. (1968). *American piety.* Berkeley: University of California Press.

Stark, R., Kent, L., & Doyle, D.P. (1982). Religion and delinquency: The ecology of a lost relationship. *Journal of Research in Crime and Delinquency, 19,* 4–24.

Stark, R., Kent, L., & Finke, R. (1987). *Sports and delinquency.* In T. Hirschi & M. Gottfredson, eds., *Positive Criminology: Essays in Honor of Michael J. Hindelang,* Beverly Hills: Sage.

Tittle, C.R., Villemez, W.J., & Smith, D.A. (1978). The myth of social class and criminality: An empirical assessment of empirical evidence. *American Sociological Review, 43,* 643–656.

Chapter 4

Religion, Responsibility, and Victims of Crime: The Return to Conservative Criminology

David Giacopassi

Department of Criminal Justice
Memphis State University

Ross Hastings

Department of Criminology
University of Ottawa, Canada

Crime and the criminal justice system are political phenomena. They subside, grow, and wane as the political tides ebb and flow, and neither has a life distinct from that imparted to it by the state. Crime and the policies of the criminal justice system, therefore, can only be interpreted by viewing them in the context of the socio-political arena in which they occur.

In the last decade, there has been an upsurge in fundamentalist religiosity and new right politics. However, criminologists and policy makers have failed to fully appreciate the impact of this movement on criminological theory, policy, and practice. This paper will examine the new right and its relationship to the conservative religious organizations that support the new right in an attempt to determine their effect on criminology.

Our contention is that there has been a regression towards conservatism in some key areas of criminological policy and practice. To illustrate, we will focus on the victims of crime movement, and more specifically, on the issue of who is responsible for repairing the injuries suffered by the innocent victims of criminal injury. We will argue that, under the influence of the religious and political right, there has been a tendency to focus the blame and the burden on the criminal offender, and to absolve society of any significant responsibility in this matter. The result is a tendency in most jurisdictions to recognize the needs of victims, but not to repair them.

THE HISTORICAL RELATIONSHIP OF LAW AND RELIGION

In *Religion and Politics,* Michael Malbin (1978) examines the intentions of the authors of the First Amendment. After studying the records of the debates of the First Congress, he concludes that the current legislative and judicial policy of the United States which embodies a "wall of separation" between church and state is the result of an erroneous interpretation of the intentions of the First Congress. His speech by speech analysis of the First Congress leads him to argue that, consistent with contemporary judicial policy, the First Amendment prohibits the government from favoring any particular religion or from interfering with the practice of religion in the state. However, and contrary to present judicial interpretation, the First Amendment does not prohibit the state from recognizing the value of religion and encouraging these values when it serves a societal need. In effect, the state need not be "religion-neutral," simply not "religion-specific."

This type of argument as to the intent of the authors of the First Amendment is becoming increasingly common, and serves to bolster the attempt of organized religion to influence the state in such areas as school prayer and the strengthening of "morality laws." These attempts are not novel to the 20th century and are, in fact, more reactionary than revolutionary.

A brief review of the factors influencing the development of law in the United States makes evident the close historical relationship of law and religion in early American society. Parallels of the early fundamentalist religions to the current religiously inspired attempts to reform criminal law and the practices of the criminal justice system are also apparent.

The desire for freedom to practice their religion served as the impetus for the Puritans to leave England and brave the dangers of settling in the New World. The Puritans left England as "aggressive malcontents" (Kammen, 1972, p. 60) and, predictably, their religion played an exceedingly important role in determining the culture and laws of the "holy commonwealths" they sought to establish. Although the Puritan theocracy declined, the Puritan tradition remained strong and vital: by 1776, three-fourths of the colonists shared a Puritan heritage and adhered to the traditional Puritanic moral code (Ahlstrom, 1973). Despite the formal separation of Church and State, Puritanism was still the dominant force in law well into the 19th century (Mueller, 1969).

The enduring effect of the Puritan religious orientation on American law is documented by Roscoe Pound who listed Puritanism as one of seven factors shaping American law (Pound, 1921). Further, three of the remaining six forces important in the formulation of American law (the contests between the courts and the crown in the 17th century, the political ideas of the 18th century, and the philosophical premises that helped remake English common law into the American legal system) have evident Puritan influences (DeWolf, 1975). Several characteristics of the Puritan belief system made its effects on the law especially strong. Among these was the belief that, given the weakness and depravity of the human spirit, a strict and all-encompassing system of law was necessary to restrain the deviant impulses found in humans (DeWolf, 1975). In the Puritan world view, there were only two classes of people: the saved and the unsaved, doomed to ever-lasting hellfire. This latter group would "drift sullenly into the lower echelons of society, highly susceptible to deviant forms of behavior" (Erikson, 1966, p. 190). Yet, the Puritans had great faith in the powers of the law to restrain and redirect the deviant impulses of the people (DeWolf, 1975, p. 76) and passed one of the most severe and restrictive legal codes known to man.

A second characteristic of the Puritan belief system that greatly influenced American law was the belief that the law should reflect Devine will as revealed in the Bible (DeWolf, 1975). These "Godly laws" often reflected a self-rightious intolerance of diversity and a vindictiveness historically reserved for infidels. According to Erikson, the punishment of the deviant had a three-fold function: it reassured the individuals of their goodness, it reaffirmed the authority of the Scriptures, and it was an act of fealty to God. These benefits combined to justify the legendary severity of the law. However, "the most terrifying thing about punishment. . . was not its fierceness, but its cold rightiousness. . . justice was governed by relentless certainty" (Erikson, 1966, p. 190). The moral certainty of Puritanism was based on a religiously inspired faith that resulted not only in the molding of the legal philosophy but also in more intangible consequences. Hofstadter (1962) believes that the fundamentalist religions of early modern Protestantism helped plant the seed of anti-intellectualism in the new world. The anti-intellectualism developed as a result of the tension between rationalism and the requirements of unquestioning faith in the religious realm.

> To the extent that it becomes accepted in any culture that religion is largely an affair of the heart or the intuitive qualities of mind, and the rational mind is irrelevant or worse, so far will it be believed that the rational faculties are barren or perhaps dangerous. . . In modern culture, the evangelical movement has been the most powerful carrier of this kind of religious anti-intellectualism. . . (Hofstadter, 1962, p. 47)

If the fundamentalist religions planted the seed of anti-intellectualism, the seed was fertilized and nurtured by business and commerce. Hofstadter characterizes the business ethic as dominant in American society. It values pragmatic action as opposed to the realm of the intellect, which is abstract and theoretical. Thus, business and fundamentalist religion share a distrust of intellectualism and its tendencies to questioning and critical reflection.

This affinity for business of fundamentalist religions is not as paradoxical as it might initially appear. The earliest Puritans in the new world came to establish holy commonwealths, but they realized that any degree of permanency would require mercantile success. This was sought not simply to maintain their base of religious freedom, but also to provide a beacon to guide others from England to the proper path of religion and prosperity. Further, as Weber explained in *The Protestant Ethic and the Spirit of Capitalism* (1958), worldly success came to be viewed in those fundamentalist religions that held to the dogma of predestination as a sign of God's favor. Worldly success then came to be valued not for materalistic reasons alone, but also as a sign of doing good and having gained the favored status of predestined salvation.

Both fundamentalist religions and the business segment historically have large and powerful constituencies. However, when their interests meld, they combine in a force capable of producing dramatic changes in law and the criminal justice system. Prohibition is an example of what can result when such a coincidence of businesss and religious interests occur.

According to one school of thought, the 18th Amendment resulted from the campaign of a coalition of businessmen and members of conservative Protestant religions. For the latter, prohibition was primarily a "symbolic crusade" by members of white, rural, middle class conservative Protestant denominations against the poor, urban, Catholic immigrants who threatened their way of life (Gusfield, 1962). Gusfield has characterized the temperance movement as reflecting an obsession with "moral perfectionism" by "devoted sectarians. . . unable to compromise with human impulse" (1962, p. 1). Using the activities of the Women's Christian Temperance Union as an example, he illustrates the concerns of a dominant social group for the urban immigrants whom they wished to "americanize and Christianize." The campaign that developed against drinking was based on "moral disapproval" (Bell, 1976, p. 153). "For a significant portion of the population prohibition meant stamping out sin. . ." (Quinney, 1979, p. 151). For the businessmen, prohibition carried not only symbolic value, but was also an attempt to insure an honest, sober, and industrious workforce. Some historians have written that financial support by businesses was crucial to the success of the temperance movement (Humphries & Greenberg, 1981). Together, these two interest groups, conservative religion and business, combined to accomplish what has been called the most effective single-issue political movement in recent times.

We have seen that conservative religious and business groups, far from being adversarial, often can join ranks and dramatically transform societal law. It is our contention that present "latter-day Puritans" (Rhodes, 1981) are mobilizing with business interests to attempt to influence the law and, indirectly, criminological thought just as their historical forebears attempted to do.

THE NEW PURITANS AS MORAL ENTREPRENEURS

In the United States, the "religious right" is composed of a diversity of groups that defy neat categorization. They have been called "latter day Puritans" because of their conservative religious philosophy and their desire to transform this moral code into societal law. Included in its numbers are fundamental Protestants, Roman Catholics, and Orthodox Jews. The largest, most active and most politically powerful group on the religious right is the Moral Majority, an educational and lobbying organization founded in 1979 by the Rev. Jerry Falwell. The Moral Majority leads a loose alliance of independent groups that includes the National Christian Action Coalition, the Christian Voice, and the Religious Roundtable.

As with the original Puritans, the Moral Majority believes it has a duty to transform the law so as to make it consistent with their moral code. Consequently, the Moral Majority and other conservative religious groups have been actively engaged in the debates over such diverse issues as the Equal Rights Amendment, abortion, school prayer, and various provisions of the criminal code, especially those dealing with "morality crimes" such as pornography, prostitution, and drugs. By lobbying for harsher penalties or stricter enforcement of existing laws, they are fulfilling the role of the crusading reformer:

> . . . there is some evil which profoundly disturbs him. He feels that nothing can be right in the world until rules are made to correct it. He operates with an absolute ethic; what he sees is truly and totally evil with no qualification. Any means is justified to do away with it. The crusader is fervent and righteous. It is appropriate to think of reformers as crusaders because they typically believe that their mission is a holy one. (Becker, 1963)

This combination of religion and moral entrepreneurship can result in a number of negative consequences for the criminal justice system. The first of these is a tendency to elevate "morality crimes" such as pornography, prostitution, and drug offenses to a primary level of concern for the criminal justice system. As a result, these proposals introduce a disproportionality of penalty to demonstrable harm caused by the criminal act. In addition, since most of these acts are victimless crimes, they are difficult if not impossible to enforce and divert resources that might be more effectively employed to combat predatory crime (President's Commission, 1968).

A second negative consequence of the religiously inspired crusading reformer is a result of their unwillingness to compromise their religiously based principles. As a result, the position presented is frequently absolutist and thus obstructs and divides the normal political process and negates the functionality of law. The proposals of the religiously inspired entrepreneur reflect a narrowness that discourages pluralism. While fundamentalist religions tend to argue against "secular supremacy," they are in fact often intolerant of religious groups that hold differing beliefs. As a consequence, there is a very real danger of the state becoming "religion specific" by elevating the morality inherent in a specific religious philosophy to the status of law.

A final danger is that by attempting to impose a particular moral perspective on a populace characterized by a diversity of moral codes, society departs from law with unanimous or near-unanimous support. To the degree that law is supported by a minority of the population, yet is intrusive into the lives of the majority, that law is transformed from a "public good" to a "public bad" (Rhodes, 1981).

Despite these dangers, fundamental religions have become increasingly active as moral entrepreneurs, merging with business interests to form a powerful conservative alliance. To appreciate the implications of this merger, we must link these religiously inspired themes to the concerns and interests of the wider political and social movement generally referred to as the "New Right." While general agreement exists as to the nature of these trends, it does not extend to a common analysis of why this "community" of religious and political interests has emerged at this point in time, nor to a shared view of probable consequences of this marriage of socio-political and religious interests.

To put the disagreement in simple terms, the right and the left disagree on the issue of why this trend would emerge now. Advocates of the right tend to see their views as a necessary counterbalance to the permissiveness and demoralization which have resulted from excessive government intervention in social and community life, and to the consequent moral degeneration and loss of family and community stability which we have experienced over the last few years. In this perspective, a criminological focus on the failures of discipline and the importance of control is a necessary part of the movement towards a renewal of family and community solidarity, and societal well-being. On the other hand, advocates of the left tend to see the religious and political expressions of the new right as predictable strategic responses in the larger attempt to manage the current national and international crises of capitalism. In this view, the moral and religious views of the new right are essentially instruments or weapons in a wider network of class conflicts. Obviously, the outcome of this debate has tremendous implications in any attempt to establish the validity of competing criminological analyses, or to specify appropriate directions for criminal justice policy and practice.

There is a community of political and ideological interests which links the new right and conservative criminology. More specifically, we would argue that the recent popularity and successes of the religious right have given considerable impetus and public support to the re-emergence of what are essentially conservative and repressive forms of criminology and criminal justice.

Our view is founded on our understanding of some of the basic trends in criminology over the last few years, trends which reflect the emergence and successes of the religious and political right. To begin, there has been a renewed tendency to argue that criminology has failed to discover the factors or causes which differentiate criminals from non-criminals. The common sense expression of this failure is the popular (though arguable) notion that "nothing works," and that criminology has failed to generate the kinds of theories or data which could contribute to the prevention or reduction of crime, or to the rehabilitation of offenders. The result, within criminology, has been the recent emergence and popularity of the "new realists" and their focus on the impact of the failure of socialization and social control (e.g, Wilson), or of bio-psychological theories of criminal behavior (e.g, Jeffrey). The practical consequence of such right wing views is to shift both criminological theorizing and policy thrusts away from the social reconstruction mandate of left wing criminology, and towards a concentration on improved social defenses against criminals (e.g., notions such as "defendable space" or crime prevention through environmental design.)

It is precisely this theme of prevention through "defensive" strategies which links right wing criminology and the religious right. The two reinforce each other in a number of ways, but most importantly is their insistence that analysis and policy should focus on the responsibility of the "truly criminal," that is, on those who constitute the principle and direct threat to the essential societal requirements of order and community. The dichotomy between the "truly criminal" and the non-criminal directly reflects the tendency of the religious right to divide all social reality into good (biblical morality) and evil (the devil's work). The common ground is a perspective which sees evil (crime) emerging out of immorality (permissiveness). The embodiment of this evil is to be found among abortion advocates, homosexuals or other purveyors of sexual permissiveness (pornography, televised sex), union or labour organizations, advocates of women's liberation, or the "uncivilized" mass of urban poor (usually members of racial or ethnic minorities) who are seen as responsible for predatory or street crime. These desperate sinners are lumped together under the universal and absolutist morality of the religious right: they constitute the modern version of the "dangerous classes" against which society must defend itself.

These fundamentalist religious views form the moral basis for the current war on crime. In an address before the International Association of Chiefs of Police, President Reagan states:

The solution to the crime problem will not be found in social worker's files, the psychiatrist's notes, or the bureaucrat's budget; it's a problem of the human heart, and it's there we must look for the answer. . men are basically good but prone to evil; and society has a right to be protected from them. . .
Our deep moral values and strong social institutions can hold back that jungle

and restrain the darker impulses of human nature. (*New York Times*, Sept. 29, 1981, p. 13).

There can be little doubt that such ideas have struck a responsive chord among the general population. These views have found fertile ground in the current frustrations of the lower and middle class, and in the traditional tendency of the American public to react to bad times by blaming economic problems on moral degeneracy and permissiveness. In the same way that the early 20th century moral beliefs concerning the wrongfulness of divorce erroneously led criminologists to judge the broken family as the major cause of delinquency (Wilkinson, 1974), we now find the major cause of criminality to be permissiveness and moral pluralism. The solution is to blend religion and politics in a moral crusade to save America. It is in this light that one can argue that a significant portion of the new religiosity is actually an old fashioned politics of scapegoating—new wine in an old bottle, if you will. Nor is the conjuction purely fortuitous.

The coincidence of interests of fundamental religion and business has led some to argue that groups such as the Moral Majority were actually formed to accomplish the political purpose of drawing "born again" Christians away from Jimmy Carter and toward conservative Republicans (Woodward, 1983). In addition, opposition to big government and fear of federal intervention—whether in family, schools, or businesses—encouraged business and religion to join forces. It would seem that if "the business of America is business," then only the morally upright are qualified to engage in this work.

Our contention is that one cannot consider the orientations to crime and criminal justice policy of contemporary religious crusaders without focusing on their relationship to current economic and fiscal crimes. Thus, it may be most accurate to view the political involvement of the religious right as a "satellite" in a wider conservative firmament.

There is no accident in the irony that the enemies of capitalism are also the incarnation of the work of the devil! Nor is it purely fortuitous that the capitalist state's focus on tightened social control over, and reduced welfare entitlements to, the victims of recession and austerity happen to the very same groups that the religious right has identified as epitomizing moral degeneracy and the failure of discipline. Ryan (1971) terms this the fallacy of "blaming the victim," whereby the politically and economically disenfranchised become blamed for their own condition. The only difference now is that they also bear responsibility for the condition the country is in.

The result of the operationalization of these views is doubly beneficial to the interests of capital. First, the reduction of entitlements and the elimination of social programs have liberated money for tax cuts for the wealthy, and for increased military spending in order to protect foreign investments. Second, the deterioration of conditions in the labor market has the benefit of increasing social discipline and making workers more subservient to the demands of industry.

THE CASE OF VICTIMS OF CRIME

There has been a great deal of interest in recent years in the plight of victims of crime. Much attention has been paid to the physical, emotional, and financial costs of crime, and to the secondary injuries victims may suffer as a result of their participation in the criminal justice process. Moreover, a great deal of energy, though not necessarily of resources, have been directed at attempts to improve the lot of victims of crime.

The problem in the case of victims is not so much to decide what should be done: there seems little real argument as to the need for entitlements for victims of crime. Rather, the difficulty is in deciding who should be responsible for operationalizing and (more importantly) financing new initiatives in this area. It is here that the distinctions between left and right wing approaches are clearest and most significant. A left orientation will favor a collective responsibility or insurance approach. Its proponents would argue that crime is a reflection of social and cultural arrangements, and that the political system (through the collective mechanism of taxation) should be responsible for responding to the needs of victims. A right orientation, on the other hand, will tend to focus on the responsibility of the guilty party to repair the damage done to the innocent victim of crime. The focus here is on individual restitution or on mediation, rather than on collectively financed "welfare-type" arrangements.

In our view, the policy and program operationalizations of victims' initiatives tend to reflect a right orientation, one that is consistent with the general tendency to austerity and a reduction in real entitlements during periods of fiscal restraint. An overview of initiatives in this victims of crime area indicates that:

1. Relatively few new financial resources have been directed to victims of crime initiatives: there has been more recognition than action.
2. The tendency has been to invest what few resources there are in programs designed to increase the efficiency and the speed of the legal process (largely by keeping victims better informed of their rights and responsibilities). This is clearly of some benefit to victims, but the justification for such initiatives is primarily that they serve to reduce costs to the system and to increase cooperation by victims.
3. The increase in the use of reparative sentencing is more a function of a belief that this best serves the goals of punishment, denunciation, and rehabilitation than it is a result of a concern for victims of crime.

4.   The little funding for reparation to victims which does exist tends to come not from general revenues but from offender based sources such as fine surtaxes. This reflects a commitment to the notion of the responsibility of individual offenders ("sinners") to repair the costs of crime.

5.   The whole notion of victims of crime has been restricted to traditional forms of "street crime" or predatory crime by individuals. No attention has been paid to the victims of corporate or political crime.

6.   Only "innocent" victims of crime are likely to get any sympathy. Those who contribute to their plight are generally thought to be relatively unworthy of our sympathy.

The result of all this is that a very good idea is not being given the support it would need to fulfill its promise. Rather, initiatives on behalf of victims of crime are being systematically (though often not consciously) reformulated and operationalized within the parameters of conservative or fundamentalist religious and political values. The victims of crime initiative has emerged concurrently with, and is being largely taken over by, a right conception of social organization and criminal justice. A wonderful idea is thereby being subverted and compromised.

CONCLUSION

The consequences of the politics of the religious right lend support and lend credibility to the policies and practices of the political right: the political drive to decrease social entitlements marries perfectly with the religious right's insistence on the responsibility of the individual, and on the importance of the moral renewal of the individual as the basis of improvements in wider social conditions. We are dealing here with a new social Darwinism, one which both emerges from and provides support to the current forms of classism, racism, and sexism which underlies much current welfare and control policy.

Moreover, and perhaps more importantly, these views help to popularize a reactionary politics and yet to divert the awareness of the public from the class basis of these politics. This is done by redirecting the focus and the energy underlying much of contemporary politics onto another, and less threatening, ideological terrain. In this way, the religious right aids in the reproduction of current social arrangements by sustaining and reproducing their moral and cultural forms. The religious right thus contributes to the ideological support of capitalism, and the capitalist state contributes to the religious right by certifying (through policy implementation) the legitimacy of their values.

All of this brings us full circle to the correspondence of the religious right and of the current forms of conservative criminology. It is our contention that there is a risk of criminology being caught up more or less unwittingly in a partnership in what is essentially an ideological rather than a scientific task. We don't necessarily wish to impune the motives of right wing criminologists. Rather, our concern is with the consequences of their work. Our contention is that science is being sacrificed to ideology. The challenge of unravelling the dialectical relationship of social factors and agents to social situations and wider structures has been neglected in much recent work. In its place, we are seeing a great deal of attention directed towards an analysis of the problem of permissiveness which is the cause of moral degeneracy of certain types of individuals, and to the need to deal with crime and criminals through the moral regeneration of the dangerous classes. These individuals are viewed as the authors of their own (and of society's) misfortune, and as requiring discipline and control if progress is to be assured.

The result is a criminology which ideologically transforms the plight of the unfortunate, ignores the criminality of the fortunate and the larger realities of social control, and generally turns the clock back to earlier social pathology or social disorganization approaches. Criminals are to be controlled rather than understood. Unfortunately, it is a criminology which has not even begun to recognize its own failures, substituting religious and extreme capitalistic ideology for value neutrality and the scientific method. As a result, a neo-Puritanic moral code is looked to for answers to crime and criminal justice policy issues when, in fact, it may be part of the problem.

REFERENCES

Ahlstrom, S. (1973). *A religious history of the American people.* New Haven: Yale University Press.

Becker, H. (1963). *The outsiders.* New York: Free Press.

Bell, R. (1976). *Social deviance.* Homewood, IL: Dorsey Press.

DeWolf, L. (1975). *Crime and justice in America.* New York: Harper & Row.

Erikson, K. (1966). *Wayward Puritans.* New York: Wiley.

Gusfield, J. (1962). Status conflicts and the changing ideologies of the American temperance movement. In D. Pittman and C. Synder (Eds.), *Society, culture and drinking patterns.* New York: Wiley.

Hofstadter, R. (1962). *Anti-Intellectualism in American life.* New York: Alfred Knopf.

Humphries, D., & Greenberg, D. (1981). The dialectics of crime control. In D. Greenberg (Ed.), *Crime and capitalism.* Palo Alto, CA: Mayfield Publishing Co.

Kammen, M. (1972). *People of paradox.* New York: Vintage Books, Random House.

Malbin, M. (1978). *Religion and politics.* Washington, DC: American Enterprise Institute of Public Policy Research.

Mueller, G. (1969). *Crime, law and the scholars*. Seattle: University of Washington Press.

Pound, R. (1921). *The spirit of the common law*. Francestown, NY: Marshall Jones.

Presidents Commission on Law Enforcement and Administration of Justice. (1968). *Task force reports: Courts*. Washington, DC: U.S. Government Printing Office.

Quinney, R. (1979). *Criminology*. Boston, Little, Brown.

Reagan, R. (1981, September). [Speech before International Association of Chiefs of Police in New Orleans]. *New York Times*, Sept. 29, p. 13.

Rhodes, A. (1981). Religious groups use of and resistance to legal change. Paper presented at 1981 American Society of Criminology Annual Meeting.

Ryan, W. (1971). *Blaming the victim*. New York: Vintage Books, Random House.

Weber, M. (1958). *The protestant ethic and the spirit of capitalism*. New York: Charles Scribner.

Wilkinson, K. (1974). The broken family and juvenile delinquency: scientific explanation or ideology? *Social Problems, 21*, 726–739.

Woodward, K. (1983, May). Jerry Falwell as a leader of men. *Notre Dame Magazine*, pp. 35–38.

Chapter 5

Criminals' Responses to Religious Themes in Whitman's Poetry *

John A. Johnson

Department of Psychology
Pennsylvania State University, DuBois

Lloyd D. Worley

Department of English
Pennsylvania State University, DuBois

Dr. Jack J. Leedy, first president of The National Association for Poetry Therapy and editor of two books on poetry therapy, defines "bibliotherapy" (of which poetry therapy is a part—cf. Hynes, 1981) as "the process of assimilating the psychological, sociological, and aesthetic values from books into human character, personality, and behavior" (1969a, p. 11). This definition would apparently include the assimilation of religious and moral values from poetry (Brown, 1975; Bell, 1982; Christensen & Moss, 1981). This chapter describes research on criminals' perceptions of religious themes in the poetry of Walt Whitman.

The use of poetry therapy in correctional institutions has been advocated by numerous psychiatrists, including such notables as Theodor Reik (1969). Clinical psychologist Maurice Flock notes that most prisoners have an extraordinary interest in themselves and their own mental processes. He quotes two inmates (cited in Brown, 1975, p. 155):

We know that somewhere we have taken a wrong turn, and we want books to help us understand where and why.

---

* This study was partially supported by a grant from the DuBois Educational Foundation to the authors.

We thank Warden Robert S. Dombrosky and the Clearfield County Prison Board for their permission to test the prisoners, the staff of the prison for helping us administer the questionnaires, and the participants who volunteered to be tested.

Books can sometimes change a man's life, especially his way of thinking. My incarceration and reading good books here have done this for me. I have plans for a much better and more wholesome life.

According to Dr. Bill Barkley, Chief Staff Clinical Psychologist at the California Men's Colony at San Luis Obispo in 1973, "Poetry therapy is not only possible, but a most important adjunct to the other psychiatric treatments offered in a correctional setting" (1973, p. 1). If this claim is true, then "poetry therapy" is not only useful, but important in the rehabilitation of criminals.

Barkley insists that "No matter how sick, hardened, and institutionalized an individual is there resides a heart, and that heart needs to be heard" (p. 1). He continues with an example (pp. 14–15): "Compassion, empathy, sensitivity, and fear all are expressed in a poem dealing with the gas chamber at San Quentin. The following poem was written many years ago, but it expresses the marked degree of empathy that is supposedly beyond the capacity of the anti-social personality."

RED LIGHT OF DEATH

Behind the high gray walls of Quentin
   Trying to beat the still hot air
I gazed into a Summer sky
   Saw a red light shining there.

Down below walked a dear old Padre
   Slowly walking down the hall
While behind him strolled a convict
   His foot-steps very slow.

The convict's eyes were filled with tears
   So full he could not see
As the dear Old Padre sang his song
   Nearer my God to thee.

Not far ahead stood a great steel door
   The color, it was green
The gates of hell stood behind that door
   For a convict, whom we'll call Gene.

They sat him in a big arm chair
   Strapped his arms down nice and tight
Now all he had to do is wait
   As the gas shut out the light.

In my hand I hold a paper
   On front page, you'll find his name
Yes, the Governor sent his pardon
   But the postman never came.

They dug a hole on yonder mountain
    Three foot wide and six feet deep
They carved his name upon an oaken board
    To mark where this convict sleeps.

As I set here, how I wonder
    How many tears he cried
As he watched the creeping darkness
    Fold around his [sic] as he died.

Now who can say I'm sorry
    His innocence plainly seen
Just who now stands in judgment
    Of a convict we'll call Gene.

Now I know what the red light meant
    Against the clear blue sky
I did not know the man who died
    But a tear fell from my eye.

I no longer set in the big big yard
    Trying to bear the Summer air
I don't like to gaze into a Summer sky
    And see a red light shining there.[1]

Not everyone would agree with the claims of Leedy and Barkley, however. Although research has demonstrated that poetry therapy can relieve certain psychiatric conditions (Edgar & Hazley, 1969), to our knowledge the effectiveness of poetry therapy in the rehabilitation of criminals has not been tested empirically. Yochelson and Samenow (1976) present arguments for why poetry therapy would *not* work for criminals. They first state that criminals' thinking is too simplistically concrete and literalistic (pp. 297–298). They claim, for example, that criminals believe that a few concrete acts, such as going to church and praying, make them religious. For criminals, the rituals of religion may satisfy certain emotional needs without providing an ethical or moral system. They may be impressed by the power of fundamentalist, hell-fire preachers, or may simply feel nostalgia upon hearing the music and psalms from their childhoods. (It is interesting to note that psychologist William James (1929, p. 258) came to the same conclusion 80 years ago).

Yochelson and Samenow do agree with psychologists like Barkley that underneath a tough exterior, many criminals are sensitive and sentimental (pp. 289–297). Prison publications often contain high quality poetry expressing idealistic and humanitarian values. Criminals have been observed

---

[1] Reprinted by permission of J.B. Lippincott Company from POETRY THE HEALER edited by Jack J. Leedy. Copyright © 1973 by J.B. Lippincott.

reading Kipling, Baudelaire, existential philosophy, and religious works. At the same time, Yochelson and Samenow claim, the concrete, literalistic thought patterns of felons cause them to miss the subtler conceptual points in literature. Rather than act as a deterrent to crime, sentimentality may instead contribute to its continuation. Yochelson and Samenow state that any kindness, charity, and aesthetic interests and talents a criminal might have only add to his belief that he is a good person and ultimately give him greater license for crime. Therefore, sensitivity and sentimentality do not form a basis for rehabilitation. If these claims are true, then poetry therapy may not only be a waste of time, it may even be dangerous. Brown (1975) in fact devotes an entire chapter of her book to possible adverse effects of bibliotherapy.

Yochelson's and Samenow's work has in turn been criticized. Their conclusions were based upon interviews with inmates, and many persons dismiss this kind of phenomenological methodology for being too subjective. We agree with Yochelson's and Samenow's critics about the subjectivity of their methods. On the other hand, as far as we know, persons advocating poetry therapy in prisons are working on faith and intuition rather than upon research evaluating the rehabilitating effectiveness of poetry.

Clearly, only large-scale, expensive, program evaluation research can definitively assess the effectiveness of poetry therapy in prisons. Our research is much less ambitious. It is predicated on the assumption that, in order to have a rehabilitating effect, the essential meanings of the poetry must be understood by the reader. Part of our research consisted of presenting passages of poetry to prisoners for their interpretation. Finding that criminals do not see the subtler interpretations in the passages would suggest that Yochelson and Samenow are correct that criminals' concrete thinking precludes instilling moral values through the use of poetry.

Our research corrects for the subjectivity in Yochelson and Samenow's research by evaluating their claims with objective questionnaire methodology. We constructed the Whitman Poetry Questionnaire to assess whether criminals see the subtler religious themes in poetry and also administered Hogan's (1969) Empathy Scale to objectively assess the sensitivity of criminals.

Even before we conducted our research, we were somewhat more optimistic than Yochelson and Samenow concerning criminals' ability to perceive subtle religious concepts in poetry and in the possible therapeutic value of poetry. An earlier literature review by the first author (Johnson, 1983) has shown that the personality and thought patterns of criminal and creative persons are similar, indicating that criminals may respond to certain poetry.

Johnson's argument is that a small percentage of the general population is born with a predisposition to deviance, but that the deviance can be expressed in constructive or destructive ways. Criminality is unacceptable deviance; artistic creativity is acceptable deviance. The key to reform, under this view, is not to make criminals conformists. Rather, successful reform would entail resocializing criminals into careers that are on the one hand consistent with their deviant personalities, yet on the other hand socially acceptable (e.g., art). Poetry, as an art form, may therefore play a useful role in the resocialization process.

Whitman's poetry was chosen for the present research for three reasons. First, Whitman's works appear on a list of poems that Leedy (1969a, p. 280) describes as suitable for use in poetry therapy. Second, we followed Leedy's (1969b) "isoprinciple" of poetry selection, which means that the most useful poems will reflect the feeling and mood of the population being treated. Though not a criminal, Whitman certainly was a nonconformist and in his time was considered deviant; therefore, he might appeal to a criminal population. Finally, critics generally agree that Whitman was a mystic and that he expressed his religious mysticism in his work. Whitman scholar Gay Allen (1957) has compiled a number of Whitman passages that illustrate mystical religious themes; Allen's book guided our selection of Whitman passages. Whitman scholarship indicates that his poetry has multiple layers of meaning from the commonplace to the sublime. Thus, Whitman's poetry seemed ideal for testing whether or not criminals will actually perceive subtle religious themes in poetry.

METHOD

The Whitman Poetry Questionnaire

Nearly all critics agree that Walt Whitman was a mystic, and that some sort of mystical experience was responsible for his sudden acquisition of creative power in the 1850s (Allen, 1957). While Whitman did not intend to express a formal philosophical doctrine of mysticism in his poetry, he nonetheless felt compelled to express his mystical insights through his poetry. (William James, 1929, describes "noetic quality"—the desire to communicate the mystical experience—as one of the four major characteristics of a person who has had a mystical experience.)

Allen devotes a chapter of his book to describing the characteristics of mysticism and the related doctrine of pantheism. He illustrates Whitman's affinity for these doctrines by citing relevant passages of poetry. We chose among these passages ten that represented the essential points of mysticism and pantheism and then wrote two alternative interpretations for each passage. The "correct" interpretation was based on Allen's explanation. The "incorrect" interpretation was constructed along three guidelines. It either (a) stated some obvious, superficial, concrete meaning of the passage; (b) presented a cliché from Judeo-Christian thought; or (c) reflected a personality trait that Yochelson and Samenow (1976) said is common in a criminal population.

Below we present the ten passages, their alternative interpretations, and explanations for each interpretation.[2]

I

There is something that comes home to one now and perpetually,
It is not what is printed, preach'd, discussed, it eludes discussion and print,
It is not to be put in a book, it is not in this book . . .

A.   Knowledge can not always be put into words.
B.   Certain thoughts are so bad that you can't talk or write about them.

This passage (lines 44–46 of "A Song for Occupations") reflects what William James calls the *ineffability* of a mystical experience (Allen, 1957, p. 243); thus "A" is the correct answer. If criminals are preoccupied with sin (Yochelson & Samenow, 1976, pp. 297–298), however, they may be more likely to choose option "B."

II

I sing the body electric,
The armies of those I love engirth me and I engirth them,
They will not let me off till I go with them, respond to them,
And discorrupt them, and charge them full with the charge of the soul.

A.   Love is power.
B.   All souls are connected through love.

This passage ("I Sing the Body Electric", lines 1–4) reflects what Bertrand Russell calls the doctrine of *unity* in mysticism (Allen, 1957, p. 246). The principle of unity states that plurality, division, and opposites are illusory, that all things, both spiritual and physical, are connected in God. Option "B' is therefore correct. Interpretation "A" was designed to tap criminals' alleged preoccupation with power (Yochelson & Samenow, 1976, pp. 276–289).

III

I mind how once we lay such a transparent summer morning,
How you settled your head athwart my hips and gently turn'd over upon me,
And parted the shirt from my bosom-bone, and plunged your tongue to my
    bare-stripped heart,

---

[2] Reprinted by permission of New York University Press from Walt Whitman: Leaves of Grass, Reader's Comprehensive Edition, edited by Harold W. Blodgett and Scully Bradley. Copyright © 1965 by New York University.

And reach'd till you felt my beard, and reach'd till you held my feet.

A. I am being held by a greater spiritual power.
B. I am letting a woman make love to me.

This passage (lines 87–90 of "Song of Myself") reflects William James's principle of *passivity* in the mystical experience (Allen, 1957, p. 243; pp. 249–250). The experience of passivity involves the sensation of being penetrated and permeated by the supernatural; thus "A" is the correct answer. Response "B" simply reflects a more superficial, obvious, concrete interpretation for the passage.

IV

Divine is the body—it is all—it is the soul also.
How can there be immortality except through mortality?
How can the ultimate reality of visible things be visible?
How can the real body ever die?

A. The body dies, but the soul lasts forever.
B. We know the soul through the body.

This passage ("Divine is the Person", lines 1–3) reflects the doctrine of *materialistic pantheism* (Allen, 1957, p. 261). This doctrine states that because God is all, indivisible, and immanent, matter and spirit are one; therefore the body is the soul and the soul is the body. Option "B", the correct answer, was adapted from a quotation by Goethe, "We know the soul only through the medium of the body, and God only through Nature" (Allen, 1957, p. 259). Interpretation "A" reflects the traditional Christian view concerning the relationship between soul and the body.

V

Omnes! omnes! let others ignore what they may,
I make the poem of evil also, I commemorate that part also,
I am myself just as much evil as good, and my nation is—and I say there is in fact no evil,
(Or if there is I say it is just as important to you, to the land, or to me, as any thing else.

A. Almost everyone has some sin in them.
B. All real things are equally valuable.

This passage ("Starting from Paumanok", lines 98–101) again illustrates the mystical notion of *unity*. God [read good] is all, therefore the perception of all opposites, including good and evil, is an illusory construction of our imagination. "The key to Whitman's attitude is the above *omnes*; he is the poety of *all*—all life, all existence, every object and particle in the universe equally necessary, perfect and therefore good" (Allen, 1957, p. 273). This means that option "B" is correct. Option "A" was designed once again to assess whether criminals are preoccupied with sin.

VI

I see something of God each hour of the twenty-four, and each moment then,
In the faces of men and women I see God, and in my own face in the glass,
I find letters from God dropt in the street, and every one is sign'd by God's name,
And I leave them where they are, for I know that wheresoe'er I go,
Others will punctually come for ever and ever.

A.   God made man in his own image.
B.   God is in everything.

This passage ("Song of Myself," lines 1284–1288) reflects the mystical and pantheistic doctrine of *signatures*, seen also in the writings of Emerson, Goethe, and Carlyle (Allen, 1957, pp. 261–262). The notion of signatures states that every object in nature bears the imprint or sign of God; this makes "B" the correct answer. The parallel and more well-known Hebraic teaching appears in option "A."

VII

One world is aware and by far the largest to me, and that is myself,
And whether I come to my own to-day or in ten thousand or ten million years,
I can cheerfully take it now, or with equal cheerfulness I can wait.
My foothold is tenon'd and mortis'd in granite,
I laugh at what you call dissolution,
And I know the amplitude of time.
And as to you Life I reckon you are the leavings of many deaths,
(No doubt I have died myself ten thousand times before.)

A.   I have had many past lives.
B.   People try to kill or control me, but I am too strong—I'll survive.

This passage (lines 416–421 and 1297–1298 of "Song of Myself") expresses the doctrine of *pantheistic transmigration* or reincarnation of the soul (Allen, 1957, pp. 267–268). Option "A" reflects this interpretation. Interpretation "B" reflects the "number one everywhere" aspect of the criminal power motive (Yochelson & Samenow, 1976, pp. 281–283). This aspect of the power motive is a criminal's strong need to come up on top in every situation.

VIII

The soul is of itself,
All verges to it, all has reference to what ensues,

All that a person does, says, thinks, is of consequence,
Not a move can a man or woman make, that affects him or her in a day,
   month, any part of the direct lifetime, or the hour of death, but the same
   affects him or her onward afterward through the indirect lifetime.

A.   Whether you are good or bad depends on how pure your soul is.
B.   Good and bad deeds affect the development of the soul.

This passage ("Song of Prudence," lines 5–9) refers to *karma*, the mystical law of cause and effect (Allen, 1957, pp. 274–275). Karma, reflected in interpretation "B," states that the choices one makes affect the evolution of the soul through birth and rebirth. Choice "A" deals with criminals' concern with purity and preoccupation with sin (Yochelson & Samenow, 1976, p. 298).

IX

Sex contains all, bodies, souls,
Meanings, proofs, purities, delicacies, results, promulgations,
Songs, commands, health, pride, the maternal mystery, the seminal milk,
All hopes, benefactions, bestowals, all the passions, loves, beauties, delights
   of the earth. . .

A.   Some people choose sex instead of religion.
B.   A person can feel very religious during sex.

This passage ("A Woman Waits for Me", lines 3–6) clearly contains both a mundane and a mystical meaning. The mundane interpretation ("A") polarizes the material and spiritual, such that one can choose only one or the other. Interpretation "B", on the other hand, carries with it the notion that sex is holy. Interpretation "B" derives from the mystic belief that the soul receives its identity from sex and thus "perpetually fulfills the cosmic plan" (Allen, 1957, p. 269).

X

Silent and amazed even when a little boy,
I remember I heard the preacher every Sunday put God in his statements,
As contending against some being or influence.

A.   As a boy I felt the power and influence of God.
B.   As a boy I felt God in harmony with everything.

The correct interpretation of the final passage ("A Child's Amaze") is obvious if one reads it carefully. Whitman's amazement about the preacher's words show that, even as a boy, he saw God in loving harmony with everything (interpretation "B"). This is part of the *unity* doctrine of mysticism. The alternative ("A") plays both upon the criminal's preoccupation with power (Yochelson & Samenow, 1976, pp. 276–289) and upon criminal's fear of God as an "all-powerful, all-knowing being" (Yochelson & Samenow, 1976, p. 297).

In essence, the Whitman Poetry Questionnaire is a semi-projective personality test. Like any projective personality test, it contains ambiguous stimuli, that is, stimuli that that can be interpreted in more than one way. Technically, the test is semi-projective because interpretations are limited beforehand to two alternatives. A complete review of the major journal of projective personality testing, *Journal of Personality Assessment,* did not reveal any previous studies using poetry in projective assessment. However, one article (Bailey & Edwards, 1973) described research using proverbs as a projective test. The proverbs successfully elicited a number of interpretable responses, including concrete thinking, psychotic thought processes, displacement hostility, and many other features of personality.

If Yochelson and Samenow are correct, criminals will tend to choose the incorrect interpretations on the Whitman Poetry Questionnaire for two reasons. First, criminals supposedly read aesthetic literature concretely and literalistically, which will cause them to overlook the subtler, mystical interpretation. Second, they possess certain "criminal" personality traits (preoccupation with power, sin, etc.), and would tend to project these traits onto the incorrect answers, just as passive-aggressive patients project their hostility onto inkblots. On the other hand, if criminal and creative thought processes are similar (Johnson, 1983), criminals should be able to perceive the correct, subtler interpretations.

The Empathy Scale

Hogan (1969) developed his Empathy Scale by comparing the responses of 57 men with high ratings and 57 men with low ratings for empathy across the combined item pool of the California Psychological Inventory (Gough, 1975), Minnesota Multiphasic Personality Inventory (Hathaway & McKinley, 1943) and a set of items used at the University of California's Institute of Personality Assessment and Research (IPAR). The 64 items that best discriminated between the high-empathy and low-empathy groups were retailed as the final Empathy scale. A three-month test-retest reliability of .84 was found for the scale, and substantial correlations were found with social acuity ratings, likability ratings, communication competence, level of moral maturity, and effective social functioning (Greif & Hogan, 1973; Hogan, 1969).

A further review of the literature by Johnson, Cheek, and Smither (1983) showed that Empathy Scale scores correlated with sociopolitical intelligence, therapist effectiveness, effective parenting, freedom from anxiety, tendency to feel what others feel, and accuracy in person perception. Noting that measurements of internal consistency for the scale are not extremely high (from .61 to .71—see Cross & Sharpley, 1982; Hogan, 1969), Johnson et al. performed a factor analysis of the scale and found four unique factors. They labeled these factors Social Self-Confidence, Even Temperedness, Sensitivity, and Nonconformity. Of the four factors, Sensitivity and Nonconformity best discriminated between the high- and low-empathy groups in Hogan's original sample, though all four components accounted for unique variance in the empathy criterion.

The evidence for the validity of Hogan's scale suggests that it is one of the best available measures of empathic sensitivity. Administering the scale to a group of criminals would objectively assess Yochelson and Samenow's claim that criminals essentially are sensitive. In his original article, Hogan (1969) found that, contrary to Yochelson and Samenow's position, prison inmates scored lower on his Empathy Scale than all non-criminal groups tested. The 92 inmates tested had a mean score of 30.4 compared to 42.4 for 70 medical students, 39.1 for 90 college students, 37.7 for 100 military officers, and 31.0 for 51 junior high school students. The present study seeks to replicate that finding.

In addition to comparing Empathy Scale scores of criminals and non-criminals, this study examines whether scores on the Empathy Scale predict scores on the Whitman Poetry Questionnaire. Because the Empathy Scale measures the tendency to imaginatively place one's self in another's position high scorers should be able to identify with Whitman and see his meanings.

The present study also looks at the four factor components of the Empathy Scale separately. For several reasons, the Sensitivity and Nonconformity factors were of particular interest. First, these factors accounted for the most variance in empathy ratings in Johnson et al.'s analysis. In addition, the Sensitivity factor seemed important because it is closest to Yochelson and Samenow's conception of criminal sensitivity or sentimentality. Two items in this factor refer to poetry. They are: "I like poetry" and "I have at one time or another tried my hand at writing poetry." The Nonconformity factor seemed particularly relevant to the present study because high scorers on this scale have an open, perceptive, intraceptive cognitive style, while low scorers have a biased, judgmental, projective cognitive style. This means, among other things, that high scorers on this factor should be more open to Whitman's mystical meanings in his poetry, while low scorers will project their own personalities into the interpretation task.

Subjects

Ninety-six male subjects participated in the study. The first group consisted of 50 freshman and sophomore college students enrolled in the authors' courses at the Pennsylvania State University's DuBois Campus. The second group consisted of 46 prison inmates at the Clearfield County Prison in Clearfield, Pennsylvania. The offenses of the inmates were as follows: theft (11), drug offenses (7), robbery (6), burglary (5), assault (3), driving under influence (3), rape (3), forgery (2), attempted murder (1), murder (1), escape (1), criminal trespass (1), and unknown (2).

All subjects volunteered to complete the questionnaires. The purpose of the study was explained to all subjects as an investigation of the way prison inmates and non-prison inmates interpret poetry. The students were tested in two groups; the prisoners, in three groups. The students completed the entire procedure on their own. The poetry passages were read orally to the prisoners as they followed along on their questionnaires to help overcome the poorer reading skills of some of the prisoners. (The Empathy Scale items are at a 6-grade reading level and presented no problems.) After subjects completed the Whitman Poetry Questionnaire and the Empathy Scale, they responded to the following demographic items on the last page: age, education, and religious preference. They were also encouraged to respond freely to the question, "Is there anything else you would like to say?"

RESULTS

Influence of Demographic Variables

The criminals and students differed on all three demographic variables. A chi-square value of 14.95 (4 degrees of freedom) indicated that the two groups differed in their religious affiliation. The criminal group showed 15% Catholic, 28% Protestant, 4% other denominations, 35% religious without denomination, and 18% nonreligious. The student group showed 44% Catholic, 32% Protestant, 6% other denominations, 12% religious without denomination, and 6% nonreligious. Thus, a relatively higher proportion of students were Catholic, and a relatively higher proportion of criminals were either nondenominationally religious or nonreligious. The age of the prisoners ranged from 19 to 49 ($M = 26.8$, $SD = 7.4$), while the age of the students ranged from 18 to 38 ($M = 20.5$, $SD = 4.1$). This difference was significant at the .0001 level ($F(1,94) = 27.07$). Obviously the students were better educated than the prisoners. All students but 3 (who were high school students sitting in on the course) had at least a year of college; only 5 prisoners had attended college. Of the remaining prisoners, 8 had grade school educations, 24 had high school educations, and 9 had completed technical school.

To determine whether the demographic differences between the two groups might influence group differences in poetry or empathy scores, the relationship between demographic variables and poetry and empathy scores was assessed within each group. Because the Poetry Questionnaire covered a wide range of religious themes, separate chi-square analyses for religion were computed for each item. For the students, only one significant result was found. On passage number five, which dealt with evil, 75% of the Catholics chose the wrong answer ("Almost everyone has some sin in them"), while 75% of the Protestants chose the right answer ("All real things are equally valuable"). The criminals showed the same trend for this item, though the result of the chi-square was not quite statistically significant ($p = .109$). None of the responses to other items were related to religious affiliation; overall, these results suggest that religious affiliation did not affect responses to the Poetry Questionnaire. Analyses of variance showed that religious affiliation was not related to scores on the Empathy Scale or its four factor-subscales. One can therefore conclude that the different religious composition of the criminals and students does not confound interpretation of group differences on the Poetry Questionnaire and Empathy Scale.

Age and level of education were correlated with total scores on the Whitman Poetry Questionnaire and with the full Empathy scale and its four factor-subscales. To determine whether using a total score on the Poetry Questionnaire was justified, an alpha reliability coefficient was computed for all cases. The value of alpha measure of internal consistency was .37, which is quite low, even for a short scale. While it is possible to use a scale with such low internal consistency in research (Cheek, 1982), one should certainly interpret the results with caution.

Age did not correlate significantly with total Poetry Questionnaire scores, Empathy scores, or Empathy factor-subscale scores in the full sample or either group separately. In the full sample, level of education (1 = grade school, 2 = high school, 3 = technical school, 4 = college) correlated significantly with Empathy ($r = .34$), Social Self-Confidence ($r = .24$), Even Temperedness ($r = .22$), and Nonconformity ($r = .30$), but not with the Whitman Poetry Questionnaire nor with the Sensitivity factor-subscale. Restriction of range precluded correlating education with the Poetry and Empathy scores for students alone. When these correlations were computed for criminals, a positive relationshp was found between education and Poetry Questionnaire scores ($r = .26$, $p < .05$), full Empathy Scale scores ($r = .34$, $p < .05$), and Nonconformity subscale scores ($r = .32$, $p < .05$). This means that when testing for differences between the criminals and students on the Poetry Questionnaire and Empathy Scale, education should be statistically controlled.

Group Differences

The central statistical analyses compare criminals' and students' scores on the Whitman Poetry Questionnaire and the Empathy Scale. These results are summarized in Table 1. Table 1 shows that chi-squares indicate no difference between the percentage of correct responses in the two groups for 7 of the 10 Whitman Poetry items. The students did better on items 6 and 9, and the criminals did better on item 10. Analysis of variance replicated this result. However, when an analysis of covariance was run for items 6, 9, and 10, controlling for the effects of education level, no differences were found between the criminals and students. An analysis of variance and covariance on the total Whitman Poetry Questionnaire scores indicated no difference between the groups. We realize that finding no differences between the groups could be due to the low reliability of the Whitman Poetry Questionnaire, and, without a power analysis, one cannot make

TABLE 1. Comparison of Criminals' and Students' Scores on Poetry and Empathy Scales

	Percent Choosing Correct Answer		
Poetry Item and Theme	Criminals	Students	Chi-Square (1 df)
1. Ineffability	80	82	.04 ns
2. Unity	70	67	.14 ns
3. Passivity	24	26	.06 ns
4. Pantheism	37	24	1.91 ns
5. Illusion of Evil	41	44	.07 ns
6. Signatures	72	88	3.99*
7. Transmigration	57	56	.00 ns
8. Karma	80	78	.09 ns
9. Oneness of Body & Spirit	46	72	6.90**
10. Unity and Harmony	52	32	4.01*

	Mean and Standard Deviation		
Scale	Criminals	Students	ANOVA (1,94 df) & ANACOVA (1,93 df)
Whitman Poetry Questionnaire	5.59 (1.81)	5.68 (1.68)	$F =$ .07 ns .84 ns
Empathy Scale	32.13 (6.11)	35.80 (5.98)	8.84** .26 ns
Social Self-Confidence	6.93 (2.30)	7.86 (2.60)	3.38 ns .00 ns
Even Temperedness	6.54 (3.22)	8.02 (3.15)	5.16* .91 ns
Sensitivity	5.63 (1.27)	5.56 (1.79)	.05 ns .02 ns
Nonconformity	5.07 (1.91)	6.36 (2.07)	10.09** 1.79 ns

  * $p < .05$.
 ** $p < .01$.

categorical null statements. Nonetheless, it does appear that criminals can perceive the subtle religious themes in Whitman's poetry just as well as college freshman and sophomores. Any slight differences in performance between the two groups can be attributed to educational level.

Table 1 also shows that analyses of variance indicate that the students are more empathic, even tempered, and nonconforming than the prisoners (recall that "nonconforming" refers to an open, malleable cognitive style rather than social deviance). However, when educational level is controlled in an analysis of covariance, no differences can be found between the groups on Empathy or its four subcomponents. This finding indicates that, according to an objective measure of empathy, criminals are definitely less empathic than college students (this replicates Hogan's, 1969, results). This deficit in empathy is related to a lower level of educational achievement on the part of the criminals.

Relation between Empathy and Poetry Interpretation

Table 2 summarizes the relationships between Whitman Poetry scores and scores on the Empathy, Social Self-Confidence, Even Temperedness, Sensitivity, and Nonconformity scores. For the total sample, higher scores on the Poetry Questionnaire were associated with higher scores on Empathy, Even Temperedness, Sensitivity, and Nonconformity. The same pattern was found for the students considered alone. For the criminals, higher scores on the Poetry Questionnaire were associated with higher scores on Empathy, Social Self-Confidence, and Nonconformity. Controlling for

TABLE 2. Correlations between Poetry Questionnaire and Empathy Scales

Scale	Full and Partial Correlations[a]		
	Criminals	Students	Total
Empathy Full Scale	27**	45****	35****
	20*	45****	34****
Social Self-Confidence	26**	00	12
	21*	00	10
Even Temperedness	04	38***	21**
	01	37***	19**
Sensitivity	03	29**	18**
	00	29**	18**
Nonconformity	25**	34***	29***
	18	33***	27***

[a] Decimals omitted from all correlation coefficients. Upper coefficient is regular correlation; lower coefficient is partial correlation, controlling for the effects of educational level.
  * $p < .10$.
 ** $p < .05$.
*** $p < .01$.
**** $p < .001$.

education, partial correlations show the same pattern of results, although the significance of the relationshps for the criminals was marginal (p's near .10). Overall, the results say that within both a normal and criminal population, we find a range of empathic dispositions, and that, as predicted, the more empathic individuals are more likely to perceive the subtler religious themes in Whitman's poetry.

DISCUSSION

One can summarize the results of the study briefly as follows:

1. Neither religious affiliation nor age is related to empathy or the ability to see subtle mystico-religious themes in our Whitman Poetry Questionnaire.
2. Educational level is related to both empathy and to the discernment of subtle religious themes in poetry. The better educated criminals were found to be more empathic, to be more open and perceptive in cognitive style, and to perform better on the Poetry Questionnaire.
3. College students are more empathic than criminals; this difference is related to the educational differences between the two groups.
4. The criminals as a group performed just as well as the students on the Whitman Poetry Questionnaire. Differences on three individual items were due to differences between students and criminals in educational level.
5. Level of empathy predicted performance on the Poetry Questionnaire for both students and criminals, and was partially confounded with educational level, yet apparently was real.

What are the implications of these findings? Will criminals react favorably to poetry? Will it help them in any way? Are they truly empathic enough to absorb religious and moral values from poetry into their character?

Based upon the present study, we are willing to reply to the above questions with a cautious "yes." As a group, the prisoners were just as capable as college students of perceiving the subtle religious themes in Whitman's poetry. The prisoners displayed neither the level of concrete thinking nor "criminal" personality traits that Yochelson and Samenow (1976) suggested would keep their sensitivity from manifesting into genuine empathy. This is not to say that poetry therapy would help all criminals. The prisoners who were less educated and who received lower empathy score performed more poorly on the Poetry Questionnaire. The relationship between education and empathy suports educators' contention that learning promotes a humane attitude.

The scores on the Empathy Scale indicate that criminals as a group are indeed less empathic than college students, scoring almost four points lower on the scale, and that this deficit is related to their lower educational level. Further evidence that empathy is related to socioeconomic factors can be found by comparing empathy scores from the present study to those found in Table 3 of Hogan's (1969, p. 313) original paper on the Empathy Scale. The prisoners' average score on the scale is a just point higher than the junior high school students tested by Hogan. Furthermore, the DuBois Campus students (many of whom come from working class backgrounds) scored six to nine points *lower* than three groups of socioeconomically-advantaged college students tested by Hogan at the University of California at Berkeley. This evidence, coupled with the finding that educational level *alone* predicted criminals' performance on the Poetry Questionnaire, indicates that educational level would moderate the effectiveness or usefulness of poetry therapy.

Some final comments concern our clinical impressions of the prison inmates based upon their free written responses at the end of the questionnaire and upon our discussion with them after the testing. On the whole, the prisoners were remarkably enthusiastic about responding to two short questionnaires. Some written comments included: "Come back & do this again," and "enjoyed the test. bring more to prison." Most prisoners appeared to be very interested in what was going on. A few demonstrated an empathic concern for us by writing comments such as "I hope you find what your [sic] looking for," and "I hope this test helps youn's [sic] in someway [sic], and I would like to thank youn's for letting me take part!"

Many prisoners talked openly about feelings and self-understanding. The following are some examples:

I think peaple [sic] do have the same feelings

. . . more people should have taken this, rather than just the handful that was here, for a better understanding of it for your benifent [sic].

I think this is a good thing for not just people in jail but for all the people in the world i really enjoy writing things and like to write and i can write but i done this in a hurry

I feel that if someone were to help each person individually to know themselves and there [sic] true feeling it would help prisoner's [sic] very much.

. . . I feel this test would greatly be helpfull [sic] on the understanding of prison inmates feelings.

I think it is a good Idea because Inmates are more in touch with theyre [sic] feelings cause they have more time to think.

Most people who visit prisons find that the prison environment feels uncomfortable and strange. What discomfited us was not the "criminality" of the prisoners we interviewed, but rather our inability to perceive any major differences between their personalities and the personalities of the students we teach. It is true that, as predicted by Johnson (1983) and Yochelson and Samenow (1976), many prisoners were unusually choleric, animated, and impulsive. (This was also reflected on their low scores on the Even Temperedness factor subscale.) Nonetheless, at least 20% of our students are not especially even tempered. We found the major difference between the students and prisoners to be their educational level. The above quotations from the prisoners illustrate their good intentions but lack of writing skills. Perhaps if these persons were better educated they could find a socially appropriate outlet for their choleric temperament. The problem is summed up nicely by one of the inmates: "I don't know if poetry will help *Inmates* most don't even know how to read or write."

REFERENCES

Allen, G.W. (1957). *Walt Whitman handbook*. New York: Hendricks House.

Bailey, L.W., & Edwards, D. (1973). Use of meaningless and novel proverbs as a projective technique. *Journal of Personality Assessment, 37*, 527–530.

Barkley, B.J. (1973). Poetry in a cage: Therapy in a correctional setting. In J.J. Leedy (Ed.), *Poetry the healer* (pp. 1–16). Philadelphia: J.B. Lippincott.

Bell, G.L. (1982). Poetry therapy—changing concepts and emerging questions. *The Arts in Psychotherapy, 9*, 25–30.

Blodgett, H.W., & Bradley, S. (Eds.). (1965). *Walt Whitman: Leaves of grass, reader's comprehensive edition*. New York: New York University Press.

Brown, E.F. (1975). *Bibliotherapy and its widening applications*. Metuchen, NJ: Scarecrow Press.

Cheek, J.M. (1982). Aggregation, moderator variables, and the validity of personality tests: A peer-rating study. *Journal of Personality and Social Psychology, 43*, 1254–1269.

Christensen, C.W., & Moss, D.M. (1981). Poetry as a therapeutic avenue. *Pastoral Psychology, 30*, 21–31.

Cross, D.G., & Sharpley, C.F. (1982). Measurement of empathy with the Hogan Empathy Scale. *Psychological Reports, 50*, 62.

Edgar, K.F., & Hazley, R. (1969). Validation of poetry therapy as a group therapy technique. In J.J. Leedy (Ed.), *Poetry therapy* (pp. 111–123). Philadelphia: J.B. Lippincott.

Gough, H.G. (1975). *Manual for the California Psychological Inventory* (Rev. ed.). Palo Alto, CA: Consulting Psychologists Press.

Greif, E.B., & Hogan, R. (1973). The theory and measurement of empathy. *Journal of Counseling Psychology, 20*, 280–284.

Hathaway, S.R., & McKinley, J.C. (1943). *Manual for the Minnesota Multiphasic Personality Inventory*. New York: Psychological Corporation.

Hogan, R. (1969). Development of an empathy scale. *Journal of Consulting and Clinical Psychology, 33*, 307–316.

Hynes, A.M. (1981). Some observations on process in biblio/poetry therapy. *The Arts in Psychotherapy, 8*, 237–241.

James, W. (1929). *The varieties of religious experience*. New York: Random House.

Johnson, J.A. (1983). Criminality, creativity, and craziness: Structural similarities in three types of nonconformity. In W.S. Laufer & J.M. Day (Eds.), *Personality theory, moral development, and criminal behavior* (pp. 81–105). Lexington, MA: D.C. Heath.

Johnson, J.A., Cheek, J.M., & Smither, R. (1983). The structure of empathy. *Journal of Personality and Social Psychology, 45,* 1299–1312.

Leedy, J.J. (Ed.). (1969a). *Poetry therapy.* Philadelphia: J.B. Lippincott.

Leedy, J.J. (1968b). Principles of poetry therapy. In J.J. Leedy (Ed.), *Poetry therapy* (pp. 69–74). Philadelphia: J.B. Lippincott.

Reik, T. (1969). Ne t'es-tu fais mal, mon enfant? In J.J. Leedy (Ed.), *Poetry therapy* (pp. 5–7). Philadelphia: J.B. Lippincott.

Yochelson, S., & Samenow, S.E. (1976). *The criminal personality. Vol. I: A profile for change.* New York: Jason Aronson.

Chapter 6

Criminalizing Conversion: The Legislative Assault on New Religions et al.

Frank K. Flinn

**Consultant in Forensic Religion
General Editor, New ERA Books
Paragon House, New York**

Conversion may be more American than apple pie. Today, however, there have been numerous attempts from the executive, legislative and judicial branches of civil government to bring religious conversion within the scope of criminal activity, notwithstanding the long-held legal tradition of the separation of Church and State. The first purpose of this essay is to examine the tactics being employed by legislative bodies to overcome or to sidestep the staunch principle of separation of Church and State in their effort to criminalize conversion to new religious movements. The second is to draw out the implications of these attempts for religion in general and for the relationship of the state to religious phenomena. In order to do this, however, we must first examine the character of religious conversion in America and the competing interpretations of the nature of conversion from the perspectives of theology, psychology, and sociology.

THE PHENOMENON OF CONVERSION

The word conversion is derived from the Latin *con-vertere* which, in its simplest sense, means to revolve, to turn around, to head in the opposite direction. This basic meaning also holds for the biblical Hebrew word *shub* (to turn, to return) and the Greek words *strepho* and *epistrepho* (Wallis, 1981, pp. 1–17). Two other Greek words in the New Testament associated with the phenomenon of conversion convey the overtones of repentance and regret. The first—*metamelomai* (from *meta*, after + *melomai*, to be concerned, anxious or repentant)—describes the state of the subject undergoing a conversion experience. The second—*metanoia* (from *meta*, after + *noia*, mind = change of mind)—describes the positive state or attitude of one who has undergone a conversion (Bauer, 1957, p. 513).

Closely related to, but distinguishable from, the phenomenon of conversion is the experience of a vocation or *calling*. Although it has become customary to refer to the "conversion" of Saul of Tarsus (Acts 9:1-30), Paul never refers to himself as someone who converted from Judaism to Christianity but as someone who has been called—in Greek *kletos* (Romans 1:1, 1 Corinthians 1:1). Paul models his vocation to announce the Gospel to the Gentiles on the calling of the prophets in the Old Testament (Isaiah 49:1; Jeremiah 1:5). The classical prophets portrayed themselves as having being "called from the womb," "set aside/chosen," or especially "appointed" by God to perform a mighty deed or bear the good news unto the nations (Stendahl, 1976, pp. 7-23). In contrast with conversion, which stresses the introspective aspects of consciousness, calling puts the emphasis on divine appointment and election, along with universal mission to the social community.

The notion of conversion in our time has been restricted to religious phenomena, but there is also something known as philosophic conversion. The classic text of the "conversion" of the philosopher is in Plato's *Republic*, Book VII (515a–516b). In this passage, Socrates narrates how the lover of wisdom or philosopher must be dragged from the Cave of images, shadows, and fleeting opinions, undergo a "turning around" (in Greek, *periagoge*), and be led up toward the Sun where truth, beauty, and goodness abide. The conversion is from the changing to the unchanging, from the temporal to the eternal, and from becoming to being. The example of the philosopher's conversion illustrates the cognitive or intellectual aspect of conversion.

Although it has become customary to separate the cognitive aspect of conversion from the religious and emotional aspects, such divisions appear to be false. Plato's account of the philosopher's turning around is colored with language adapted from the initiation of neophytes into Greek mystery religions. In every conversion there seem to be a cognitive aspect, a religious aspect, a moral aspect and an emotional aspect. Furthermore, popular accounts of conversion experiences such as Thomas Merton's *Seven Story Mountain* leave the impression that modern conversions are distinctly private and individual affairs. The common experience, however, is that conversion is experienced in the context of communities. Even the Great Awakening in the 1730s, often held up as the paradigm of the individualistic interpretation of conversion, was not without its social dimension. William Scheick (1974) has pointed out that the family, not the individual, is the structural motif of Jonathan Edwards's *A Faithful Narrative of the Surprising Work of God In the Conversion of Many Hundred Souls in North-*

hampton (1737). Edwards wrote: "There were remarkable tokens of God's presence almost in every house. It was a time of joy in families on account of salvation being brought unto them; parents rejoicing over their children as new born, and husbands over their wives, and wives over their husbands. The doings of God were then seen in his sanctuary; God's day was a delight, and his tabernacles were amiable" (Edwards, 1966, p. 101).

Psychological interpretations of conversion—beginning with William James's *The Varities of Religious Experience*—have consistently neglected the social dimension of the phenomenon of conversion. Josiah Royce, James's mentor and colleague at Harvard, noted that, while *Varieties of Religious Experience* began with the principle that "religious experience is a field where one must beware of defining sharp boundary lines or of showing false exclusiveness," James himself did draw one boundary line in violation of his own principle: "Religious experience, [James] insists, is. . . the experience of an individual who feels himself to be 'alone with the divine'" (Royce, 1909, II. p. 1029). Royce himself spent the latter part of his life demonstrating that conversion to faith is a spiritual phenomenon that takes place within communities of interpretation (Royce, 1968). Following the lead of James but not of Royce, American psychology has tended to see conversion in exclusively atomistic, individualistic and positivistic terms.

While the "sense of personal sinfulness" cannot be excluded from any account of the experience of conversion, Royce argued with equal force in a celebrated essay "Individual Experience and Social Experience as Sources of Religious Insight" that the meaning of that intensely private experience depends upon the *interpretation* of faith in the "wider vision" of a community (Royce, 1969, II. pp. 1015–1037). The "conversion" or "calling" of Saul of Tarsus in Acts 9 illustrates the reciprocity of individual and social experience with great lucidity. The flash of light, the voice lamenting "Saul, why do you persecute me?" and his bewildering blindness were no doubt experiences which drove Saul into the inner sanctuary of the private self. What could all this mean? The *interpretation* of this experience, however, did not come from within Saul's self but from Ananias "a disciple in Damascus" whose vision from the Lord (in close parallel to the calling of Samuel in 1 Samuel 3:1–18) contains the essence of Saul's future mission as the Lord's chosen vessel to bear my name before the nations and their kings, and before the people of Israel" (Acts 9:15). The meaning of Saul's individual experience depended upon the interpretation of the community of faith in Damascus.

MODELS OF CONVERSION

The discussion of the linguistic roots of the words used for conversion in the West tell us it is some kind of "turning." It does not tell us much about the nature or characteristics of this "turning." There have been two competing models of interpretation about the nature of conversion. Both deal with arguments about the nature of the soul (H. Richardson, 1980, pp. xlvii–xlviii).

The first model conforms to Plato's and St. Augustine's theory that the soul is something like a spiritual eye which attains perfection by *turning away* from the images of shadows of temporal life toward the eternal and unchanging realities ("Ideas," God). With this understanding of the soul, conversion is seen as a *sudden event* and an *escape* from time. This model of conversion lies behind many accounts of the experience of being "born again," and, oddly enough, behind many psychological theories of conversion as a rapid and sudden event, resulting from some kind of life crisis.

The second model conforms to Aristotle's and St. Thomas Aquinas' theory that the soul is the principle of growth in all living things by which they attain wholeness. In this view, all living things have "souls," even the lowly acorn within which resides a green "fuse" that gives rise to the whole oak tree. Thus the soul is not so much a lever for hoisting oneself out of time up to the eternal Ideas but the life-fulfilling meaning of time itself. Conversion, in this context, is not an escape from time but a turning toward the next stage in the completion of whole growth. Conversion then is not a sudden event but a process of ordered stages.

Both the Platonic-Augustinian and the Aristotelian-Thomistic interpretations of the soul and the theories of conversion derived therefrom seem to contain two partial truths. On the one hand, in the heat of the conversion process the experience seems, to subjects and observers alike, a sudden turning away from one's past life and behavior patterns, a momentous event marked by emotional upheaval, and a radical crisis in thinking, values and norms. On the other hand, conversion in the context of a full life cycle seems to be a stage of growth toward maturity, a transition from one status to another, a turning toward a fuller and more complete commitment to the wholeness of life and its ultimate meaning. The temptation is to take an either/or approach to conversion—either it is an event or it is a process. A both/and approach, however, seems to give a fuller account of the phenomenon of conversion.

The case of St. Augustine of Hippo is instructive. In Book VIII of his *Confessions* he recounts the immediate circumstances surrounding his decision to become a Christian. He found himself in inner turmoil in which his divided will struggled against himself until, sitting in a garden, he heard a child chanting over and over "Tolle, lege" ("Take up and read"). Thereupon he took up Paul's Epistle to the Romans and read one verse (13.13). "Instantly," Augustine continues, "there was infused in my heart something like the light of full certainty and all the gloom of doubt vanished away" (*Confessions*, VIII.xii). To someone who has read only Book VIII of the *Confessions*, Augustine's conversion would appear as sudden, rapid, and radical. But this would be to take away the context of his full narrative. Augustine's conversion takes place in a garden which may be likened to the Garden of Gethsemane. In two other places Augustine speaks of gardens. When he was 16 yrs. old he once stole some fruit from a garden. This experience made him conscious of his sinfulness: "And I became a wasteland to myself" (II.x). He likens it with Adam and Eve's sin and expulsion from the Garden of Eden (II.ii). Again, after his conversion and before his mother's death, Augustine and Monica, overlooking a garden in Ostia, conversed about celestial things and the Garden of Paradise (IX.x). The recurrence of the theme of the garden in the *Confessions* provides the background and context of the steps or stages in Augustine's conversion: remorse over sin, surrender leading to a change in his life pattern, and foretaste of celestial bliss spread out over a lifetime. Augustine's conversion is both a momentous event and a stage in his spiritual growth.

Contemporary developmental theory lends credence to reconciling the Platonic-Augustinian and Aristotelian-Thomistic models of conversion. In his celebrated essay "Eight Ages of Man" (1963, pp. 247–274) and now in *The Life Cycle Completed* (1982), Erik Erikson has noted that while the human life cycle unfolds in "ages" or stages, beginning with basic trust vs. mistrust and ending with ego-identity vs. despair, young adulthood (identity vs. role confusion) is particularly marked by a call to "ideological" commitment and conversion-like orientation. The conversion experience required for the transition into adulthood was the focus of Erikson's study *Young Man Luther*. Conversion is both *maturational*, i.e., a stage in the unfolding dialectic of life, and *critical*, i.e., a crucial event like Luther's *Turmerlebnis* (tower experience), that shapes the fundamental orientation of a person.

Uniting Erikson's psycho-sexual stages with Lawrence Kohlberg's model of stages of moral development, James Fowler has derived six possible relations between stage development and conversional change. Fowler builds on Lewis Rambo's definition of conversion as "a significant sudden transformation of a person's loyalties, patterns of life, and focus of energy" (Rambo, 1980, p. 22). According to Fowler, conversion entails "significant changes in the *contents* of faith." But the relation between stage and conversion is not one-to-one. There can be, argues Fowler, 1) a stage change without conversion, 2) a conversion without a stage change, 3) a conversion that precipitates a stage change, 4) a stage change that precipitates a conversion, 5) a conversion that goes hand in hand with a stage change, and 6) a conversion that either blocks or helps a stage change (Fowler, 1981, pp. 285–286). Fowler fails to mention the seventh theoretical possibility: a stage change that blocks or helps a conversion. Fowler's contribution to the discussion has been to alert us that the phenomenon of conversion is amazingly complex. This complexity is often pushed aside by those who see conversion to new religious movements simply and solely as "ego reversion," or "infantilic regression" or as a blockage to maturational growth.

Summary

Drawing together the many trajectories indicated above, we can say that conversion is an extremely complex phenomenon. What is that phenomenon? First and foremost, conversion appears as a complex process in the life cycle. This process can be broken down into three dialectical moments: (1) a turning away, (2) a state or period of suspension, and (3) a turning toward. Below I discuss these aspects in detail.

(1) Turning Away. Those who experience conversions seem to undergo something akin to "spiritual dissonance." That is, the horizon of experience within which the person is presently living, for one reason or another, is now experienced as limited or otherwise unfulfilling. This perception of the limited horizon may be both experienced and expressed on several distinct planes which are nonetheless interconnected. Psychologically the convertee may appear to suffer from "mental disturbances." William James described this phenomenon as hitherto peripheral ideas invading the habitual center of consciousness: "To say that a man is 'converted' means, in these terms, that religious ideas, previously peripheral in his consciousness, now take a central place, and that religious aims form the habitual centre of his energy" (James, [1902], p. 183). Emotionally, the about-face can be described as "losing one's grip." Intellectually, a conversion can be seen as a "radical clarification" that brings about a shift in the paradigm of knowing and acting such as the "Copernican revolution" noted by Immanuel Kant in his *Critique of Pure Reason* (Bxi-xii) or the "inverse insight" so minutely dissected by Bernard Lonergan (1958, pp. 19–25). Religiously, it may depicted as "finding oneself a sinner" (Christianity) or "entangled in the threads of existence" (Buddhism). Theologically, conversion may be elaborated as experiencing the workings of the Holy Spirit on the affections (Edwards, 1966, pp. 184–195). Morally, the experience may be one of "pangs of conscience" experienced in the conflict between self-satisfaction and universal norms. Sociologically, the experience of "turning away" may be perceived as a discrepancy between stated ideals and the status quo leading to group disillusionment and disassociation from accepted relationships with the formation of new communities such as the Quakers, Mormons, etc. Politically, a turning away may form the nucleus of a revolution leading toward the peaceful or turbulent change in the established social order such as Moses's founding of the People of Israel or the foundation of the mendicant orders by Sts. Francis and Dominic.

It is imperative to note that all the above factors—psychological, intellectual, religious, moral, sociological, and political—are latent in any conversion experience (Gelpi, 1976; Lonergan, 1972, pp. 237–244). Although each factor has its specific function, all resonate with one another. Restricting our scope of analysis to the psycho-emotional aspects of conversion arbitrarily neglects the other aspects that accompany the phenomenon of turning away. Such restriction also constricts religious conversion to a sphere all by itself and betrays a privatistic interpretation of religion as in Alfred N. Whitehead's dictum: "Religion is what the individual does with his own solitariness" (1974, p. 16). In reality, religious conversion takes place in communities and through the interaction of the public and private realms. Moreover, religious conversion partakes of a much broader set of phenomena which in scientific circles have been called "scientific revolutions" or paradigm shifts (Kuhn, 1970). Paradigm shifts in the interpretation of empirical phenomena also occur in art, such as the shift from the aspectival bifocal rule of artistic construction in medieval Gothic painting to the perspectival monofocal rule in the Renaissance (Gadol, 1969, pp. 22–37). The bell-jar approach to the turning away aspect of religious conversion inhibits the kind of far-reaching insight to be gained by becoming sensitive to the interconnectedness of phenomena. Conversion in the aspect of turning away is one species of a genus which, in general terms, may be called a change in worldview, paradigm shift or discovery of an unforeseen horizon (McGowan, 1982). Turning away is an about-face resulting from fundamental conflicts which are overcome only by an intellectual, moral or religious conversion.

(2) Suspension.   The middle phase in the conversion process is very difficult to describe and, in general, has suffered from inattention. This inattention is due to the view that conversion is an instantaneous event. Nonetheless, the gap is being filled in. I have used the term "suspension," though this is perhaps not the best term. The state of suspension can also be described as a phase of indecision, the experience of what Plato called the "In-between" (in Greek, *metaxu*), or the experience of the threshold (in Latin, *limen*) in which the convertee is not all the way out of one room ("the old man") and not yet in the other ("the new man"). This last notion refers to the "liminal phase" in rites of passage during which the initiand is statusless, anonymous, and secluded from society (Van Gennep 1960; Turner, 1969, pp. 94–130; 1970, pp. 93–111). Liminal transitions occur in modern industrial societies but they are fragmented and diffuse rather than compact and intense as they are in tribal societies (Melton & Moore, 1982, pp. 47–59).

Recent investigations into the genetic and structural aspects of development have amplified our understanding of the transitional state of suspension. E.D. Starbuck in his classic study of adolescent conversion *Psychology of Religion* (1899), a primary source for William James' *The Varities of Religious Experience*, noted the psychological features of a "sense of incompleteness and imperfection; brooding, depression, morbid introspection, and sense of sin; anxiety about the hereafter, distress over doubts, and the like" (James, [1902], p. 185). These descriptions have become almost platitudes and have led to the conviction that the conversion experience is some kind of mental disease rather than a transitional shift in the pattern of knowing, construing, and committing oneself to the horizon of ultimate concern. Starbuck and James carefully pointed out: "Conversion is in its essence a normal adolescent phenomenon, incidental to the passage from the child's small universe to the wider intellectual and spiritual life of maturity" (James, ibid.). Genetic and structural interpretations of paradigm shifts in the developmental process have lowered the emotional charge attached to purely psychological descriptions of conversion. Jean Piaget speaks of the transitional states between the stages of cognitive growth structures as marked with "cognitive disequilibrium" (1970, pp. 45–46); Lawrence Kohlberg talks about "cognitive conflict" between moral stages (1981, p. 47); Thomas Kuhn refers to the perception of an anomaly or new sort of fact which generates doubt about older scientific paradigms (1970, pp. 52–65); finally, Erik Erikson notes that transitions in general and the passage to identity in particular are signalled by a "psychological moratorium" (1963, pp. 262–263). William James depicted this phase as "the divided self" or the *homo duplex* who stands in need of being twice-born ([1902], pp. 156–176).

Another important feature about the state of suspension and the transition from one stage to another is that they are accompanied by what many psychologists and developmentalists call "ego regression" to an earlier stage. Erikson speaks of "regression in service of the ego" by which the loose ends of past experience are reassembled for the next stage (1982). Fowler describes this normal transition period as "recapitulation in service of faith development" (1981, p. 288). Anti-conversionists often highlight this aspect of the conversion process to argue that religions, especially new religions, "infantilize" their young adult converts. Developmentalists can argue that such "regressions" are normal, temporary and an expected aspect of the maturation process. This does not mean that there cannot be pathological regressions among convertees—or among the general population, for that matter. Melton and Moore suggest that "chronic liminality" exists among *some* members of new religions but add that the same holds true for traditional congregations (1982, pp. 59–60). To date, there exist no solid statistical studies on permanent ego regression or chronic liminality in any religion, much less the new religions. The transitional stage of suspension can be compared to what L.S. Vygotsky (1978, pp. 84–91) called the "zone of proximal development" during which the developmental process lags behind the learning process. Each of us experiences this when we know that our old patterns of knowing and construing no longer work but we do not fully sense the new horizon. Vygotsky compared it to the "buds" and "flowers" as opposed to "fruits" in biological development.

(3) *Turning Toward.* Many contemporary theories of conversion tend to stop with the *terminus a quo* of the conversion sequence. The experiences accompanying the initial "turning away" are often colorful, dramatic and even traumatic. The modern mind is well tempered to decipher origins and causes and less suited to find purposes and consequences. Likewise, modern therapies have precise definitions of disease—psychosis, neurosis, dementia, praecox, etc.—and vague conceptions of health—"normality," "averageness," etc. (Grant, 1962). That conversion experiences produce long-term effects can hardly be denied. Moses's conversion from a life in the Egyptian court ended with the founding of a people. Gautama's turning away from royal life resulted in the founding of a monkhood. Augustine's conversion led to a life-long membership in the Catholic Church of North Africa. I once heard a psychiatrist compare the experience of conversion to an alcoholic bender, i.e., something that might be ok once in a while, but best gotten over quickly. Many of the legislative bills discussed below compare conversion to and membership in the new religions to being "under the influence." William James, without doubt one of the originators of modern psychology, never deceived himself with such quick-fix similes. That is why over one-half of *The Varieties of Religious Experience* is devoted not to the "turning away" and "suspension" aspects of conversion but to the third phase of "turning toward."

The third phase of the conversion process has been characterized with terms like commitment, revitalization, renewal, regeneration, a sense of sanctification or blessedness, etc. (James, [1902], pp. 239–341). If the first two phases of the conversion process may be said to be inner-directed, the third may be seen as other-directed in the sense that the convertee dedicates himself or herself to new ideals, new codes of behavior, spiritual disciplines such as prayer and mediation, works of charity, or evangelization. The social impact of conversion is felt through the public expression of new modes of life in the third phase. That impact is perceived even when the stated aim of conversion is to "withdraw from the world." Here we can point to the social and political impact of hermits and monks during the Byzantine era, the most notable example of which is Simeon Stylites who is said to have wielded enormous political power while living atop a pillar in the desert.

The third phase is also the seedbed of religious innovation. The turn toward the goals and ideals of sanctification and regeneration often flows into the revitalization of a traditional religious belief (Moses), the founding of a new religion based on an earlier religion (Christianity, Islam, Mormon), the founding of new types of religious orders (St. Francis of Assisi, St. Dominic, St. Ignatius of Loyola), the reformation and reformulation of established religion (Martin Luther, John Wesley, John Calvin), and the generation of religious movements within traditional religious bodies (Pentecostalism, Charismatics). It is hard to underestimate the innovative impulse which religious conversion nurtures and motivates. Yet this innovative impulse is what makes conversion controversial and questionable to a majority who have become quite satisfied in their comfortable pews. What a new discovery is to scientific theory, conversion is to religion. It unsettles the perception of sacred reality, not only for individuals but also for whole civilizations. Conversion also responds to different needs of history. As the Roman empire was collapsing from the weight of its own earthly concerns people turned to the "contemplative life" for the rediscovery of God's self-gift in love. When the contemplative life itself became jaded, the Protestant reformers justified the "active life" as an arena for sanctification. Today, philosophers and historians almost universally speak of the pervasive "meaninglessness" which has infected post-industrial society. Conversion to the new religions is in no small part a conversion to the restoration of ultimate meaningfulness of human life.

DELEGITIMIZING CONVERSION

Conversion has been legitimized and delegitimized on different grounds throughout history. In this essay I will concentrate on the western experience and the grounds given for delegitimizing innovative religious movements. The first method was outright physical persecution, i.e. imprisonment, torture, and execution, such as the Roman execution of Christian converts, the elimination of the Albigensians by the Inquisition in the Middle Ages, and the burning of the Salem witches. Physical persecution is most likely in instances where the religion of the state is the state itself (e.g., Rome) or when civil and ecclesiastical polity coincide as in the high Middle Ages or Puritan New England. The second method is economic and social, such as the ostracism of the Mormons, the Oneida community, the Amish, and the Irish Catholics in late 19th-century Boston ("No Dogs Allowed; No Irish Need Apply"). Social persecution takes place even in societies upholding a constitutional separation of church and state. The third method of persecution, one which is currently in vogue, is psychological. Instead of killing converts, or applying pressures to drive them into unpopulated places, people are claiming that converts have undergone "brainwashing" or "mind control." The grounds for delegitimating religious conversion and justifying religious persecution can be divided historically into the political, the ecclesiastical, the social and the psychological.

(1) Political Delegitimization. When Christians first came under the scrutiny of Roman authorities, they were accused of *superstitio*. The term *superstitio*, as used by the Roman authors Suetonius, Pliny, and Tacitus, did not refer to odd folkways, such as tossing spilled salt over the right shoulder, but to foreign religion as such (Wilkin, 1984, pp. 48–50, 60–67). A foreign religion was one which forbade its members to participate in public games, during which sacrifices to the gods were made, in official worship of the state gods, and in military service. To the Romans, the Christians were impious and the Christian associations were perceived as "political clubs" (*hetaeriae*), traditional hotbeds for political unrest. In the treatise *De Superstitione*, attributed to Plutarch, superstition was seen as the "seed from which atheism springs" (167 d-e).

For the Romans religion was intimately bound up with the maintenance of the social order. To refer to Jean-Jacques Rousseau, the Romans had what may be called "civil religion" which stressed "sentiments of sociability" (*Social Contract* 4.8). Romans were wary of all groups and associations which might weaken such social sentiments. The many cults imported from the empire to the capital were cautiously tolerated because most asked only "adhesion" of the believer, but Christianity was not simply a cult of adhesion but a counter-religion which called for personal, individual "conversion" and conversion "demanded a new life for a new people," i.e., an all-encompassing radical change in behavior as well as belief (Nock, 1933, p. 7). It is not difficult to see in conversion, so conceived and so perceived, an imminent danger to the web of social solidarity. The actual legal charges brought against the Christians were not allegations of promiscuity or infant cannibalism but "obstinacy" (*contumacia*), i.e., contempt and defiance of magistrates in judicial inquiries (Barnes, 1968; Wilkin, 1984, pp. 22–24).

The example of Roman "civil religion" is not without application in the contemporary situation, even with respect to societies like the United States which profess a constitutional prohibition against the establishment of religion by the state. Some students of American religion have suggested that there is indeed an implicit "civil religion" in the United States (Bellah, 1967). Others have pointed up the dangers of the state arrogating to itself ultimate reality. They argue that the American constitution specifically insures the "countersovereignty of *special* groups," most especially of universities, families, professions, businesses and churches, which limits absolutist claims on the part of the state and guarantees inviolable human rights (H. Richardson: 1974, pp. 174 ff.). Proponents of American civil religion seem to want to claim that "In God We Trust" suffices as a "minimal creed" for the body politic; their opponents want to assert that "I pledge allegiance..." needs to be hedged by "I believe in God...." Although advocates of civil religion want to argue that American civil religion is meant to be "tolerant," they seem to forget that Rousseau, the first proponent of the "religion of tolerance," was remarkably intolerant toward true believers:

> Now that there is not, and can no longer be, an exclusive national religion, all religions which themselves tolerate others must be tolerated, provided only that their dogmas contain nothing contrary to the duties of the citizens. But anyone who dares to say "Outside the church there is no salvation" should be expelled from the state, unless the state is the church and the prince the pontiff. (*Social Contract* 4.8)

Rousseau is saying that the "religion of tolerance" is tolerant only toward those who do not claim to possess the true way of life. In his quest to subsume the "will of all" into the "general will" of the state, Rousseau ruled out sectarian differences of opinion about religious questions.

In the United States, the First Amendment forbids constitutional establishment of religion: "Congress shall make no law respecting an establishment of religion, or prohibiting the free exercise thereof..." (Amendments to the Constitution, Article the First). Mr. Justice Black, speaking for the court, wrote in *Everson v. Board of Education* 330 U.S. 1 (1947):

> The "establishment of religion" clause of the First Amendment means at least this: Neither a state nor the Federal Government can set up a church. Neither can pass laws which aid one religion, aid all religions, or prefer one religion over another. Neither can force nor influence a person to go to or remain away from church against his will or force him to profess a belief in any religion. No person can be punished for entertaining or professing religious beliefs, for church attendance or non-attendance.

In short, the tradition of the Supreme Court has been to prohibit *entanglement by legislation* in religious affairs. Notwithstanding this prohibition, there has been considerable entanglement in religious affairs, if not by legislation, then by *regulation* through various regulatory agencies (IRS, INS, FBI, etc.) of the executive branch, as well as by *investigation* under the aegis of the legislative branch (Worthing, 1982; Stumbo, 1982; Boettcher, 1980, pp. 307–324). Entanglement by investigation and regulation has become the backdoor to entanglement by legislation. That federal agencies have their fingers in the religion pie is beyond cavil. For example, the FBI published an investigative report in their Law Enforcement Bulletin on the "cult" question entitled "Cults: A Conflict Between Religious Liberty and Involuntary Servitude?" (Lucksted & Martell, 1982) which derives its image of the cults from anti-cult literature. This Bulletin is sent to every law enforcement agency in the United States.

Entanglement by regulation has been further complicated by confusion about the power of government agencies, and even the courts, to "characterize" an activity as secular or religious. The celebrated case of Rev. Sun Myung Moon hinged on this very point, for the defense was inhibited by the trial judge in producing evidence to the effect that Rev. Moon received assets—characterized by the IRS to be for personal and, therefore, secular uses—as a trust for religious purposes. Commenting on the implications of this case and the Bob Jones University case, Brent Marshall (1984, p. 1004) has written:

> If the state, even the judiciary, were given the power to define the contents of a religion, then the freedom of religion would become meaningless: the government could suppress any activity simply by defining the activity as secular and applying a rational basis test.

The state legislation discussed below attempts to do just that. First, it secularizes the phenomenon of conversion in behaviorist language—"a sudden and abrupt change in behavior and lifestyle"—and then gives a color of rationality—"mind control," "manipulation," etc.—justifying legislation which would suppress proselytizing and conversion. Some members of the U.S. Congress have become alarmed at the amount of entanglement by regulation. In 1983, Congressman Dymally introduced a resolution (U.S. HR217, June 2, 1983) to hold hearings "on the subject of governmental intervention in religious affairs."

(2) Ecclesiastical Delegitimization.   After the establishment of Christianity in the age of Constintine (313 A.D.), the question of conversion per se became a moot point. The new problem was the relation of various sectarian Christian groups—Arians, Nestorians, Sabellians, Gnostics, etc.— to what the early Fathers of the church called the *regula fidei* or "rule of faith." Conversion to a sectarian branch became "apostasy," depending on one's preferred branch. The teaching of the apostates came under the label of "heresy" and their practices were called "abominations." It is interesting to note that the charges of perverse sexual practices and ritual murder attributed to various libertine Christian groups do not appear in the pagan Roman critics of Christianity but in the Christian authors themselves (Wilkin, 1984, p. 22).

The concept of heresy grew to encompass more and more matters over time. Among the 2nd century Fathers of the church, such as Irenaeus of Lyons and Hippolytus of Rome, it meant denial of ecclesiastical and biblical teaching; for 4th century Cyril of Alexandria it meant fragmentation of the Body of Christ (the church) through schism; and finally in the 11th-century church-state controversy between Holy Roman Emperor Henry IV and Hildebrand, Pope Gregory VII, heresy came to mean rejection of spiritual authority by temporal rulers (Seeberg, 1964, II p. 51, n. 1). With the ever-waxing temporal might of the church in the Middle Ages, the concept of heresy, monopolized by the stern Inquisition, was wielded as a bloody mace against reformist groups such as the Cathars, Joachimites, Wycliffites, Hussites, and other millennial sectarians (Russell, 1971; Cohn, 1961). The same type of force was unleashed against the "witches" of Salem, Massachusetts, in 17th century New England. It is worth noting that twenty persons (mostly women) and two dogs were executed for witchcraft in 1692 (Miller & Johnson, 1963, 2.735).

Heresy trials seem to be coming back into fashion. The most notable example in recent times is "A Critique of the Theology of the Unification Church as Set Forth in *Divine Principle*" by the Faith and Order Commission of the National Council of the Churches of Christ (NCC, 1977). This report was used by the NCC as the basis for denying the Unification Church membership as "a Christian Church." The criteria for the denial of membership are a) the affirmation that Jesus of Nazareth is the Lord, b) that Jesus' life, death and resurrection are "the ground and means of salvation," c) belief in the Trinity, and d) the doctrine of the church as the "believing community" (NCC, 1977, p. 11). I have no quarrel with the NCC's right to deny the Unification Church membership. It is, after all, a voluntary association. But a certain irony does appear in the judgment that the Unification Church is not Christian, The NCC report was written by Sr. Agnes Cunningham, a Roman Catholic, Drs. J. Robert Nelson and Jorge Laura-Braud, Presbyterians, and Dr. William L. Hendricks, a Southern Baptist. Not so long ago Catholics, Presbyterians, and Southern Baptists labelled one another as "heretics" and "apostates," to use only the mildest of epithets once wielded. The NCC report does warn that their critique is not to be used "for arbitrary or punitive purposes" (NCC, 1977, p. 1). However, Dr. Hendricks was listed in 1976 a member of the Committee Engaged in Freeing Minds (CEFM), one of the anti-cult groups which have pushed for the "punitive" legislation I discuss in the next section (H. Richardson, 1977, p. 174). The conclusions of the NCC report seem to have spilled over into the legislative arena. One sentence of Mr. Justice Douglas comes immediately to mind: "Heresy trials are foreign to our Constitution" (*U.S. v. Ballard* 322 U.S. 78 [1944]).

(3) Social Delegitimization. Along with the separation of church and state and the autonomy of civil affairs in modern societies, the political and ecclesiastical grounds for delegitimizing conversion lost their persuasive force. This did not mean that efforts at delegitimization stopped. The

emperor simply put on new clothes, namely, forms of social ostracism. Often religious groups were behind these attempts, but the power wielded was mainly social rather than political or ecclesiastical. Though there are many types of social ostracism—rumor, allegations of conspiracy, promiscuity, or criminality, etc.—I will discuss only two types which have been recently employed to delegitimize religious conversion: the stereotype and the apostate story.

The religious stereotype is like a reusable mold into which ever new substances (unpopular groups) can be poured. The groups stereotyped change according to the whims of the times but the mold remains pretty well fixed. Thus in the 19th century, the Know-Nothings sought to prove that the Pope ("The Whore of Babylon") was seeking to take over the world, especially the United States. After W.W. I, the new candidates for the "conspiracy slot" of the stereotype were the Jews, who were accused to seeking a stranglehold over the world ("The Protocols of Zion"). Today the candidate is the Unification Church and Rev. Sun Myung Moon, who according to one author, is in league with the Korean CIA and seeks to control American foreign policy (Boettcher, 1980, pp. 307–324). H. Richardson has charted an illuminating map of "religious conspiracy" as it has been applied to Catholics, Jews, and Unificationists (Table 1). What is remarkable about these categories is that they are well nigh eternal and can be applied to any unpopular group that appears on the scene. The sum total effect of the stereotypical formulas can be effectively used to delegitimate the methods of gaining and retaining membership, esp. the methods of conversion. In our time the media have reinforced the stereotypes by lumping all "cults" together and reproducing "olds" not "news," i.e., printing information off the wire services without seeking first-hand information about how members of innovative religious groups actually live and worship (Willoughby, 1979; Testa, 1980). Rumors or authentic facts about one group have been recycled to fit others. The most notable example of this occurred after the Jonestown massacre, which was indeed a tragedy. Rumors soon spread that members of other new religions had entered "suicide pacts" and gone through "suicide drills" in the manner of the Jonestown group until the evidence proved skimpy (Bromley & Shupe, 1981, pp. 66–67).

Closely related to the religious stereotype is what has come to be called the "apostate stories." As noted above, such stories can be found already in the early Christian Fathers' writings about heretical groups, and the genre type has continued up to the present day. A notorious 19th century example of this was the anti-Catholic tract lugubriously entitled *The Aweful Disclosures of Maria Monk, as Exhibited in a Narrative of Her Sufferings at the Hotel-Dieu Nunnery at Montreal*, first published under the title, *The Hotel-Dieu Nunnery Unveiled* in 1846 under the auspices of the noted

TABLE 1. Stereotype of "Enemy" Religion

Anti-Catholicism	Anti-Semitism	Anti-Cultism
The pope is seeking to take over the world.	The Jews are seeking to take over the world. (The Protocols of the Elders of Zion)	Moon is seeking to take over the world.
Catholicism is not a true religion, but a political system.	Judaism is not a religion, but a political system.	The Unification Church is not a church but a political front group.
Catholics aren't loyal Americans, but are really loyal to Rome—a foreign power.	Jews aren't loyal Americans, but are really loyal to Israel.	Moon teaches Americans to fight for Korea.
The Catholic church exploits the poor in order to build rich churches and buy land.	Jews are really only after money.	Moon claims to be a prophet, but is really only after profit.
The priests enslave the minds of young people, inculcating irrational superstition.	Judaism is a legalistic, tribalistic system, ritualistic and antirational.	Moon brainwashes his converts.
Catholics control their young people's lives by teaching that sex is evil.	Jews control their young people's lives by making them feel guilty about marrying a non-Jew.	Moon controls young people's lives by making them remain chaste and then arranging their marriages.
Catholics justify lying by "mental reservation."	Jews always lie.	Moonies don't tell the truth but practice "heavenly deception."
Catholics entice children, while too young to decide for themselves, to become nuns and priests.	Jews kidnap gentile children for vile purposes.	Moon entices the young to leave their families.
Catholics are swarthy (Latin) and have too many children.	Jews have crooked noses and are verminious.	Moonies have glazed-eyes and are undernourished.

(H. Richardson, 1980, p. 1, xxvii)

publishers Harper Bros. (Billington, 1963, p. 100 ff.; Shupe, 1981, pp. 207–228). Maria Monk allegedly escaped from this convent after being subjected to cruelties by nuns and impregnated by the chaplain. Subsequent investigation proved that Maria Monk was really an Albany woman of ill-repute who had never graced the doors of a convent and that her "aweful disclosures" were ghosted by George Bourne (1780–1845), a Presbyterian minister of noted anti-Catholic sentiments. This apostate story did much to enhance the legends of tunnels running between rectories and nunneries, infanticide, child seduction, etc., on the part of Catholics. In similar vein, but less salacious in content, is *Convent Cruelties or My Life in the Convent* by Helen Jackson (1919), which boasted the promotional subtitle "A providential delivery from Rome's Convent Slave Pens: a sensational experience." In this titillating booklet real fact is fused with rumor and hearsay to produce a picture of Roman Catholic convent schools as prisons or asylums and their pupils as "inmates."

Today there is a growing literature of apostate genre stories by ex-cult members (Bromley & Shupe, 1979; 1981, pp. 243–244). Although one is loathe to deny real experiences to ex-cult members, the degree to which the stories participate in ageless stereotypes (deception and coercion in recruitment, heretical or strange beliefs, sexual perversion, political subversion and financial exploitation) points up the rhetorical nature of a standard genre. As Bromley and Shupe have written, "Each individual story reinforces the stereotype of the enemy, and the overall stereotype in turn makes each story believable" (1981, p. 11). Stereotyping and apostate stories in turn have served to rally the anti-cult organizations (Flinn, 1979; Shupe & Spielmann, 1980; Beckford, 1983) and to legitimate the delegitimizing efforts of psychological and psychiatric opinion, which, again in turn, was mustered for the legislative assault on conversion to the new religions.

(4) Psychological Delegitimization. This topic brings up a web of complex issues which cannot be fully untangled in this essay. But the nub of psychological delegitimization is condensed in the ambiguous term "brainwashing." The term came into common use in the 1950s but has no precise definition. Webster's New World Dictionary (College Edition, 1962), noting that the term is "journalese," gives the following definition: "to indoctrinate so intensively and thoroughly as to effect a radical transformation of beliefs and mental attitudes." The journalist in question was E. Hunter, whose *Brainwashing in Red China* (1951) was somewhat of a sensation. The word "brainwashing," however has been used in three widely different contexts (Flinn, 1981b).

The term is derived from the colloquial Chinese phrase *hsi nao* which literally means "wash brain" but which has Confucian roots that mean "to purify (cleanse) one's thoughts." The phrase was current among Communist Chinese during the political re-education programs after 1949. The more technical phrase for political re-molding was *szu-hsiang-kai-tsao* (lit., "thought-reconsider-change-previous") which has been variously translated as "ideological remolding," "ideological reform" or "thought reform" (Lifton, 1969, p. 4). During the Korean war the term "brainwashing" was recycled to refer to the techniques, both psychological *and* physical (torture), the Communist captors used on Allied prisoners of war. The aim was not so much political reindoctrination but military and ideological propaganda. Finally, during the 1970s deprogrammers and deprogramming groups made use of the term to refer to the methods of conversion employed by new religious groups. The analogy between "brainwashing" techniques and traditional religious conversion was first suggested by Robert J. Lifton in *Thought Reform and the Psychology of Totalism* (1969, pp. 419–437). Lifton's categories for "ideological totalism" (milieu control, mystical manipulation, the demand for purity, the cult of confession, the "sacred science," loading the language, doctrine over person, dispensing of existence) were claimed by deprogrammers, anxious parents and anticult organizations to apply equally to new religious movements. Conversion to new religions soon became classified as a new form of mental illness in the popular mind.

The person most responsible for spreading the idea that members of new religions suffer from mental disorders was Ted Patrick, a community organizer for Ronald Reagan in San Diego during the early 1970s. Patrick is the arch-deprogrammer who went by the code name "Black Lightening." He claimed that cult members had been "brainwashed." Potential members could "zapped" by their leaders with a single glance and turned into "zombies" (Patrick, 1976; Flinn, 1982, pp. 29–38). Patrick also claimed that cult members could be spotted by their "glazed eyes." When subjected to deprogramming, cult members had tendencies of "floating" between their new (normal) and old (abnormal) lifestyles. With the exception of the term "brainwashing," such voodoo-psychiatry terminology would not hold up in any meeting of the American Psychological or Psychiatric Associations, yet many accredited members of professional mental health associations came to the conviction that cult members suffered from psychological disorders and that conversion to them was a new form of mental disease (Clark, 1977, 1979; Singer; 1979; E. Levine, 1980). However, conclusions that members of new religions have been brainwashed was based mostly 1) on information provided by those who had been forcibly abducted and deprogrammed (75% of Singer's sample had been deprogrammed) and 2) on personal interviews with psychologists and psychiatrists which are prone to subjective "impressions." Objective tests tend to show that both cult and ex-cult members display the normal curve of mental competence (S. Levine & Slater, 1976; Kuner, 1981). Ungerleider and Wellisch (1979, p. 281), using the Minnesota Multiphasic Personality Inventory, concluded their study thus:

> No data emerged from intellectual, personality, or mental status testing to suggest that any of these subjects are unable or even limited in their ability to make sound judgments and legal decisions as related to their persons and property.

Another label falling within the umbrella charge of brainwashing is the metaphoric term "snapping" (Conway & Siegelman, 1979). Conway and Siegelman have gone on to elaborate their hypothesis, now claiming that entrance into and exit from religious cults constitute a new form of mental illness which they call "information disease" (1982). Steven Chorover, professor of brain science at M.I.T., has warned against those who find new mental illnesses. His favorite example is "drapetomania," an illness discovered by white southern doctors during the days of slavery and which supposedly diagnosed a black slave's "insane desire to run away from home" (1977, p. 194). James Lewis (1984, p. 7) has pointed out that studies of ex-cult members seldom include those who have *voluntarily* left groups. One study of voluntary exit members of the Unification Church concluded: "But the indications from my research at present are that people who have withdrawn from the Unification Church without being deprogrammed in any obvious way do not usually adopt a fervently hostile attitude towards it. Rather, as has already be stressed above, their feelings are generally confused and ambivalent" (Beckford, 1978, p. 113). Voluntary ex-members tend to view their experience in both plus and minus terms, whereas deprogrammed ex-members take a negative view. Hence, claims of "brainwashing" and hostility by ex-members is closely correlated with having been "deprogrammed." The so-called post-cult involvement "syndrome" (disorientation, guilt, hallucinations, disassociative states, etc.) is much like typical post-traumatic stress disorders, such as those experienced after the death of a loved one, military combat, or a divorce. Lewis concludes that "information disease" is not a new mental disorder unique to cults, that the stress entailed results not so much from membership in the cult but that it is "a reaction to a traumatic exit experience" itself, i.e., the forcible abduction of the cult member and the recantation of faith under duress. My own estimate of membership in the Unification Church has it attaining 35,000 members from 1960 to 1980. Of these, only a few hundred have been deprogrammed. Today, there are between 3000 and 4000 full-time members. If the Unification Church is indeed "brainwashing" members, it is doing a bad job of it. In reality, many young adults have joined new religions as a stage in life. Some remain, but most move on. Membership for most is a phase in what J. Richardson (1980) has called "conversion careers." In *The Making of a Moonie* Eileen Barker (1984) has dispelled once and for all the myth that the Unification Church is using "brainwashing." Her first-hand statistics demonstrate that people who join are "seekers" in the first place, that the retention rate is stunningly low, and that members can leave at any time with relative ease.

There can be no doubt that psychological and psychiatric opinion has had direct influence on the legislative process with respect to the anti-conversion bills proposed over the last decade. In particular, the psychiatrists John Clark and Margaret Singer have been cited as authorities confirming the effects of "destructive conversion" techniques used by the proselytizers of the new religions. Some social analysts contend that that the hidden motive behind psychiatrists (the number is few) claiming converts are mentally ill is that psychiatry and religion are in competition for the same clientele (Robbins & Anthony, 1980). The father of modern psychoanalysis, after all, argued that religion was a manifestation of infantile wish-fulfillment and a systematic illusion, which he distinguished from error and delusion (Freud, 1961, pp. 30–33). Few seem to notice that Freud simply replaced the old gods with some very old gods, which he called Ananke (Necessity) and Logos (Reason) and, later, Eros and Thanatos, perhaps in unconscious recognition that psychoanalysis was going to have to compete with religion on religion's own terms.

CRIMINALIZING CONVERSION

The various forces of political, ecclesiastical, social, and psychological de-legitimation of new religious movements have percipitated into a variety of legislation introduced into state legislatures and assemblies since the mid-1970s. Whatever overt name these bills went by, their not-so-covert intention was to either destroy, restrict, or investigate conversion to the "cults." The bills can be broken down into four categories: (1) bills seeking to restrict the fundraising activities of religious groups (e.g., Pennsylvania, Massachusetts); (2) bills allowing relatives or others to get conservatorships or guardianships over cult members (e.g., New York, Connecticut, Oregon, Texas), (3) bills allowing people to seek damages against "organizations promising religious or philosophical self-fulfillment" (e.g., Minnesota), and (4) bills creating legislative committees to investigate new religious movements (e.g., Pennsylvania, Maryland, Ohio). The welter of legislation has been staggering; a tabulation of the bills is in order before further discussion (Table 1).

TABLE 2. Anti-Cult Legislation

State & Bill #	Name and Description
CT SB1429	An Act concerning conservatorship. This bill grants conservatorships over persons "incapable of managing his or her own affairs," including mental illness resulting from "ASSOCIATION WITH A GROUP WHICH PRACTICES THE USE OF DECEPTION IN THE RECRUITMENT OF ITS MEMBERS *AND* WHICH ENGAGES IN SYSTEMATIC FOOD OR SLEEP DEPRIVATION OR ISOLATION FROM FAMILY OR UNUSUALLY LONG WORK SCHEDULES. . ." (Sec. 1.d; caps, in the original). Sponsors: Sens. Owens, Ciaroni, R. Smith. Date: Jan., 1981.

TABLE 2. (Continued)

State & Bill #	Name and Description
DL SB263	A Bill amending the Delaware Criminal Code relating to kidnapping. An additional criminal kidnapping offense of the first and second degrees is: "To subject such individual to any mental or physical procedure or activity with the intent of undermining or attempting to destroy or change such individual's religious, political, ideological, or any other beliefs." This bill was aimed at cults, but oddly would apply equally to deprogrammers. Sponsors: ? Date: May 28, 1981.
KA HB2688	An Act providing for the appointment of temporary guardians for certain persons. The "certain persons" includes one who has "undergone substantial behavioral change" (Sec. 1.a). A "behavioral change" is noted by "(a) abrupt and drastic alteration of basic values and life-style. . . , as contrasted with gradual change which might result from maturation or education; (b) blunted emotional responses; (c) regression to child-like levels of behavior; (d) physical changes, including but not limited to drastic weight changes, cessation of menstruation, diminished rate of facial hair growth and cessation of perspiration and (e) reduction of decisional capacity, including impairment and inability to make independent informed decisions" (Sec. 1.a.1.A-E). These five behavioral changes form the standard stereotype of conversion to the new religions and stem from the "source" bill against new religions in New York, AB11122/SB9730 proposed by Assemblyman Howard Lasher and Senator Joseph Pisani, beginning in 1980 (see below New York AB11122). Sponsors: Committee of Judiciary. Date: 1982.
IL HR121	A Resolution to set up a committee to "examine the relationship between cultism and religious freedom. . ." The resolution purports to give 14 "characteristics" of "pseudo-religious cults." Sponsors: Reps. Hoxey, Capparelli. Date: 1979.
IL HB908	An Act concerning charitable money handled by religious organizations, amending certain Acts therein named. This bill attempts to remove the exemption of religious organizations from the Charitable Trusts Act (Jan. 26, 1963) in order to find a way to get at new religious movements. Sponsors: Rep. Hoxey. Date: Mar. 14, 1979.
IL HB1083	A Bill appropriating funds to the Attorney General's Charitable Trust Division "to look into the conduct of organizations posing as religious groups to see if such organizations are engaging in fraud in the solicitation of funds or the use of funds, or criminal misconduct in the recruitment or treatment of members" (Sec. 1). Sponsors: Rep. Hoxey. Date: Apr. 3, 1981.
IL HB1084	An Act in relation to preventing illegal organization practices to prevent interference with family relationships. The bill states "the need for a remedy in situations where certain unreasonable forms of peer-group or psychological pressure can be used to persuade a person to join a religious or philosophical organization or where techniques are used which improperly prevent relatives, who might legitimately wish to counsel the new converted person about his or her adherence to the group from communicating with such a person" (Sec. 1). The bill creates torts and criminal

(continued)

173

TABLE 2.   (Continued)

State & Bill #	Name and Description
IL HB1084 (continued)	offenses for "malicious interference with the family," including anyone who "entices a person under the age of 18 to leave or avoid the custody of his or her parents or guardian and to enter into a communal or other close association with any religious or philosophical organization" (Sec. 2.a.1) or who "commits illegal organizational practices when he uses any methods to gain or keep adherents to any religious or philosophical organization which: (1) unreasonably deprive a person of proper sleep, food, health facilities, or contact with other people or (2) rely on coercive psychological techniques" (Sec. 3.a). Sponsors: Rep. Hoxey. Date: Apr. 3, 1981.
IL HB1085	An Act providing a private cause of action for a person or persons who are deceived into joining a religion or philosophical organization. This bill is a "Public Policy" statement aimed at inhibiting "deceitful practices": (a) the use of "false names" in "early contacts with potential converts and converts"; (b) the use of "menticide techniques...such as deprivation of sleep, continual observance, interference with privacy, group peer pressure to discourage contrary thoughts and questioning, monotonous chanting and singing, and inadequate diets..."; and (c) malicious interference with "normal family relationships between potential converts and their families..." (Sec. 1.a-c). Damages can be for "mental pain and suffering" (Sec. 3.a), loss of income by converts, "lost schooling or lost business opportunities" (Sec. 3.c), amount of funds collected by converts, "deceitful interference with family relationships" (Sec. 5.a), "loss of companionship" of convertees (Sec. 5.c), expenses incurred to establish contact by families, and attorney's fees. Compare with MN HB293, below. Sponsors: Rep. Hoxley. Date: April 3, 1981.
IL HB1086	An Act to require identification badges by persons soliciting funds for religious charities. This law states: "No person may solicit funds for any religious organization or group affiliated with a religious organization directly from members of the general public whether in a public place or by going door-to-door unless such a person obtains and is wearing the badge required by this Act" (Sec. 1). Application for solicitation badges require "(a) The name of the organization soliciting funds. (b) Names of the persons who will be soliciting funds. (c) The name of any organization with which the soliciting organization is affiliated. (d) The dates, time, and places the soliciting is to occur and whether the solicitation will be door-to-door. (e) Any other information which the Attorney General requests" (Sec. 2.a-e). Penalties include perjury and forgery. Sponsors: Rep. Hoxey. Date: Apr. 3, 1981.
IL HB1087	An Act to add Section 9a to "An Act to regulate the solicitation and collection of funds for charitable purposes." This amendment provides penalties for fraudulent solicitation practices by "a religious or charitable organization." In effect, this bill removes the exemption of religious organizations from the Charitable Trusts Act of Illinois (July 26, 1963). See IL HB908 (Mar. 14, 1979), above. Sponsors: Rep. Hoxey. Date: Apr. 3, 1981.
MD HJR67	A House Joint Resolution concerning "Cults in Maryland." The resolution empowers the Committee on Constitutional and Administrative Law to appoint a special joint committee "to study and report to the Maryland

TABLE 2. (Continued)

State & Bill #	Name and Description
MD HJR67 (continued)	Legislature on the recruitment and membership retention techniques and fundraising techniques of such cults and other entitites and the possible need for remedial legislation" (lines 87–90). "Such cults" refer to those "attracting significant numbers of youth to nontraditional, totalistic, and sometimes harmful and bizarre life styles" (lines 50–51), which "attempt to destroy family ties by turning children against their parents" (lines 60–60), which "recruit or retain their membership by way of techniques which undermine voluntary consent" (lines 65–66), or which engage "in improper and deceptive fund raising practices" (line 77). Sponsors: Delegates Ruben, Bromwell, Miedusiewski, Hagner, Campbell, Athey. Date: Feb. 13, 1981.
MN HB293	A Bill for an act relating to civil actions. The bill allows for civil damages against "organizations promising religious or philosophical self-fulfillment" (Sec 1). Among "the deceptive misrepresentations and deceitful practices" which give grounds for civil action are the "use of false names" and other attempts to cover-up an organization's "true nature and purpose . . . including rules of the organization designed to: (1) alter or destroy the convert's style of life, (2) radically interfere with the rights of a convert's family to keep the family intact; and (3) restructure a convert's psychological processes by use of subtle psychological techniques of behavior modification and manipulation . . ." (Sec. 1.a.1-3). The damages are the same as in IL HB1085, above. Sponsors: Reps. Reding, Kalis. Date: Feb. 9, 1981.
MO HB218	An Act relating to the appointment of a temporary guardian in certain circumstances. This bill contains similar wording and provisions as the NY AB11122-A (see below).
NB LR108	A Resolution stating: "The problem of cult activity is one which affects Nebraska and the United States. Several cults are active in Nebraska. These cults exercise mind control over their recruits causing radical personality changes, as well as psychological changes. In response to cult activities, parents of recruits have undertaken rescue operations often at a tremendous financial cost and some risk of injury" (Nebraska Legislative Reports, 1983, pp. 33–34). The resolution seeks to authorize a committee to investigate the cults in order to answer the following questions: "(1) How widespread cult activity is in Nebraska? (2) What rights the parents of cult members have to rescue their children for deprogramming under Nebraska Law? (3) What duties law enforcement personnel have respecting the capture and deprogramming of cult members? (4) What civil liabilities parents and deprogrammers face respecting deprogramming activity? (5) What First Amendment rights cults and cult members have? (6) What legislation is needed which would clarify the respective rights of parents, deprogrammers, the State, and the cult and cult members and protect parents and deprogrammers from lawsuits from cult members and cults" (p. 34). Sponsors: Rep. Goll. Date: 1983.
NV SB108	An Act relating to cults. This bill states: "Any person who is a member of a cult may bring civil action against the cult (whether or not it calls itself a religion) or against one or more of its practicioners and recover treble the

(continued)

TABLE 2. (Continued)

State & Bill #	Name and Description
NV SB108 (continued)	amount of any damage the person has suffered as a result of his membership if: (a) The cult held itself out as providing psychological benefits; (b) Neither the leader of the cult nor any of its other practitioners was a licensed psychologist or psychiatrist and available to provide those benefits to the aggrieved member; and (c) The cult demanded a fee or contribution at or before the time of the person's entry into the cult or before those benefits were to be realized" (Sec. 1.1.a-c). It is noteworthy that the sponsor of the bill had his daughter "deprogrammed" from the Church of Scientology and recovered a large sum of money (Beller, 1983). Sponsors: Sen. Hernstadt. Date: Feb. 3, 1983.
NV SB6	An Act relating to guardianship. This act seeks to amend Nevada law (NRS, Chap. 159, Secs. 2–17) by providing temporary guardianships for "any person 18 years of age or older" (Sec. 2) who has lost the capacity to make independent decisions "as a result of a systematic course of coercive persuasion" (Preamble); exemptions from civil and criminal activities for court appointed persons seeking to extricate someone; prohibition of flight or concealment; and penalties. The bill defines "coercive persuasion" as: "(a) Manipulation and control of the proposed ward's environment; (b) Isolation of the proposed ward from his family and friends; (c) Control over information and channels of communication; (d) Physical debilitation of the proposed ward through such means as deprivation of sleep, inadequate diet; unreasonably long hours of work or inadequate medical care; (e) Performance of repetitious tasks; (f) Lack of physical and mental privacy; (g) Use of intense pressure from others in the organization to induce feelings of guilt and anxiety; fear of the outside world and a childlike dependence upon the organization; and (h) Encouragement of a simplistic, polarized view of reality and the renunciation of self, family and previously held values" (Sec. 3.1.a-h). The categories are obviously derived from Lifton (1969). With open contradictoriness, the bill has the boldness to add: "The temporary guardianship is not requested for the purpose of altering the political, religious or other beliefs of the proposed ward" (Sec. 5.2.e.3). Sponsors: Committee of the Judiciary. Date: Jan. 23, 1985.
NY AB9666	A Bill dealing with "Promoting a Pseudo-religious Cult." Sponsors: ? Date: Oct. 5, 1977.
NY	"Public Hearing on Treatment of Children by Cults." Sponsors: ? Date: Aug. 9–10, 1979.
NY AB11122-A	An Act to amend the mental hygiene law, in relation to temporary conservatorship. This bill adds a new article to the NY Mental Hygiene Act. It is the "mother load" legislation for most of the conservatorship/guardianship bills which have spread around the nation since 1980. The bill allows for the appointment of "one or more conservators of the person and property of any person over 15 years of age, upon a showing that such a person for whom the temporary conservator is to appointed has become closely and regularly associated with a group which practices the use of deception in the recruitment of members and which engages in systematic food or sleep deprivation or isolation from family or unusually long work schedules; and that such person for whom the temporary conservator is to be appointed has undergone a sudden and radical change in behavior, lifestyle, habits, and attitudes; and has become unable to care for his welfare and

TABLE 2.   (Continued)

State & Bill #	Name and Description
NY AB11122-A (continued)	that his judgment has become impaired to the extent that he is unable to understand the need for such care" (Sec. 77.50,). The bill also stipulates provisions for preliminary hearings (not later than 72 hours after the preliminary order—a sufficient amount of time for "deprogrammers" to get to the convert first) as to the mental competence of the conservatee. As in NV SB6 (1985), the bill contradictorily states: "A temporary conservatee shall not be deprived of any civil right solely by reason of that appointment of a temporary conservator" (Sec. 77.68). Noting the opposition of the National Council of Churches, the New York State Catholic Conference, the New York Bar Association, and the New York Civil Liberties Union, Gov. Hugh Carey vetoed this bill after it passed the New York Assembly for the following reasons: "Although this bill represents a sincere effort by its sponsors, it places in jeopardy constitutionally guaranteed rights and raises false hopes by appearing to create an acceptable procedure—but one which would ultimately prove to be both unworkable and unconstitutional" (Message to the Assembly, July 1, 1980). This bill is commonly referred to as the "Lasher Bill." Sponsors: Reps. H. Lasher, Connelly, Larkin, Sanders, Wertz, A. Cohen, Greco. Harenberg, Kisor, Lipschutz, Sholer, Wilson, Yevoli. Date: March 25, 1980.
NY SB7912	The New York State Senate version of NY AB11122-A. Sponsors: Sens. Pisani, Mega, Nolan, Tauriello. Date: May 6, 1980.
NY AB7912	An Act to amend the Mental Hygiene Law by adding a new article (art. 80). This 1981 bill is virtually the same as NY AB11122 of 1980. It adds a characterization of "a sudden and dramatic personality change": "1. Abrupt and drastic alteration of basic values and lifestyle, as contrasted with gradual change such as that which might result from maturation or education; 2. Lack of appropriate emotional responses; 3. Regression to child-like behavior; 4. Physical changes which may include: (i) weight change; (ii) cessation of menstruation; (iii) loss of facial hair; (iv) wooden, mask-like expression; (v) dilated pupils; (vi) cessation of perspiration; (vii) constant and frenetic activity resulting in extreme fatigue; 5. Reduction of decisional capacity, which may include impairment of judgment and inability to make independent informed decisions; 6. Psychopathological changes which may include: dissociation, obsessional ruminations, delusional thinking, hallucinations and various other psychiatric signs and symptoms" (Sec. 80.01.a). The bill also seeks to protect conservators and their agents from charges of "false arrest, false imprisonment, unlawful detention, assault, trespass or invasion of civil rights;; and to protect other provisions of the act if single parts are found "unlawful" (Sec. 80.19). Like its predecessor this act was vetoed by Gov. Hugh Carey because "the bill would allow for the deprivation of rights of some or all members of a group because of the fraudulent activities of the few," because it would "subject people to the deprivation of their liberty and civil rights solely because of their affiliation with a particular group," and because the bill "would also authorize, in certain circumstances, the physical seizure of a person under warrant of attachment which a court might issue even though no criminal action is involved" (Message to the New York Assembly, July 17, 1981). Sponsors: Rep. Lasher. Date: May 10, 1981.

(continued)

TABLE 2. (Continued)

State & Bill #	Name and Description
NY SB5119	Senate version of NY AB7912. Sponsors: Sen. Pisani. Date: May 10, 1981.
OH HB250	A Bill to set up a committee to investigate the Society of Krishna Consciousness and the Unification Church. Sponsor: Rep. Cruze. Date: 1976.
OH HR32	A Resolution to form a committee to investigate "the activities of the religious bodies whose international leader is the Rev. Sun Myung Moon and which is generally named as the Unification Church and related organizations." Sponsor: ? Date: Apr. 26, 1977.
OH HB498	An Act "to provide for the appointment of temporary guardians for persons who have become incapacitated because of the influence of an individual or a cult." Sponsors: ? Date: July 1981.
OR SB524	An Act relating to guardianship. The bill would grant temporary guardianships for persons incapacitated "by reason of undue influence of a person" (Sec. 1.1.6). Undue influence results when a person or group fails to allow its members or associates: "(a) Information sufficient to form informed consent to membership in the group; (b) Freedom to associate with relatives and friends; (c) Reasonable personal privacy; (d) Reasonable and adequate rest; (e) Reasonable communication with relatives and friends; (f) Reasonable access to medical care and treatment; (g) Retention of income assets; (h) Reasonable independence of thought and action; and (i) Reasonable opportunity for travel" (Sec. 1.1.a-i). A person is considered under "undue influence" if he or she shows "(a) Loss of spontaneity or originality in language and behavior; (c) Sudden changes in personality, values, goals or associations with nongroup members; (d) Regression to child-like dependence on group leaders, members or associates for making personal decisions; (e) Failure to assert needs for personal health or welfare; and (f) Impairment of ability to critically evaluate information and form independent conclusions" (Sec. 1.1.a-f). Sponsors: Committee on Justice at the request of Peter S. Rudic and Sen. Day. Date: 1981.
PA HR20	A Resolution referred to the committee on rules to set up a committee to investigate "the Unification Church, and the following religious societies; Scientology, Children of God, International Society of Krishna Consciousness, Divine Light Mission, Church of Bible Understanding, Council for Social Development, Neo-American Church and The Way International" which allegedly "utilize improper mind control techniques in their recruitment and retention of members" (p. 1, lines 2–8). The committee is to have full subpoena powers and can inflict penalties on anyone "who willfully neglects or refuses to testify before the committee or to produce any books, papers, records, or documents" (p. 3, lines 8–9). Sponsors: Reps. Goebel, Lashinger, Pott. Date Mar. 6, 1979.
PA HB406	An Act creating a temporary study commission to study groups which seek to unduly exert control over children and youth. The unnamed groups to be studied seek control over youth and children "which is hazardous and detrimental to their general and mental health, freedom and life style and which seek to induce, by undue pressure . . . through the use of inappropriate suggestions, hypnosis, drugs, unethical physical or social inducements and any other coercive or unacceptable methods" (Sec. 1). Sponsors: Reps. Lashinger, Maiale, Salvatore, Pratt, Mackowsdi, Alden, Telek, Freind, E.Z. Taylor. Date: Feb., 3, 1981.

TABLE 2. (Continued)

State & Bill #	Name and Description
TX HR35	A Resolution passed by the House of Representatives Committee on Criminal Jurisprudence to examine cults. Sponsors: ? Date: May 10, 1977.
TX SB1058	An Act relating to guardianships for certain people who are under undue influence. This bill is identical to the Oregon bill OR SB524, above. Sponsors: ? Date: 1981.
VT	Report to State Senate on "Fraudulent and Criminal Practices of Various Organizations in the State." Sponsors: ? Date: 1977. John Clark, Jr., was called in as an expert witness for this report (Clark, 1977).

LEGEND: A = Assembly; B = Bill; H = House; J = Joint; L = Legislative; R = Resolution; S = Senate

Before discussing the implications of these bills for the relation of religion and law in the United States, a word about their repercussions on the federal level and in other countries is in order. In 1980 U.S. Congressman Richard L. Ottinger (D-NY) published a report "Cults and Their Slaves" in the *Congressional Record* (Ottinger, 1980). The report urged a federal bill on the model of the "Lasher Bill" NY A11122, above. On June 18, Ottinger introduced a resolution into the U.S. Congress entitled "A Bill to amend title 18, United States Code, to provide penalties for certain deceptive and coercive practices used by certain organizations in recruiting members, and for other purposes." The resolution did not get out of committee.

During 31st Legislature (1980) in the Province of Ontario, Canada, a bill entitled "An Act to monitor and regulate the activities of Cults and Mind Development Groups" (H. Richardson, 1980, pp. 33–36) was introduced by Member of Parliament Sweeney. The introduction of this bill provoked the legislatively authorized study by Daniel Hill (1980) entitled *Study of Mind Development Groups, Sects and Cults in Ontario.* The Hill report, which gleaned information from law enforcement, mental health professionals, and religious experts, concluded:

That being the case, the study can identify no legitimate grounds on which to base substantive recommendations for government action. In the light of the evidence and the bulk of the advice at hand, none seems warranted.

As a result of the study, the Ontario bill was tabled.

The latest ripple from New York Assemblyman Lasher's "mother lode" bill is being felt in France, where anti-cult and deprogramming activity (including the deprogramming of a female convert to Islam) is at a peak. Membre de Parliament Alain Vivien has presented a report to the Family Ministry of France on *les sectes* which just been made public (Vivien,

1983). (The French term "secte" is equivalent to the English "cult.") Mssr. Vivien is promoting a version of the Lasher bill for France (Stein, 1984). Influence of the U.S. legislation is also being felt throughout Europe via the report of Englishman Richard Cottrell (1984) to the Committee on Youth, Culture, Education, Information and Sport of the European Parliament. The recommendations of the report, entitled "Report on the Activity of Certain New Religious Movements within the European Community," follow along the lines of the U.S. legislation and were adopted by the European Parliament. It appears that the Europeans are not yet aware that the constitutionality of such legislation has been seriously challenged in the United States. Nor do the Europeans seem to be aware that their legislative recommendations, which target the Unification Church as it was targeted in the U.S. in the middle 1970's, is in violation of both the letter and spirit of the U.N. "Declaration on the Elimination of All Forms of Intolerance and of Discrimination Based on Religion or Belief" (Jan., 18, 1982), to which all the European countries and the United States were signatory. Article 1, Secs. 1 and 2, of the U.N. Declaration (U.N., 1982) reads:

1. Everyone shall have the right to freedom of thought, conscience and religion. This right shall include freedom to have a religion or whatever belief of his choice, and freedom, either individually or in community with other and in public or private, to manifest his religion or belief in worship, observance, practice and teaching.
2. No one shall be subject to coercion which would impair his freedom to have a religion or belief of his choice.

There can be no doubt that this wealth of legislation raises countless questions about conversion to new religions—and old religions—as it pertains to the Establishment and Free Exercise Clauses of the First Amendment in the United States. As the issues and topics are complex, I shall enumerate my concluding statements.

1. Constitutionality. Although some of the legislation above is still pending, on the whole the four types of bill are coming to be recognized as unconstitutional and in violation of freedom of religion. The legislative acts have either been a) withdrawn or tabled, b) defeated in committee or assembly, c) vetoed as "unworkable and unconstitutional" or d) found unconstitutional by the courts. The recognition of the unconstitutionality of such legislation has come about in no small part by the role played by civil rights organizations and mainline churches in opposition to restricting freedom of belief. Responding to the New York AB7912/SB5119, the Commission on Law and Social Action of the New York and Long Island chapters of the American Jewish Committee (AJC, 1981, p. 1) commented:

The New York and Long Island Chapters of the American Jewish Committee are concerned about and recognize the problems and strains in family relations and the deep feelings of those whose children and other family members are attracted by groups espousing unorthodox religious beliefs and spiritual practices. The proposed legislation, however, is a mistaken and misguided approach to the challenge of these groups and jeopardizes constitutionally guaranteed rights of freedom of religion and association.

This statement correctly notes the seamless garment of freedom: freedom of religion cannot be separated from freedom of speech or freedom of association. Noting the novel notion of "temporary conservatorship" in the New York AB11122, the Committee on Mental Hygiene of the New York State Bar Association (NYSBA, 1980, p. 2) stated: "The bill could also be used by a spouse in a matrimonial dispute or by an adult child against his parents. To the extent that this bill permits a temporary conservator to be appointed when an adult associates with persons not liked by a family member or other defined persons, it unconstitutionally restricts the temporary conservatee's freedom of association." J. Allan Davitt, Executive Director of the New York State Catholic Conference noted the vague wording in his opposition to the bill: "The language is such that a parent could, for example, with the assistance of a sympathetic judge have his child taken from virtually any group with which the child associates, religious or otherwise" (NYSCC, 1980, p. 1). It is on constitutional grounds that the New York AB11122—known as the "Lasher Bill" and the primary "mother lode" of legislation in other states—was opposed also by the the the NAACP, the National Council of the Churches of Christ, Americans United for the Separation of Church and State, the New York Civil Liberties Union, etc. Gov. Carey specifically cited this opposition in his veto of New York AB11122.

2. *"Cults"*.   A number of bills used the words "cults" or "cultism" (e.g., Illinois HR121, Maryland HR67, Nebraska LR108, Nevada SB108, New York AB9666). Whether explicity stated so or not, the clear implication is that a "cult" is a "pseudo-religion" or a religious fraud. The word "cult" is fraught with ambiguity. The ancient Romans used it, along with the term *superstitio*, to designate the rites of the mystery religions, including Christianity. As the saying goes, "Yesterday's 'cult' is tomorrow's religion." Roman Catholics speak of the "cult of the Blessed Virgin Mary" and mean by the term the acts and rites of devotion to God through the intercession of Mary. The slipperiness of the term is further complicated by such phrases as "the Manson cult," "the Elvis cult" or a "diet cult," etc. After the Jonestown tragedy, the term "cult" became associated with a deranged, tyrannical leader, "brainwashing" of converts, bizarre beliefs, and practices. It was used to lump all the new religious movements—and some of the old,

such as Jehovah's Witnesses, Mormons, and Seventh Day Adventists—into one gunny sack, neglecting the genuine differences between the various religious movements.

The original term is derived from the Latin verb *colere* and means to till the ground, as in "cultivation," to worship the gods who bestow fertility on the soil, and finally to worship in general. In sociological terminology, the word cult is differentiated from church, denomination and sect (Flinn, 1983, pp. 89–92):

FIGURE 1. Religious Groupings

CHURCH	DENOMINATION
—claims sole possession of truth	—pluralistic truth ("many paths")
—active role in society	—active role
SECT	CULT
—exclusive truth	—multiplistic truth
—set against "corrupt" society	—indifferent or inactive in society

The classic example of a church is Roman Catholicism, of a denomination is Presbyterianism or Congregationalism, of a sect is Jehovah's Witnesses, of a cult is Madame Blavatsky's Theosophical Society. Today this classification system has broken down because the term "cult" has become a legal buzz word. Some anti-cultist organizations believe that they have *ipso facto* established a group as a "pseudo-religion" if they have managed to get a group labelled a "cult" in judicial or legislative proceedings. Elsewhere I have argued (Flinn, 1981b) that the constitution uses only one word for all the phenomena included under the above classification system —*religion*. Legislative and executive branches of government are specifically prohibited from determining religious questions ("no laws" in the First Amendment). If the question comes before the courts, and it has many times, the courts can determine solely *that* a group is, or is not, a religion but not *how* a group is to be a religion in terms of its beliefs, ritual practices, ethical codes, and religious organization. (If a group has practices which lead to crimes, then those crimes are to be prosecuted as civil and not religious crimes.) In other words, whether a religious group is a church, synagogue, temple, congregation, meeting (as with the Quakers), fellowship, sect, cult, association, etc., is constitutionally irrelevant. For the judiciary to give preference, for example, to the term "church" as against "cult" is to establish certain religions (the traditional ones) over others (the innovative ones). The oft-stated principle of "benevolent neutrality" was most clearly phrased in *Everson v. Board of Education* 330 U.S. 1 (1947) by Mr. Justice Black, speaking for the court:

The "establishment of religion" clause of the First Amendment means at least this: Neither a state nor the Federal Government can set up a church. Neither can pass laws which aid one religion, aid all religions, or prefer one religion over another.

3. Temporary Conservatorship/Guardianship.   The great preponderance of the legislation above is aimed at allowing relatives and others to get temporary guardianships over their adult offspring or acquaintances. The Nevada bill states that "the temporary guardianship is not requested for the purpose of altering the political, religious or other beliefs of the proposed ward" (NV SB6, Jan. 25, 1985, Sec. 5.2.e.3). Yet the common acknowledgement by those for and against this type of legislation is that its purpose is to put family members under the power of their guardians precisely for the purpose of breaking their faith in their new-found religion, most often with the assistance of deprogrammers. This is the reason for providing a temporary guardianship lasting 30 or more days. That is time enough for the deprogrammers to incarcerate a member of the new religions, make mockery of their beliefs, and harass them physically and verbally so that they give up their faith. Jeremiah Gutman, president of the New York Civil Liberties Union and attorney in more deprogramming cases than any other lawyer known to me, has given a detailed run-down of just what takes place in a deprogramming (Gutman, 1982). The family seeking guardianship and the deprogrammers seeking a healthy fee claim they are "rescuing" but what they are really doing are depriving the kidnappee of his or her civil liberties and, in effect, victimizing the alleged victim (Drakeman, 1984, p. 164; NYSBA, 1981:2). Many noted attorneys have commented that the use of conservatorship laws to *deprive* rather than to *protect* a person's liberties and property is both an abuse and misapplication of Fourteenth Amendment guarantees and a perversion of the intent of conservatorship laws themselves (Baker, 1977; Brandon, 1982, pp. 44–46). In order to justify a conservator- or guardianship, the parties involved must necessarily rely on the testimony of mental health professionals. But in *Addington v. Texas* 441 U.S. 418 (1979), the Supreme Court established a rigid standard of proof in cases of civil commitment and specifically placed doubts about psychiatric diagnoses:

> The Court in recognizing the limitations of psychiatric diagnosis said, "The subtleties and nuances of psychiatric diagnosis render certainties virtually beyond reach in most situations. . . . Psychiatric diagnosis. . . is to a large extent based on medical "impressions" drawn from subjective analysis and filtered through the experience of the diagnostician."

In other words, the "facts" of psychiatric analysis can be presumed to be "colored" and fail the test of hard evidence in cases of civil commitment.

4. Solicitation and Proselytizing.   Some bills, such as Illinois HB1085 and Minnesota HB293, seek to inhibit solicitation and proselytizing. This legislation, especially in the provisions requiring registration and identification badges, in effect puts prior restraint on the free exercise of religion. In *Cantwell v. Connecticut* 310 U.S. 296 (1940) the Supreme Court determined that the right to speak religiously cannot be inhibited by licensing even if there is the suspicion that the speaker may commit fraud: "Such a censorship of religion as the means of determining its right to survive is a denial of liberty protected by the First Amendment and included in the liberty which is within the Fourteenth. . . ." The Minnesota bill, in particular, is addressed against reputed fraudulent promises, but that would put religious beliefs to legislative test and empower the state to distinguish between what is believed and what is believable. In *U.S. v. Ballard* 322 U.S. 28, Mr. Justice Douglas, speaking for the court, wrote:

> Men may believe what they cannot prove. They may not be put to the proof of their religious doctrines or beliefs. Religious experiences which are as real as life to some may be incomprehensible to others. Yet the fact that they may be beyond the ken of mortals does not mean that they can be made suspect before the law. Many take their gospel from the New Testament. But it would hardly be supposed that they could be tried before a jury charged with the duty of determining whether those teachings contained false representations. The miracles of the New Testament, the Divinity of Christ, life after death, the power of prayer are deep in the religious convictions of many. If one could be sent to jail because a jury in a hostile environment found those teachings false, little indeed would be left of religious freedom.

The *Ballard* decision in no way inhibits the state from prosecuting *civil* frauds, e.g., shortchanging someone buying a religious tract. It does restrict the state in judicially examining religious promises or beliefs. Calling in psychologists and psychiatrists to determine whether or not a religious conversion is a fraud is like calling in a chemist to test the bread and wine before and after Consecration in the Catholic Mass to determine whether the elements are truly "transubstantiated" into the Body and Blood of Jesus Christ.

5. Conversion. Finally, we come to the most important theme of this essay: conversion. The legislative bills do not use the word "conversion" as that would be patently unconstitutional. Instead they refer to "substantial behavioral change" or an "abrupt and drastic alteration of basic values and lifestyle" as opposed to gradual, maturational, or educational change (Kansas HB2688); "radical personality changes" (Nebraska LR108); "change in behavior, lifestyle, habits and attitudes" (New York AB11122); or "a sudden and dramatic personality changes" (New York AB7912). It is obvious that the anti-cult sponsors of these bills single out one type of conversion model, namely what I described above as the classic Platonic-Augustinian model, and claim it takes place under criminal influence. This is to prefer one type of religious experience over another, and, consequently, to put those religions which recognize sudden "born-again" religious experiences as central to their faith at a disadvantage before the law. Furthermore, scholars of religious experience, including William James, have noted that conversion can take place either suddenly or gradually, and that even sudden conversion has subsequent stages (James, [1902], pp. 190–213). James summed up the difference between the two types of conversion with the sentence: "The value of conversion depends not on the process, but on the fruits" (ibid, 7) Secondly, the research of Fowler demonstrates that sudden conversion is not necessarily incompatible with maturational growth. Constitutionally, the Supreme Court has recognized the validity if not the credibility of sudden conversion. In *U.S. v. Ballard* 322 U.S. 78 (1944), Mr. Justice Douglas, speaking for the Court, wrote:

> Religious Scriptures overflow with instances of unusual and astonishing spiritual experiences, experiences that are incomprehensible to the rational and unbelieving mind—visions of burning bushes and miraculous and immediate conversions to a new system of belief. These experiences, which are inherently personal and ineffable are often accompanied by behavior that seems bizarre (or even delusional) to outsiders.

Yet, the contention of *Ballard* is that just such experiences and changes in "values" and "lifestyle"—to use the language of the legislation are protected by the First Amendment. Such beliefs and lawful yet "bizarre" practices may not be put to political, criminal, civil or psychiatric tests.

In the linguistic legerdemain to avoid the obvious target of the legislative intent—conversion to the new religions—the bills end up being hopelessly vague. They seem to legislate against change itself on the part of young adults. When the "target cults" are removed from the wording of the legislation, its unconstitutional vagueness becomes immediately apparent. The description of "sudden" or "radical" changes in "behavior," "lifestyle" or even "ideals," "goals," and "associations" can be applied to countless secular and sacred circumstances. Certainly, a draftee entering boot-camp experiences all of the above. So does any young Catholic who enters a monastery or convent. Thomas Brandon, Jr., writes: "The bills, while attempting to target only certain groups, could be applied to many mainline religions and denominations. The Ohio bill [HB498], for example, on its face, would certainly be applicable to a 'born-again' Christian conversion, to the Charismatic movement, certain Roman Catholic orders or certain branches of Chassidic Judaism . . ." (Brandon, 1982, pp. 51–52). Anyone who has read Thomas Merton's *Seven Story Mountain* can discover that he went through "sleep deprivation" (called vigils by the monks), "food withdrawal" (called fasting), "monotonous chanting" (called choir), "loss of facial hair" (called tonsure), "manipulation of the environment" and "control over information and channels of communication" (called cloister and rules of silence). One commentator not-so-jokingly noted that the criteria for a cult in the New York AB11122 applied to the Legislature itself in terms of behavior and lifestyle (Shaffer, 1980). There can be no doubt that deprogramming has been applied indiscriminately to, besides members of the new religions, converts to Roman Catholicism, Old Catholicism, Hasidic Judaism, Islam (in France), as well as Episcopalians, feminists, and political activists FOD, 1982, pp. 44–69; Bencheikh El Hocine, 1985). Aside from the denial of equal protection to "target cults," the bills, if enacted, are almost certain to entangle the state in the quagmire of a second Inquisition, an eventuality the Fathers of the Constitution looked upon with abhorrence.

Another aspect to the criminalization of conversion is to limit proselytizing, described in the Delaware SB263 as the attempt to "destroy or change such individual's religious, ideological, or any other beliefs." The preposterousness of this provision has been pointed up by Thomas Brandon: "It appears to prevent any conversion from one religion to another or from being a Democrat to a Republican or from being a Marxist to a capitalist" (Brandon, 1982, p. 43). Yet this type of provision has its legal advocates (Delgado, 1980). The arguments boil down to the question whether conversion is a form of "religious thought-control" or whether "thought reform" or "mind control" is in fact a mental illness or even a crime. The New England Psychological Association issued a declaration (H. Richardson, 1977, p. 183) stating: "We assert that the terms 'mind-control' and 'brainwashing' as applied to the practices of the Hare Krishna devotees, or any legitimate religious minority, are colloquial, non-professional terms which should not be wielded as legal weapons for religious or social persecution." Proselytizing, evangelizing, "carrying the message," persuasion to belief, etc., are religious practice long sanctioned by the Supreme Court as part and parcel of the essence of religious freedom and cannot be gainsaid. In *Cantwell v. Connecticut* 310 U.S. 296 (1940), Mr. Justice Roberts, speaking for the court, wrote:

> In the realm of religious faith, and in that of political belief, sharp differences arise. In both fields the tenets of one man may seem the rankest error to his neighbor. To persuade others to his own point of view, the pleader, as we know, at times resorts to exaggeration, to vilification of men who have been, or are, prominent in church or state, and even to false statement. But the people of this nation have ordained in the light of history, that, in spite of the probability of excesses and abuses, these liberties are, in the long view, essential to enlightened opinion on the part of citizens of democracy.

In numerous cases in the last ten years the Supreme Court has stated that statutes must pass three tests: 1) they must have a secular legislative purpose, 2) they must have a principal or primary purpose that neither advances nor inhibits religion, and 3) they must not foster excessive entanglement with religion (see esp. *Lemon v. Kurtzman* 403 U.S. 602 [1971]). The anti-cult legislation which has cluttered the legislative docket for the past ten years fails on all three counts.

Although "deprogramming" gained a patina of legality, the courts in recent decisions have come to see it as a violation of fundamental constitutional rights. First, courts have upheld pleadings as stating a cause of action under the U.S. Code 1985(3) against deprogrammers. Paragraph 1985(3) of the U.S. Code is popularly known as the "Ku Klux Klan Provision" and allows redress against those conspiring to deprive "any person or class of persons of the equal protection of the laws, or of equal privileges and immunities under the laws. . . ." Among the most important court rulings that can be cited in this regard are *Ward v. Connor*, 657 F.2d 45 (4th Cir. 1981), *cert. denied*, 455 U.S. 907 (1982); *Cooper v. Molko*, 512 F. Supp. 563, 568-71 (N.D. Cal. 1981); and *Taylor v. Gilmartin*, 686 F.2d 1346, 1357-61 (10th Cir. 1982), *cert. denied*, 495 U.S. 1147 (1983). In *Columbrito, et al. v. Kelly, et al.*, United States Court Appeals, 2d Cir., No. 84-7672 at 16 (June 12, 1985), the court, citing *Taylor v. Gilmartin*, stated that "deprogramming" is "odious and has the effect of depriving the victim of important rights—his liberty, his freedom, his right to practice his religion among other rights." In effect, the highest courts in the nation are stating in unequivocal terms that, what the KKK has been to the political rights of blacks and others, the "deprogrammers" are to religious rights of unusual religious groups.

Perhaps it is time for Americans to consult the light of history for a longer view of enlightened opinion. This era is not the first time that conversion has created controversy. The young adults who joined the medieval urban youth movement known as the mendicant orders—such as the Dominicans, Franciscans and Augustinians—were called *dementes* ("insane") and *filii diaboli* ("sons of the devil") by clerics of the establishment (Chenu, 1964, pp. 340–343; Pieper, 1957, pp. 3–17). Both St. Francis of Assisi and St. Thomas Aquinas were kidnapped and imprisoned by their parents and relatives who tried to "deprogram" them out of their bizarre beliefs and lifestyles as "mendicants," i.e., beggars (Flinn, 1981a). Similar charges and epithets were hurled by the established Harvard divines against the principals and participants in the Great Awakening (Lane, 1979). I will leave it to the reader as to whether or not St. Francis, St. Thomas and Jonathan Edwards were a boon to the spiritual history of humanity. For those who take time to consult the light of history there is the illuminating fact that the first treatise against "conservatorship" and "deprogramming" on religious grounds was written by St. Thomas himself. It was called in Latin *Contra pestiferam doctrinam retrahentium homines a religionis ingressu*—"Against the Pernicious Teaching of Those Dragging Youth Away from Entering the Religious Life" (Aquinas, 1954).

REFERENCES

AJC (American Jewish Committee, New York & Long Island Chapters) (1981). Statement in Opposition to Proposed Bills A. 7912, S. 6614. New York, May 27, 1981.

Aquinas, St. T. (1954). Contra pestiferam doctrinam retrahentium homines a religionis ingressu, *Opuscula Theologica* II.159–90. Raymundus N. Spiazzi (Ed.), O.P. Romae: Marietti.

Augustine, St. (1961). *Confessions* (2 vol.). Tr. William Watts. Cambridge, MA: Loeb Classical Library.

Baker, R.L. (1977). Abuse and misapplication of conservatorship law in H. Richardson, pp. 159–63.

Barker, E. (1984). *The making of a moonie*. London: Blackwell.

Barnes, T. (1968). Legislation against the Christians. *Journal of Roman Studies, 58*, 32–50.

Bauer, W., Arndt, W.F., & Gingrich, F.W. (1957). *A Greek-English lexicon of the New Testament and other early Christian literature.* Chicago: University of Chicago Press.

Beckford, J. (1978). Through the looking-glass and out the other side: Withdrawal from Reverend Moon's unification church. *Archives de sciences sociologiques des religions,* (Jan.–Mar.) *45*(1), 95–116.

Beckford, J. (1983). The 'cult problem' in five countries: The social construction of religious controversy. *Of Gods and men:* New religious movements in the west, Eileen Barker (Ed.), pp. 195–214. Macon: Mercer University Press.

Bellah, R. N. (1967). Civil religion in America. *Daedulus* (Winter), *96* 1, 1–20.

Beller, M. (1983). Bill targets cults that fail to save souls. *Los Angeles Herald Examiner* (Feb. 5, 1983) A5.

Bencheikh El. H. (1985). Letter addressed to Mssr. Kurt Herndl, Director of the Center of the Rights of Man, United Nations, Geneva, on the deprogramming of Sehra Salim (nee Caroline Banks). January 3, 1985. (Bencheikh El Hocine is the Director of the Institut Musulman of the Mosque of Paris.)

Billington, R. (1963). *The Protestant crusade*. Gloucester, MA: Peter Smith.

Boettcher, R. (1980). *Gifts of deceit: Sun Myung Moon, Tonsun Park, and the Korean Scandal.* With Gordon L. Freedman. New York: Holt, Rinehart and Winston.

Brandon, T.S., Jr. (1982). *New religions, conversions and deprogramming: New frontiers of religious liberty.* Oak Park, IL: Christian Legal Society.

Bromley, D.G., & Shupe, A.D. (1979). Apostate tales, the unification church and the social construction of evil. *Journal of Communication,* (Summer) *29,* 42–43.

Bromley, D.G., & Shupe, A.D. (1981). *Strange Gods: The great American cult scare.* Boston: Beacon.

Bryant, M.D. (Ed.). (1979). *Religious liberty in Canada.* Documentation Series No. 1: Deprogramming and Media Coverage of New Religions. Toronto: Canadians for the Protection of Religious Liberty.

Chenu, M.D. (1964). *Toward understanding Saint Thomas.* Chicago: Henry Regnery.

Chorover, S. (1977). Statement at the Harvard symposium: Krishna consciousness and religious freedom in H. Richardson 193–94.

Clark, J. (1977). Investigating the effects of *Religious Cults* on the health and welfare of their converts. *The American Atheist,* (May) *19/5,* 5–7.

Clark, J. (1979). Cults. *Journal of the American Medical Association,* (July 20) *242,* 279–81.

Cohn, N. (1961). *The pursuit of the millennium.* New York: Harper & Row.

Conway, F., & Siegelman, J. (1979). *Snapping* (2nd ed.). New York: Lippencott.

Conway, F., & Siegelman, J. (1982). Information disease: Have cults created a new mental illness? *Science Digest* (January), 86–92.

Cottrell, R. (1984). Report on the activity of certain new religious movements within the european community. Committee on youth, culture, education, information, and sport. European Parliament. Mar. 22, 1984.

Edwards J. (1966). *Jonathan Edwards: Basic writings*. Ola Elizabeth Winslow (Eds.), New York: New American Library.

Erikson, E.H. (1963). *Childhood and society*. (2nd ed.). New York: W.W. Norton.

Erikson, E.H. (1982). *The life cycle completed: A review*. New York: W.W. Norton.

Delgago, R. (1980). Limits to proselytizing. *Society* (March/April) *17*(3), 25–33.

Drakeman, D.L., Esq. (1984). Cult members: Converts or criminals? *Christian Century* (Feb. 15), 163–65.

Flinn, F.K. (1979). Deprogramming and the deprogramming network in Bryant, pp. 3–10.

Flinn, F.K. (1981a). Deprogramming in the middle ages. *New ERA Newsletter 1*, 1, 4.

Flinn, F.K. (1981b). Law, language and religion. *New ERA Newsletter 1*(2), 3–4, 6.

Flinn, F.K. (1982). *Law v. Religion:* Cults, brainwashing, deprogramming, conservatorship. St. Louis: Frank K. Flinn

Flinn, F.K. (1983). Scientology as technological buddhism in *Alternatives to American Mainline Religions*, Joseph Fichter (Ed.), (New York: Rose of Sharon, 1983), pp. 89–110.

FOD (Facts on Deprogramming) (1982). A collection of articles, reports, and court decisions on facts relating to deprogramming. New York: ICARRI.

Fowler, J. (1981). *Stages of faith: The psychology of human develoment and the quest for meaning*. San Francisco: Harper & Row.

Freud, S. (1961). *The future of an illusion*. New York: W.W. Norton.

Gadol, J. (1969). *Leon Battista Alberti: Universal man of the early renaissance*. Chicago: University of Chicago Press.

Gelpi, D.L. (1976). *Charism and sacrament: A theology of christian conversion*. New York: Paulist Press.

Grant, G.P. (1962). Conceptions of Health. *Psychiatry and Responsibility*, Helmut Schoeck & James W. Wiggins (Eds.), (Princeton: Van Nostrand), pp. 117–34.

Gutman, J. (1982). *Deprogramming: Step by Step. New ERA Newsletter* (Mar.-Apr.) *2*(1), 1, 4.

Hill, D. (1980). *Study of mind development groups, sects and cults*. A Report to the Ontario Government. Toronto: The Queen's Printer.

Hunter, E. (1951). *Brainwashing in Red China: The calculated destruction of men's minds*. New York: Vanguard.

Jackson, H. (1919). *Convent cruelties or my life in a convent*. Toledo, OH: Helen Jackson.

James, W. (1902). *The varieties of religious experience*. Garden City, NY: Doubleday, n.d.

Kelley, D.M. (Ed.). (1982). *Government intervention in religious affairs*. New York: Pilgrim Press.

Kohlberg, L. (1981). *Essays on moral development* (Volume 1). The philosophy of moral development, moral stages and the idea of justice. San Francisco: Harper & Row.

Kuhn, T.S. (1970). *The Structure of Scientific Revolutions*. (2nd ed.). Chicago: University of Chicago Press.

Kuner, W. (1981). Ein Sammelbecken für Verruchte? *Psychologie Heute* (Sept.), 53–61.

Lane, B.C. (1979). Brainwashing and conversion, *The Reformed Journal*, (April), 9–12.

Levine, E.M. (1980). Deprogramming without tears. *Society* (March/April) *17*(3), 34–38.

Levine, S.V., & Salter, N.E. (1976). Youth and contemporary religious movements: Psychological findings. *Canadian Psychiatric Journal, 21*(6), 411–20.

Lewis, J.R. (1984). Information Disease and the Legitimation of Repression. Paper presented at the Annual Meeting of the Association for the Sociaology of Religion. San Antonio, TX, Aug. 25–27.

Lifton, R.J. (1969). *Thought reform and the psychology of totalism: A study of brainwashing in China*. New York: W.W. Norton. First published in 1961.

Lonergan, B.J.F. (1958). *Insight: A study of human understanding.* London: Longmans, Green & Co.

Lonergan, B.J.F. (1972). *Method in theology.* New York: Herder and Herder.

Lucksted, O.D., & Martell, D.F. (1982). Cults: A conflict between religious liberty and involuntary servitude? *FBI Law Enforcement Bulletin.* Part I, April, 16–20; Part II, May, 16–23; Part III, June, 16–21.

Marshall, B.E. (1984). The unseen regulator: The role of characterization in first amendment free exercize cases, *Notre Dame Law Review* 89(4), 798–1004.

McGowan, T. (1982). Conversion: A movie version, *New ERA Newsletter* 2(1), 5, 4.

Melton, J.G., & Moore, R.L. (1982). *The cult experience.* New York: Pilgrim.

Miller, P., & Johnson, T.N. (1963). *The Puritans: A sourcebook of their writings.* (2 vols.). New York: Harper & Row.

NCC (National Council of Churches) (1977). A critique of the theology of the Unification Church as set forth in *Divine Principle.* 11 pp. New York: Commission on Faith and Order, National Council of Churches of Christ in the U.S.A., June, 1977.

Nock, A.D. (1933). *Conversion: The old and the new in religion from Alexander the Great to Augustine of Hippo.* Oxford at the Clarendon Press.

NYSBA (New York State Bar Association) (1981). Committee on Mental Hygiene Report No. 11122-A. June 23, 1980.

NYSCC (New York State Catholic Conference) (1980). Letter from J. Allan Davitt, Executive Director, to Richard A. Brown, Counsel to the Governor. Albany, July 1, 1980.

Ottinger, R.L. (1980). Cults and their slaves. *Congressional Record,* July 24, E3578.

Patrick, T. (1976). *Let our children go.* With Tom Dulack. New York: Ballentine.

Piaget, J. (1970). *Main trends in psychology.* New York: Harper & Row.

Pieper, J. (1957). *The silence of Saint Thomas.* Chicago: Henry Regnery.

Plutarch (1962). *Moralia.* Frank Cole Babbit (Ed.). Cambridge, MA: Loeb Classical Library.

Rambo, L. (1980). Psychological perspectives on conversion. *Pacific Theological Review, 13*(2), 22 ff.

Richardson, H.W. (1974). Civil religion in theological perspective. *American Civil Religion,* Russell E. Richey & Donald Jones (Eds.). New York: Harper & Row.

Richardson, H.W. (1977). *Deprogramming: Documenting the issue.* Conferences on Religious Deprogramming, February 5, 1977 (New York), March 18–20, 1977 (Toronto). Toronto School of Theology & American Civil Liberties Union.

Richardson, H.W. (1980). *New religions and mental health: Understanding the issues.* Lewiston, NY: Edwin Mellen.

Robbins, T., & Anthony, D. (1980). Cults vs. shrinks: Psychiatry and the control of religious movements in H. Richardson, 48–64.

Rousseau, J.J. (1968). *The social contract.* Tr. Maurice Cranston. Baltimore: Penguin.

Royce, J. (1968). *The problem of christianity.* John E. Smith (Ed.). Chicago: University of Chicago Press. Originally published 1913.

Royce, J. (1969). *The basic writings of Josiah Royce* (2 volumes). John J. McDermott (Ed.). Chicago: University of Chicago Press.

Russell, J.B. (1971). *Religious dissent in the middle ages.* New York: John Wiley.

Scheick, W. (1974). Family, conversion, and the self in Jonathan Edwards A *Faithful Narrative of the Surprising Work of God, Tennessee Studies in Literature 19,* 79–89.

Seeberg, R. (1964). *Text-book of the history of doctrines.* Tr. Charles E. Hay. Grand Rapids: Baker Book House.

Shaffer, D. (1980). Cult definition may even apply to Legislature. *The Times Record,* Albany, NY, June 5.

Shupe, A.D. (1981). *Six perspectives on new religions: A case study approach.* Lewiston, NY: Edwin Mellen.

Shupe, A.D., Spielmann, R., & Stigall, S. (1980). Cults of anti-cultism. *Society* (March/April) *17*(3), 43–46.

Singer, M. (1979). Coming out of the cults. *Psychology Today* (January) *12*, 72–82.

Starbuck, E.D. (1899). *Psychology of religion*. New York: Charles Scribner's.

Stein, S. (1984). Sectes a l'index, *L'express* (March). Paris, France.

Stendahl, K. (1976). *Paul among Jews and Gentiles*. Philadelphia: Fortress.

Stumbo, J.E. (1982). The IRS cracks down on coalitions, in Kelly, 77–83.

Testa, B. (1980). It would have been nice to hear from you.....On *fifth estate's* Moonstruck in H. Richardson, 74–80.

Turner, V. (1969). *The ritual process*. Chicago: Aldine.

Turner, V. (1970). *The forest of symbols:* Aspects of Ndembu ritual. Ithaca: Cornell University Press.

U.N. (United Nations) (1982). Declaration on the elimination of all forms of intolerance and of discrimination based on religion or belief. Resolution adopted by the General Assembly, Jan. 18, 1982.

Ungerleider, J.T., & Wellisch, D.K. (1979). Coercive persuasion (brainwashing), religious cults, and deprogramming. *American Journal of Psychiatry* (March) *136*(3), 279–82.

Van Gennep, A. (1960). *The rites of passage*. Chicago: University of Chicago Press.

Vygotsky, L.S. (1978). *Mind and society: The development of higher psychological processes*. Cambridge, MA: Harvard University Press.

Wallis, J. (1981). *The call to conversion: Recovering the gospel for these times*. San Francisco: Harper & Row.

Whitehead, A.N. (1974). *The making of religion*. New York: New American Library.

Wilkin, R.L. (1984). *The Christians as the Romans saw them*. New Haven: Yale University Press.

Willoughby, W. (1979). Religious journalism and new religions (Interview) in Bryant, 43–55.

Worthing, S.L. (1982). The potential in recent statutes for government surveillance of religious organizations, in Kelly, 111–28.

Chapter 7

Religious Commitment within the Corrections Environment: An Empirical Assessment

Byron R. Johnson

Department of Criminal Justice
Memphis State University

> I'm reminded of an inmate who spent ninety percent of his time in disciplinary confinement until he got "saved." The change in his life was so dramatic that that institution was never the same. He never got into another fight after that. He started writing people while he was in prison in order to make restitution.[1]

This statement was made by the Chaplaincy Services Coordinator of the Florida Department of Corrections, during a conversation about the role of religion in the lives of prison inmates. His position represents one side of a debate that has centered around the topic of religion and crime. There have been studies claiming religion is an important factor in the prevention of crime and delinquency while others have claimed that religion is not an influence (see Johnson, 1984, for an in-depth review of this literature).

The relationship between religiosity and deviance has long been a topic of interest among sociologists, criminologists, and religionists. While theoretical and commonsensical reasons suggest that religion should enhance social conformity (Davis, 1948; Erikson, 1966) and inhibit various types of social deviance, the empirical evidence has often been less than convincing and at times contradictory (Albrecht, Chadwick, and Alcorn, 1977; Benson, 1960; Fitzpatrick, 1967; Knudten and Knudten, 1971; Tittle and Welch, 1983; Stark, Doyle, and Kent, 1979, 1982). Several studies have reported that various measures of religiosity or religious commitment are related to the nonoccurrence of deviant activities (Healy & Bronner, 1936;

---

[1] Statement made on August 1, 1984, by William E. Counselman, Chaplaincy Services Coordinator for the Florida Department of Corrections in Tallahassee, Florida.

Travers and Davis, 1961; Miller, 1965; Rhodes & Reiss, 1970; Rohrbaugh & Jessor, 1975).

Others, however, have found that religiosity is essentially unrelated to deviance (Kvaraceus, 1944; Hirschi & Stark, 1969). Hirschi and Stark's (1969) research was widely cited and quickly became the cornerstone of studies examining the religiosity-deviance relationship and set the standards by which both present and future studies would be compared.

Various measures of religiosity and deviance have been utilized in many different settings to determine the relationship between religious commitment and deviance. They have essentially attempted to discover the degree to which religiosity may act as a social control mechanism in preventing delinquency and criminal activity.

The present research takes an area that has been completely neglected in the religiosity-deviance literature as a point of departure. This area bypassed by researchers is the study of religious commitment among prison inmates. Studies in the religiosity-deviance literature have typically dealt with samples of juveniles, delinquents, students, and other noncriminal groups. The whole idea behind studying religion and crime would seem to logically lead to the study of those who are the most criminalistic in society, the prison inmate. The goal of the present research is to examine religious characteristics of prison inmates and to discover the differences in religiosity among prison inmates.

DATA

Obtaining data that have been collected on religious variables within the correctional setting is not an easy task. However, an interview with the Director of Chaplaincy Services for the Florida Department of Corrections, proved to be helpful with regard to locating such data. He reported that there is much variation among different institutions in the state and the data (if any) they collect. Chaplains are encouraged to collect data but it is done only on a voluntary basis.

Subsequent interviews with the director revealed one prison where a particular chaplain had an interest in keeping records of some type. This was the Apalachee Correctional Institution (ACI), in Chattahoochee, Florida. At this prison records had been kept on all inmates who attended any religious functions during their imprisonment.

Data were collected on the inmate population ($n = 782$) released from 1978 through 1982, at ACI. Data were collected on 30 religious variables contained within an inmate's religious folder, which represents only one section of the overall institutional file. Twenty-five of the 30 religious variables on which data were collected came from a religious interview form which is completed for all inmates entering the Florida prison system.

Questions from this religious interview form deal with the religious background of the inmate and that of his family. Questions are also designed in order to determine an inmate's self-reported religiosity, and for staff (i.e., chaplains) to make their evaluation of the inmate's religiosity.

The remaining five religious variables came from data in the same religion section of the central file but were unique to inmates from ACI. These five religious variables pertain to participation in religious activities at ACI.

INDEPENDENT VARIABLES

Two of the three independent variables examined in this analysis are indexes. Researchers in the social sciences commonly construct different kinds of indexes in the course of data analysis (Duncan, 1966). An index refers to any measure which combines the values of several variables or items into a composite measure. Indexes allow more accurate measurement of something which can only be partially measured by any single item or variable which is included in the index.[2]

The first independent variable is the inmate's perceived family religiosity. This variable came from data obtained on the religious interview form which was completed during an inmate's initial classification. Four of the variables on this form were used to create an index which would give a more complete measurement of the inmate's perceived family religiosity: church membership status of mother, church membership status of father, church attendance of mother, and church attendance of father. Each of these four ordinal level variables was weighted equally in the construction of the index of the inmate's perceived family religiosity.

A second independent variable is the church attendance of the inmate prior to incarceration. This variable also comes from the religious interview form and was created with the variables: church attendance of subject as an adult and church attendance of subject the last two years prior to incarceration. Responses to these two ordinal level variables were divided into three equally weighted categories and used to create an index of the subject's church attendance throughout his life.

A third independent variable deals with the conversion experience of the inmate. It was determined that if any inmate accepted a new faith during their incarceration this would be deemed a religious conversion. This information came from the progress reports and updates in the religious section of an inmate's file which address religious experiences during an inmate's incarceration. Updates are usually short and to the point. The

---

[2] For a thorough explanation of the logic and method of indexing see Warren S. Torgerson, *Theory and Method of Scaling*, Wiley, New York, 1958.

subject matter for updates usually consists of statements relative to some religious experience. "Shared gospel with subject and he accepted Jesus as his Savior." "He accepted Christ as his Savior tonight and has been reading the Bible and praying." Only conversions that occurred during their incarceration were analyzed. This two category nominal level variable was used as a dummy variable in the subsequent analysis.[3]

DEPENDENT VARIABLES

Eleven variables were utilized to construct three different religiosity indexes in the analysis. One religiosity index is the institution's perception of an inmate's religiosity. This variable comes from data obtained on the religious interview form. An index was created with the variables: religious background and religious attitude. Responses to these two ordinal level variables were divided into five equally weighted categories and used to create an index of the institution's perception (as perceived by the chaplains) of an inmate's religiosity.

A second religiosity index is the self-reported religiosity of an inmate. Data for this variable also comes from the religious interview form. An index was constructed with the variables: Do you believe in the Bible? Do you believe in God? Is Jesus Christ your personal Savior? How often do you plan to attend chapel services? Responses to each of these four ordinal level variables were divided into two equally weighted categories and used to create an index of the inmate's self-reported religiosity.

A third religiosity index is an objective measure of religiosity based on actual church attendance records of inmates at ACI. Data for this variable were provided from ACI church attendance records that were contained in the religious section of an inmate's institutional file. Attendance sheets are checked at the time of the specific religious activity, insuring the most accurate process of keeping records. Attendance is not only taken for the entire group, but more importantly, is marked on the attendance sheet of each individual's file. Therefore, it is possible to tell exactly how many times a particular inmate attends any religious service or activity. An index was created with the variables: Chapel attendance, Tuesday night Bible study attendance, Evangelism Explosion (class) attendance, and Sunday night Bible study attendance. These four variables were equally weighted and were divided by the number of days served in the institution (in order to control for time) to create an index of the inmate's institutional church attendance.

---

[3] Dummy variables are most commonly used when a researcher wishes to insert a nominal-scale variable into a regression equation.

Studies that comprise the religiosity-deviance literature usually incorporate a single measure of religiosity based on self-reported church attendance. Only a few of the studies reviewed used more than one measure of religious commitment and none of them utilized an objective measure of religiosity based on verifiable records of actual church attendance and participation. The present research improves on prior measures of religiosity by using three distinct measures of religiosity. One addresses the inmate's self-reported religiosity, a second probes the institutional perception of the inmate's religiosity, and the third examines objective records of inmate attendance at religious services and functions during the period of their incarceration.

Another significant contribution is that the present research improves upon prior measures of religiosity through the utilization of indexes as measures or religious commitment. Each of the three measures of religiosity used in the study are indexes created from a number of variables. The individual variables used to construct the indexes only represent one aspect of the inmate's religiosity. The indexes, however, provide a more precise measure by combining the relative influence of individual variables into a new variable, the index.

CONTROL VARIABLES

Five control variables are examined in this analysis: race, age, maximum length of sentence, class of felony, and church denomination. The variable church denomination refers to the religious affiliation or preference of the inmate. The following denominational breakdown was used: Catholic, Methodist, Baptist, Pentecostal, Other Protestant, and All Others. The Catholic, Methodist, and Baptist, denominations are straightforward and need no explanations; Pentecostal, Other Protestant, and All Other categories do need clarification.

The Pentecostal grouping was comprised of Pentecostal or Charismatic churches (e.g., Holiness, Assembly of God, Church of God, etc.). It was thought this particular grouping would be of interest because Pentecostals are considered by some as the most fundamental of fundamentalist denominations. The Other Protestant grouping consisted of all other protestant denominations not already included (e.g., Nazarene, Church of Christ, etc.). The All Other category consisted essentially of non-Christian religions (e.g., Islam, Zen Buddism, Judism, etc.). Traditionally, studies in the religiosity-deviance literature have not appropriately studied denominational breakdown. Most of the studies which examined religious affiliation simply looked at Protestant, Catholics, and Jews. The goal of the present study was to look at a wide range of denominational breakdowns to more precisely determine the affects different affiliations might have upon religiosity. Unfortunately, the present research was only partially successful in this regard. Due to the fact that only a few inmates belonged to some of the denominations, several denominational preferences had to be collapsed to form a single category large enough to be statistically analyzed. While lumping Jews and Muslims into one category presents obvious problems, the denominational breakdown advanced nonetheless represents a marked improvement over prior research.

STATISTICAL PROCEDURES

A number of statistical procedures are used at various stages of the analysis and for different levels of data. Frequency distributions were used on nominal and ordinal level data to make decisions in regard to the elimination of variables that lacked appropriate distribution. Crosstabulations of ordinal level data allowed trends in the variables to be compared and subsequently aided in the construction of the religiosity indexes by determining if individual variables which were combined in the construction of the indexes were equally weighted.

The present research utilizes path analysis to examine the relative contribution of selected religious variables upon each of the three religiosity indexes. The use of path analysis in the present research is an effort to fill a methodological void in the religiosity-deviance literature and to give some direction to the field.

FINDINGS

In the analysis the independent variables index of the inmate's perceived family religiosity, index of the subject's church attendance throughout his adult life, and religious conversion, are included in three path analytic models. This is done in order to determine their relative contributions in explaining the variance in the three religiosity indexes, the institutional perception of inmate religiosity, the inmate's self-reported religiosity, and the inmate's institutional church attendance.

Model of Institutional Perception of Inmate Religiosity

The tentative model of institutional perception of inmate religiosity proposes a total of five direct and one indirect paths among four variables (see Figure 1). The tentative model assumes direct links exist between the index of the inmate's perceived family religiosity and the other two independent

FIGURE 1.   The Tentative Path Analytic Model of Selected Religious Variables
Upon Institutional Perception of Inmate Religiosity

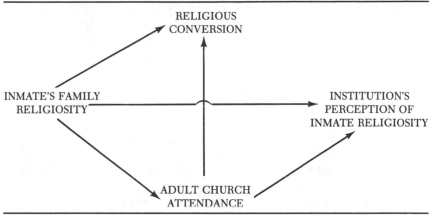

variables: the index of the subject's church attendance throughout his
adult life and religious conversion. The underlying assumption is the
greater the perceived family religiosity of the inmate the greater the likelihood that the inmate will have attended church more frequently as an
adult, and the stronger the possibility of the inmate experiencing a religious conversion during his incarceration.

The tentative model also assumes a direct link between the index of the
subject's church attendance throughout his adult life and religious conversion. The presumption is the more frequent the church attendance of the
subject during his adult life the better the chances are that he will experience a religious conversion during his incarceration. The reasoning here is
that the more exposure a person may have had to religious teaching and
training the easier it would be for them to turn to religion for some "spiritual" help and to possibly undergo a religious conversion.

The last two direct paths in the tentative model are from two of the
three independent variables to the dependent variable, the index of the institution's perception of inmate religiosity. The tentative model holds that
the index of the inmate's perceived family religiosity, and the index of the
subject's church attendance throughout his adult life, are directly related
to the index of the institution's perception of the inmate's religiosity. In
other words, the more the tendency of an inmate to perceive his family as
being religious, and to have reported frequent church attendance as an
adult, the more enhanced are the chances that the institutional perception
of an inmate's religiosity will also increase.

The indirect path in the tentative model runs from the index of the inmate's perceived family religiosity to the index of the subject's church attendance throughout his adult life, and then to the index of the institution's

perception of the inmate's religiosity. This indirect path claimed that the higher the inmate's perception of his family's religiosity the more likely the subject will have attended church frequently during his adult life, which in turn will be related to the institution's perception of inmate religiosity.

The tentative model does not propose a direct path from the independent variable, religious conversion, to the dependent variable, index of the institutional perception of inmate religiosity, because this would violate the time-order assumption of path analysis.[4] This is due to the fact that the institution's perception of inmate religiosity occurs before the inmate could experience a religious conversion. In other words, if a religious conversion occurs during incarceration it could not enhance the index of the institution's perception of inmate religiosity because this conversion experience would have occurred after the institution's evaluation had been complete.

Of the five direct and one indirect paths proposed in the tentative model, three direct and one direct paths are found to be significant in the analyzed model of institutional perception of inmate religiosity (see Figure 2). The proposed links between the index of the inmate's perceived family religiosity with the index of the subject's church attendance throughout his adult life, and also with the index of the institution's perception of inmate religiosity are indeed significant in the final model. The direct path between the index of subject's church attendance throughout his adult life, and then to the index of the institution's perception of inmate religiosity is supported by the analysis.

Two proposed direct paths in the tentative model were not significant in the analysis. The two independent variables, index of the inmate's perceived family religiosity and the index of the subject's church attendance throughout his adult life, were not significantly related to the third independent variable religious conversion.

The following conclusions can be drawn from this path analytic model of institutional perception of inmate religiosity. First, the inmate's perceived family religiosity does influence the inmate's church attendance as an adult prior to his incarceration. Second, the inmate's perceived family religiosity and his church attendance as an adult are significantly related to how the chaplains perceive an inmate's religiosity. Third, neither the inmate's perceived family religiosity or church attendance as an adult have an impact upon the likelihood of an inmate experiencing a religious conversion while in prison. And finally, only 22% of the variance in the dependent variable is explained by the independent variables. Indicating that the religious variables do not explain too much of whatever it is that influences the chaplain's perception of the inmate's religiosity.

---

[4] In causal models we cannot violate the assumption of time-order (Asher, 1983).

FIGURE 2. The Final Path Analytic Model of Selected Religious Variables Upon
Institutional Perception of Inmate Religiosity

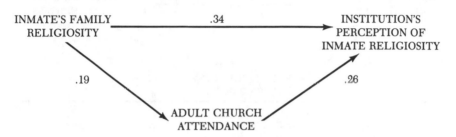

$R^2 = .22$

Decomposition of Paths: The Relationships between Religious Variables and the Institutional
Perception of Inmate Religiosity

ADULT CHURCH ATTENDANCE		INSTITUTION'S PERCEPTION OF INMATE RELIGIOSITY	
(Simple Correlation = .47)		(Simple Correlation = .39)	
Direct Path	.26	Direct Path	.34
Indirect Paths		Indirect Paths	.05
		through adult church attendance	.05

Race, age, maximum length of sentence, class of felony, and denominational affiliation were each used as control variables but did not affect the
findings from the final model. New paths were not created and beta (path)
coefficients remained essentially the same.

Due to the fact that the three independent variables in the model came
from the religious interview form and that the dependent variable also
came from the religious interview form, only two possible explanations are
available which help understand the rather small amount of variance explained in the institution's perception of inmate religiosity. Either the
chaplains were making their evaluations on the basis of unstated criteria
not covered in the interview form, or else their perceptions were made on
the basis of personal and subjective feelings.

Model of Inmate Self-Reported Religiosity

The tentative model of the inmate's self-reported religiosity also proposes
five direct and one indirect paths between three of the same four variables

FIGURE 3.   The Tentative Path Analytic Model of Selected Religious Variables
Upon the Inmate's Self-Reported Religiosity

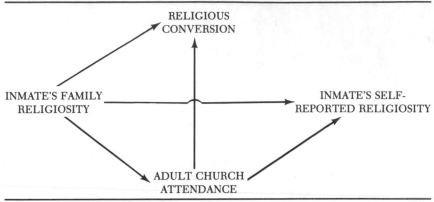

as the tentative model of institutional perception of inmate religiosity (see
Figure 3). The first three direct paths between each of the independent
variables are the same as those of the previous tentative model and will not
be repeated.

The last two direct paths in the tentative model are from two of the independent variables to (the dependent variable) the index of the inmate's
self-reported religiosity. The tentative model holds that the index of the inmate's perceived family religiosity, and the index of the subject's church
attendance throughout his adult life are directly related to the inmate's
self-reported religiosity. The tentative model claims the more the tendency
of an inmate to perceive his family as being religious, and to have reported
frequent church attendance prior to imprisonment, the more the probabil-
ity that the inmate's self-reported religiosity will increase.

The indirect path in the tentative model runs from the index of the inmate's perceived family religiosity to the index of the subject's church attendance throughout his adult life, and then to the index of the inmate's
self-reported religiosity. This indirect path proposes that the higher the inmate's perception of his family's religiosity the more likely the subject will
have attended church frequently during his adult life, which will be
related to the inmate's self-reported religiosity.

The tentative model does not assume a direct path from the independent
variable, religious conversion, and the dependent variable, index of the
inmate's self-reported religiosity. As in the previous model, the inmate's
self-reported religiosity occurs before the inmate can experience a religious
conversion. Therefore, even if a religious conversion does occur during an
inmate's incarceration it could not influence the inmate's self-reported
religiosity because the conversion experience would have occurred after
the institution's evaluation had been completed.

FIGURE 4.   The Final Path Analytic Model of Selected Religious Variables Upon the Inmate's Self-Reported Religiosity

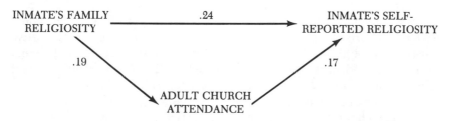

$R^2 = .11$

RELIGIOUS CONVERSION

INMATE'S FAMILY RELIGIOSITY — .24 → INMATE'S SELF-REPORTED RELIGIOSITY

.19   .17

ADULT CHURCH ATTENDANCE

Decomposition of Paths: The Relationships between Religious Variables and the Inmate's Self-Reported Religiosity

ADULT CHURCH ATTENDANCE		INMATE'S SELF-REPORTED RELIGIOSITY	
(Simple Correlation = .40)		(Simple Correlation = .30)	
Direct Path	.17	Direct Path	.24
Indirect Paths		Indirect Paths	.03
		through adult church attendance	.03

Of the five direct and one indirect paths proposed in the tentative model, three direct and one indirect paths are significant in the final model (see Figure 4). The presumed direct links between the index of the inmate's perceived family religiosity with the index of the subject's self-reported religiosity are found to be significant in the final model. The direct path between the index of subject's church attendance throughout his adult life and the index of the inmate's self-reported religiosity was also supported in the final model. As a result, the indirect path from inmate's perceived family religiosity to the index of the subject's church attendance throughout his adult life, and then to the inmate's self-reported religiosity index was confirmed in the final model.

The conclusions to be drawn from the path analytic model of inmate self-reported religiosity are virtually identical to those of the model of institutional perception of inmate religiosity, and will not be repeated. However, there were several small differences between the two models. The index of the inmate's perceived family religiosity and the index of the subject's church attendance prior to incarceration, make less of a relative contribution to the dependent variable in the present model (see Figure 4) than in the model of institutional perception of inmate religiosity (see Figure 2). Consequently, the amount of variance explained by the independent variables in the model of inmate self-reported religiosity is only 11 %.

Model of Inmate Institutional Church Attendance

The tentative model of the inmate's institutional church attendance proposes six direct and three indirect paths among the same three independent (religious) variables of the two previous models, but utilizes an objective measure of religiosity for the dependent variable (see Figure 5). The first three presumed direct paths between each of the independent variables are the same as those of the two previous models and will not be repeated.

The last three direct paths in the tentative model are from each of the three independent variables to the dependent variable, the index of the inmate's institutional church attendance. The tentative model contends that the index of the inmate's perceived family religiosity, the index of the subject's church attendance throughout his adult life, and religious conversion, are all directly related to the index of inmate institutional church attendance.[5] According to the tentative model, the more the tendency of an inmate to perceive his family as being religious, to have reported frequent church attendance as an adult, and to have experienced a religious conversion, the greater the likelihood an inmate will attend institutional religious functions.

The first indirect path in the tentative model runs from the index of the inmate's perceived family religiosity to the index of the subject's church attendance throughout his adult life, and then to the index of the inmate's institutional church attendance. This indirect path proposes that the higher the inmate's perception of his family's religiosity the more likely the subject will have attended church frequently during his adult life, which will be related to the inmate's institutional church attendance.

The second indirect path in the tentative model runs from the index of the inmate's perceived family religiosity to religious conversion, and then to the index of the inmate's institutional church attendance. This indirect path assumes that the greater the inmate's perception of his family's pre-

---

[5] It is also possible that the index of the inmate's institutional church attendance could influence the likelihood of a religious conversion. However, the present research is specifically interested in the impact of religious variables upon religiosity indexes and not the influence of religiosity indexes upon religious variables. Nonetheless, the correlation between these two variables is only .08.

FIGURE 5.   The Tentative Path Analytic Model of Selected Religious Variables Upon the Inmate's Institutional Church Attendance

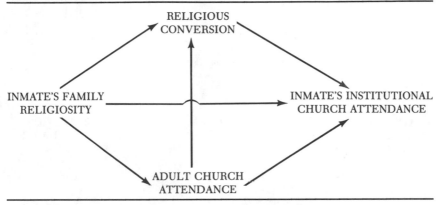

ligiosity the stronger the possibility of the inmate experiencing a religious conversion during his incarceration, and the more likely the inmate will have attended institutional church functions while in prison.

The third indirect path in the tentative model runs from the index of the subject's church attendance throughout his adult life to religious conversion, and then to the index of the inmate's institutional church attendance. This indirect path claims that the more frequent the church attendance of the subject during his adult life the better the chances are that he will experience a religious conversion during his incarceration, and that this will subsequently cause him to attend church on a more frequent basis while completing his sentence.

Of the six direct and three indirect paths in the tentative model, two direct paths and one indirect path are significant in the final model (see Figure 6). The proposed direct link between the index of the inmate's perceived family religiosity and the index of the subject's church attendance throughout his adult life with the index of the inmate's institutional church attendance is significant in the final model. Therefore, the indirect path from the index of the inmate's perceived family religiosity to the index of the subject's church attendance throughout his adult life, and then to the index of institutional church attendance is confirmed in the final model.

Four proposed direct paths in the tentative model are not found to be significant in the final model. The path from the inmate's perceived family religiosity to religious conversion was not supported in the final model or the two previous models of religiosity. Although the proposed path from the inmate's perceived family religiosity to the dependent variable in the two previous models was significant, it is not significantly related to the

FIGURE 6.   The Final Path Analytic Model of Selected Religious Variables Upon the Inmate's Institutional Church Attendance

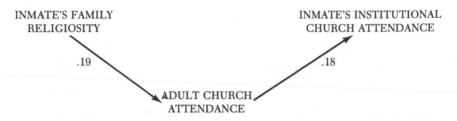

$R^2 = .04$

RELIGIOUS
CONVERSION

INMATE'S FAMILY
RELIGIOSITY

INMATE'S INSTITUTIONAL
CHURCH ATTENDANCE

.19

.18

ADULT CHURCH
ATTENDANCE

Decomposition of Paths: The Relationships between Religious Variables and the Inmate's Church Attendance

ADULT CHURCH ATTENDANCE		INMATE'S CHURCH ATTENDANCE	
(Simple Correlation = .17)		(Simple Correlation = .01)	
Direct Path	.18	Direct Path	
Indirect Paths		Indirect Paths	.03
		through adult church attendance	.03

index of inmate institutional church attendance in the present model. Finally, the presumed path between religious conversion and the index of inmate institutional church attendance was not significant.

Due to this lack of direct paths two of the three proposed indirect paths are not realized in the final model. There is no support for an indirect path from the inmate's perceived family religiosity to religious conversion, and then to the inmate's institutional church attendance. There is also no support for the indirect path from the subject's church attendance throughout his adult life to religious conversion, and then to the index of inmate institutional church attendance.

The conclusions from the path analytic model of inmate institutional church attendance are similar to those of the two prior religiosity models except for the fact that the direct link found from the inmate's perceived family religiosity to the dependent variable in the two prior models does not exist in the present model of inmate institutional church attendance. As a result, the independent variables explain only 4% of the variance in the dependent variable, the index of inmate institutional church attendance.

Supplementing the analysis with the five control variables race, age, maximum length of sentence, class of felony, and denominational affiliation, as in the case of the two prior models, does not affect the findings from the final model. The fact that only 4% of the variance is explained in the model calls into question the validity of these independent (religious) variables.

CONCLUSIONS

In the analysis it was discovered that the religious variables explained very little of the variance in the religiosity indexes. This was especially true of the objective measure of religiosity, the index of the inmate's institutional church attendance. This objective measure of religiosity is based on actual church attendance records and provided the most verifiable (and therefore the best) indicator of inmate religiosity. The religious variables explained only 4% of the variance in this objective measure of inmate religiosity.

The findings can be explained in several ways. One explanation is that the validity of the religious variables may be very poor. Two of these religious variables, the index of the inmate's perceived family religiosity, and the index of the subject's church attendance throughout his adult life, are somewhat similar to religious variables used in prior research. However, the fact that they are indexes means that they may more accurately assess religious characteristics than the more traditional variables found in the literature. To assume that religious variables should be highly related to measures of religiosity is a logical assumption. To find that these religious variables explain very little of the variance in the religiosity indexes indicates not only a validity problem with these religious variables, but possibly calls into question the validity of similar religious variables typically used in the religiosity-deviance literature.

The third religious variable, religious conversion, was thought to be effected by the other two independent religious variables the index of the inmate's perceived family religiosity, and the index of the inmate's church attendance throughout his adult life. However, neither have a significant impact upon the inmate experiencing a religious conversion. Also, religious conversion was not found to be significantly related to the objective measure of religiosity, the index of the inmate's institutional church attendance.

To assume that an inmate who experiences a religious conversion during his incarceration would be more likely to attend institutional religious services and activities would seem to be a logical assumption.[6] To find that

---

[6] It is also possible that some inmates experiencing a religious conversion might not be inclined to attend insitutional religious services if they felt their needs were not going to be satisfied at these religious services. For example, this would be true of those inmates converting to Islam. It is doubtful that a Muslim would want to attend Christian religious services.

those inmates who experience a religious conversion are no more likely than other inmates to attend institutional religious functions, causes one to either question the validity of the variable or the significance of a supposed religious conversion upon an individual in a prison setting.

Another possible explanation for the findings is that two of the religiosity indexes, the institution's perception of inmate religiosity and the inmate's self-reported religiosity, may also be lacking in validity. In other words, the chaplains' (institutional) assessment of inmate religiosity may be based on criteria unrelated to the religious interview. Similarly, inmate's may make exaggerated claims in regard to their personal religious commitment that are not accurate assessments of their real religiosity in order to enhance the way they are perceived by the institutional staff.

Although the objective measure of inmate religiosity, the index of the inmate's institutional church attendance, provides the most valid measure of religiosity, it is the religiosity index least related to the religious variables. This again casts doubts on the validity of the religious variables.

A reference to the control variables employed in this analysis may further help to explain the findings. Throughout the analysis the control variables race, age, maximum length of sentence, class of felony, and denominational preference, were entered into the path analytic models. The control variables did not effect one path in any of the models. In other words, whether an inmate is black or white, young or old, has a short or long sentence, was convicted of a relatively minor or serious offense, or belongs to any of six denominational categories has no bearing upon any of the models. Being an inmate appears to override these religious characteristics and concerns which may otherwise distinguish individuals not in prison. These religious variables and control variables do not seem to have too much of a meaning for prison inmates. Quite simply, nothing else is as important to inmates as being in prison.

REFERENCES

Albrecht, S.L., Chadwick, B.A., & Alcorn, D.S. (1977). Religiosity and deviance: application of an attitude-behavior contingent consistency model. *Journal for the Scientific Study of Religion, 16,* 263–274.

Benson, P.H. (1960). *Religion in contemporary culture.* New York: Harper and Row.

Davis, K. (1948). *Human society.* New York: Macmillan.

Duncan, O.D. (1966). Path analysis: Sociological examples. *American Journal of Sociology, 72,* 1–16.

Erikson, K. (1966). *Wayward Puritans: A study in the sociology of deviance.* New York: John Wiley.

Fitzpatrick, J.P. (1967). The role of religion in programs for the prevention and correction of crime and delinquency, in Task Force Report: *Juvenile delinquency and youth crime.* Washington, DC: Government Printing Office.

Healy, W. & Bronner, A.F. (1936). *New light on delinquency and its treatment.* New Haven: Yale University Press.

Hirschi, T. & Stark, R. (1969). Hellfire and delinquency. *Social Problems, 17,* 202–213.

Johnson, B.R. (1984). Hellfire and Corrections: A Quantitative Study of Florida Prison Inmates. *Ph.D. Dissertation,* Florida State University.

Knudten, R.D. & Knudten, M.S. (1971). Juvenile delinquency, crime, and religion. *Review of Religious Research, 12,* 130–152.

Kvaraceus, W. (1944). Delinquent behavior and church attendance. *Sociology and Social Research, 28,* 284–289.

Miller, M.E. (1965). The place of religion in the lives of juvenile offenders. *Federal Probation, 29,* 50–54.

Rhodes, A.L. & Reiss, A.J. Jr. (1970). The 'religious factor' and delinquent behavior. *Journal of Research in Crime and Delinqunecy, 7,* 83–98.

Rohrbaugh, J. & Jessor, R. (1975). Religiosity in youth: a personal control against deviant behavior. *Journal of Personality, 43,* 136–155.

Stark, R., Doyle, D.P., & Kent, L. (1979a). *Rediscovering moral communities: church membership and crime.* Seattle: Center for Law and Justice, University of Washington.

Stark, R., Doyle, D.P., & Kent, L. (1982b). Religion and delinquency: the ecology of a 'lost' relationship. *Journal of Research in Crime and Delinquency, 19,* 4–24.

Tittle, C.R. & Welch, M. (1983). Religiosity and deviance: toward a contingency theory of constraining effects. *Social Forces, 61,* 653–682.

Travers, J.F. & Davis, R.G. (1961). A study of religious motivation and delinquency. *Journal of Educational Sociology, 34,* 205–220.

Chapter 8

The Yoke of Anger: A Brief Look at the Lives of Four Inmates

Chaplain James G. Arnold, III

**with appreciation to Lorraine Fowler, Ph.d.
South Carolina Department of Corrections**

The individuals in this chapter may be seen by some, perhaps most, beyond redemption. I have tried to show through their statements that criminals are certainly in some real way a product of their environment. Certainly, genetic proclivity, biological and chemical factors and even diet are also being looked to as causes of crime. But in the lives of these individuals and countless others the past has indeed shaped the present and is responsible, at least in part, for what these men and women have become. This is not offered as an excuse for crime, but I firmly believe that until the pain of the past is neutralized, the anger which comes from these negative scripts will continue.

One way to neutralize this pain is to confess that what has been done is wrong and then by relating to the pain of others develop a degree of empathy that will cause the future to look more hopeful whereby the inmate can feel useful. The inmate needs to feel that regardless of what he has done, he can join in an accepting community of believers and achieve a kind of regeneration. Most of the things that many inmates learned as youngsters were negative given the fact that perhaps 70% of our total prison population in this country are victims of psychological, physical, or sexual abuse.

A certain percentage of inmates are so embittered by these experiences that they remain angry and never change. They merely burn out with age. For others, including hardened criminals, new learning is possible, a change of heart takes place. One of the strongest motivations for this change is found in the need to be accepted, no longer rejected as inade-

211

quate, deviant, or different. When a person can feel that he belongs to something of value inspite of his badness, he then has the chance to finally admit that he has done evil things and then find forgiveness through faith. Religious literature, particularly the Bible, is full of the life histories of individuals who went beyond that point where society can forgive. The worst crimes perpetrated by mankind are set forth in graphic detail. The history of Israel, indeed, is one of degeneration and regeneration.

I feel that this provides hope for many inmates, a hope that they often reject for years, but finally embrace. Time and experience also show the inmate how untrustworthy and fickle his convict associates are and at some level he yearns for relationships that are based on trust. This brings him to the positive side of life.

As a man on death row told me once, "I have the same emotions that everybody else has, I watch a sad movie and I cry, you know. I can't stand to see children and animals abused and things like that, you know. I'm considered a total misfit by society, just a hard case. After I did my crime (murder), I couldn't sleep without the light on for a month. I never thought about the death penalty; no one does; it is not a deterrent as some say. I was drunk and I guess nearly psychotic, in a blind rage. This doesn't make it right, but I can't stand to see myself as that kind of animal, but wishing won't bring them (the victims) back." They had formally been associates in crime. The death row inmate is the son of an alcoholic who was an escaped convict on the run. He had five different names by the time he was fifteen, living in seven states and Alaska. He still hides most of the pain of his youth. However, his sister has detailed in court just how brutal their family life was.

In the cases presented, the question of in some way giving up one's power and surrendering to a greater being to negate anger has been present. I feel that this leap of faith finally brings the inmate a permanent peace and hope.

In some of the statements the inmates reflect a kind of works righteousness in the sense that the quality of their faith is dependent upon behavior (as a necessary prerequisite). There are numerous examples in prison where an inmate "gets religious" and equates this with becoming perfect. Perfectionism is frequently tied to the authority struggle in an ingenious way. This is to say that these folks posit being perfect as an almost absolute standard. This standard is applied to all authority figures, since it is implied that these figures (the representatives of society and its institutions) are better than the prisoners (because they are not in jail). When the authority is "caught" in a "not perfect position" he is often discounted and dismissed. This means that the inmate is now free to set his own standards which may be based on selfish gain.

I believe that the men and the women in this chapter are honestly trying to move toward a Christian life and I find it rather remarkable that they have made the strides they have, given their experiences during and following childhood.

Religion primarily based on compliance with social custom (regardless of the actual ethics of this custom) may be part of the culture. This is not to say that the Biblical injunction that "faith without works is dead" should be overlooked. It would seem, however, that the sincerity of those in this chapter is most evident when they realize the impossibility of becoming perfect (working toward some idealized state which robs us of our humanity) and open themselves up to the need for unearned grace.

Somewhat abbreviated histories of the individuals involved in this chapter, as well as their personal accounts or statements concerning their feelings as they relate to their religious values and experiences are presented. With the exception of Zeb, all names have been changed to ensure anonymity.

The statements made by each inmate are given in their own words and are uncorrected.

DUSTY'S STATEMENT

Dear Brothers and Sisters:

I have been under conviction to write this testimony for some time and as we so often do, I have put it off until now. I want to tell of my experience of the New Birth and of how the Lord led me to the Church of God.

My first encounter with the Lord was at about the age of twelve-years-old. A young church man of another denomination had been visiting with me and telling me of the Lord Jesus and had wanted me to make a commitment to Him. This was very new to me. I had gone to church with my mother on occasion for we did not go except on special days like Christmas and Easter. This young man, on his last visit, took me aside and lead me through the scriptures telling me of how the Lord died and suffered for me, that I was a sinner and was condemned to a hell, and that out of God's love, He had provided a way that I could redeem life. He told me about Jesus whom God had provided to be my substitute and that he paid my sin debt for me as a substitute and that God required a perfect sacrifice and that only Jesus was perfect, being the Son of God. This all stirred my soul and I asked the Lord to come into my life and He did.

After this, I never saw this man again. I started to attend a local church each Sunday and entered a Bible study. Soon things became a struggle for me. I had problems with my step-father for he objected to my going to church. He was an alcoholic and an evil man. He demanded that I not go.

After these punishments, I soon lost courage and drifted back into the old ways. I had not really learned much through this church experience and my fellowship was not good so I was not able to gain roots that would last. My family was split and the environment in which I was raised was often unbearable. I often wondered if it were not for the Lord could I have gone on for He truly had His hand in my life, even when I was not aware.

I grew and as a young man I entered the service. While in service, I went to chapel a couple of times for I felt so distant and lost, but could not make a commitment to God.

I soon was on my own and as the world had much to offer we who are lost, I entered into drugs and all kind of vice. I was soon in trouble and ended up in prison in another state. After three years I was out. I went to church again and even tried to live the Christian life again, only to become discouraged and to slip away from God once more. During this period, I yearned for a family of God, but could not find the love that I knew could come only from God. After a while, I violated the law again and ended up in prison with a very long sentence for my deeds.

I recall when I first entered prison how cold and unfeeling it was; you could actually feel the evil in the air. Oh, what a terrible life I was leading. I fit well into this atmosphere for I had become evil. While trying to adjust to this new situation of prison, I decided that to live I must be mean and so I started to be what I thought it took to survive. I carried knives and took drugs and felt so empty inside myself. I still yearned for love, but had decided that there was no such thing and even though the idea of God was only a crutch for weak people and that I only had to be tough and smarter to have what I wanted, and if I couldn't out-smart people to get it I would just take it by force. This was my condition and this idea I sustained for many years in prison. I soon found myself on the lock-up security for nearly five years. During this five years, I was to spend sixteen months in the hole at the maximum security center. This was the lowest that a person in prison could go. It was the bottom of the degradation of prison life and the highest security for any prisoner. While here, I remember how the guards would talk about me and would not take me out of my cell without two being present for fear of my attempting to harm them. While in the hole without the amenities of life, I spent much time in meditation. I sought evil, I studied witchcraft and satanism and wanted to even exalt myself above others. I traversed many avenues of thought both in psychology and of the field of philosophy. But, God was there. My last Christmas, I was given the single copy of the book of Luke. I became angry and threw the book across my cell and under my bed where it lay for months. Finally, in what I considered a moment of weakness, I read it through. It meant nothing as I read; I had become hardened and unfeeling even more. I threw it back under the bed where it lay even longer. After another three months or so, I took it out and read it through again several times and somehow there seemed to be a flicker of hope to the words on the pages. I soon returned to the normal lock-up section, I was out of the hole.

After a few more months on general population lock-up, I was able to enter the main line of the prison population. I soon entered the prison college program and after two years I received a degree. During this period of time, I took classes in eastern religions and studied philosophy and psychology. I took two classes in world religions and gained interest in God again. I had begun to search once more. As I sought God through meditation and eastern thoughts I would have recurring visions (feelings) of Christ. This bothered me and so I soon stopped my meditations in eastern religions. I had found them empty and without substance except for this thing with Jesus that kept coming to the surface.

At this time, I became interested in helping prisoners and helping them to resolve their problems. I wanted for myself and others a better life. I had come to the end of my rebellion and wanted to make a positive change in my life. I studied intensely the field of psychology and wanted to become a therapist and help people in prisons. I searched for a way to do this and gained a job within the chaplaincy of the institution. I knew not the Lord, but my attitude had changed and I had a positive air about me. I soon was busy counseling and working with other men. Something was still missing in my life. I did not feel quite total and I felt guilty and wanted to rid myself of this pest. I found a book and read about guilt during this time because this book was directing me toward God. After reading this I began to meditate and evaluate myself and in doing this, I felt that I still needed some work in order to put my life back together more completely. As I sat in my office, a voice came to my mind, "why don't you go to church and try Jesus again."

I was not crazy about this idea, but I felt confident that I could stand it. I even felt in some way that I could settle the questions I had about Jesus so I could go on living my life without this relentless questioning of Christ so I could go on living my life as I had been.

I went that evening and sat in the last row of the chapel. There I was very relaxed and confident that I would not be stirred and that all was well with me. We had a man there that evening who was preaching what some refer to as Hell, Fire and Brimstone preaching. I found myself listening intently and after about a half hour, I was deep in meditation and searching myself. As the preaching continued, I became bent and tears were flowing down my cheeks. I was soon sobbing and in distraught condition. I felt condemned and knew I was lost. I was guilty of much and my whole life lay in front of me. While thinking these thoughts, a voice came to me and spoke to me. I could no longer hear the preaching, nor was I aware of the others around me. I felt very alone except for the voice. The voice was that of the Savior. He spoke, "I love you, come to me, I love you, I have always loved you, I never left you, come, come, come to me." I then answered, "No, I cannot, I failed you so much and I did such evil after knowing you. No, I cannot, I will fail again. No, I cannot bear the pain again." The Lord spoke ever so softly as to a small child, "Come, come to me, nothing has changed, come to me, serve me, come, I will make you strong and I will carry you, I love you, come to me, come, I say come." "Oh Lord," I spoke with voice cracked and sobbing from all that was taking place. I said, "I am so scared that I shall fail you and the hurt will be unbearable." "Come," the Lord continued to beckon me to him, "I love you, come to me."

I soon was on my feet and went forward to the alter. There I cried my heart out, and after I cried and came to myself the minister started to lead me through the scriptures. I told him that I knew these scriptures he referred to and he told me that I was already saved then and didn't need salvation. This confused me for I knew my convictions. I left the service with much to think about for there was much on my mind about all that had happened this night and I wanted to rest and sort things out. Later, I lay in my cell thinking upon the events of the past years and the voice of the Lord returned saying, "get upon your knees and pray." I obeyed and began to pray earnestly from my heart. The more I prayed, the more I needed to pray. I began to cry from deep within my self, from the soul of me. I felt so condemned and confused about life, I cried so, I cried to be saved, I asked the Lord to forgive my sins, and to heal me. At this moment, I felt a sudden peace that I had never known before and because of this, I began to cry so, but it was different now. The cry was one of a great joy, a knowing spirit within me that said all is well with you, you have not to fear, I am with you. Here in prison and on bended knees, our Lord came to me in a darkened cell. He touched me and now I live. Where once I was so dead in sin I am found cleansed by the blood of Christ our Lord.

AUTHOR'S COMMENTS

Dusty participated for several months in group counseling led by a co-therapist and myself. I have known Dusty for the past six years and first met him at a maximum security prison where we spent a good deal of time together talking about his life. We particularly talked about his youth, his anger, his guilt or his shame (I was never quite sure which it was at first) and we talked a lot about his crime. Dusty was in prison for rape.

In terms of Dusty's early adolescent years, the stepfather he mentions was most cruel to him. Much of the anger that he felt for years came from, I think, the double messages given to him by his stepfather and his mother. He was told, for example, by his mother that he must have dates, that is, go out with girls in order to be fully a man, to be potent. His father would then counter with "you can't do that, you're not really capable of going out with girls." His acceptance then depended on doing something that he was told he couldn't do. This characterized his early life along with the sad, uncertain memories of his biological father suddenly departed through divorce. Dusty vented his anger by becoming a "killer football player," a lineman who took great vengeance on the opposing team.

Dusty's presentation of himself was quite passive when I first met him. He continued in this mode for several years. I expect that the anger and the tough-guy stance he mentions, such as carrying knives, etc., was driven more by a normal fear of prison than some kind of bravado or need to be a tough guy or a "super con," as the lingo goes. Dusty's dynamic indicates that because of his early childhood and the adolescent messages of "you are not okay; you are not capable," an intense sense of inferiority was imposed. In the group in which Dusty participated, it was most important that other members like and affirm him even after he was openly insulted on several occasions.

His first marriage ended in divorce and was sexually unfulfilling. There was, at the outset of our counseling, a tremendous amount of guilt over sex. His crime actually caused fewer feelings of guilt at that point than did his anxiety over sexual matters. When I first met him he thoroughly hated himself because he felt powerless. It was this entrenched anger and feeling unable to express himself as a capable person that I believe caused him to vent his anger against women through the years. Women were seen as controlling and, like his mother, objects of dread. And yet they held the "key" to confirming his manhood, a confirmation withheld by women throughout his life.

I have long believed that sex is a biological drive which rides the back, so to speak, of other needs. Or to put it another way, sex becomes the means by which we express deeper needs. (Those needs that relate most particularly to nurture, rights of passage, confirmation as a whole and acceptable person.) Successful sexual performance, or at least the appearance of such, to the young man is one way to prove "I am capable." Dusty's life from the beginning was marked by the loss of his real father, by impossible demands and, in essence, rejection. Therefore, it is understandable that he wanted the acceptance of the group mentioned above.

His religious experiences also show a strong need to be accepted, his first encounter beginning at the age of 12. His early experiences began with severe judgment. Most youngsters who are told early on about the perils of hell will learn to relate more to a punitive god than one who truly redeems through love. His first religious mentor, it is noted, vanishes, never to be seen again, another loss in his life. He was subsequently punished for going to church by an alcoholic stepfather. This occurred at a time when he was working out ethical and moral values and needed permission to explore and test his world. This permission was denied Dusty and along with other growth denying messages served to block the normal expression of an emerging moral self. Subsequently, he was not able to claim himself but was made to feel guilty or shameful about his very existence. In instances of severe trauma or deprivation, an intense anger toward life's processes ensues which finds its expression in degrading, denouncing, and striking out at those processes that symbolically represent nurture such as motherhood (women).

Dusty's hatred of himself is finally complete and self-ordained when he states, "I went to church again only to slip away from God once more. During this period, I yearned for a family of God, but could not find the love which is nurture that I knew could come only from God." (Who, it might be added, was now unavailable because of Dusty's own sense of unworthy rejection.) After reentering prison he states, "I have now become evil." The question for Dusty became (1) How can I find a family who will love me? (2) I am unworthy, even evil. (3) Evil men don't deserve love, but they need this love. So Dusty, I believe, wound up again in a complete double bind.

This scenario, played out in Dusty's mind in prison, is a close approximation of the struggle he knew with his mother and stepfather. Herein lies a great hope for Dusty, however. In a brutal, hard prison, he lived through the judgment, the fire and brimstone found in the preaching that he mentions and was blessed, indeed accepted, by the preacher when he told him that he was *already saved and did not need salvation.* He then later cries from "deep within myself, from the soul of me." The sermon had set the tone that allowed him to truly confess his sins and feel accepted (as he cried tears of joy). He was no longer guilty or *evil as a person.* He felt redeemed as if a weight had been lifted from him. I would add that Dusty is able to own the fact that his behavior has been vile and from some human standpoints unforgiveable. With further nurture by a church that has taken him in as a member, he will, I believe, have re-enforced those values and the caring that he needs.

Dusty's story is obviously one of dependency. He is moving away from a kind of overt dependency to a stance characterized by a more independent claiming of self. All of us are dependent at some level or there would be no real need for others and hence no real human community. The dependency issue, I believe, is one of degree. The hurts of the past don't go away completely, but the riddle of the past does not need to be solved. If one can find a life now and in the future that approximates the life he would have had if he had known a normal childhood (Glasser).

The religious or faith position cannot be proved empirically. The psychological data and overtones found in this report are dominant and may lead some to assign to the faith statements contained herein the role of either wish fulfillment or fantasy. (I would submit that finally often only such a "fantasy" is available in prison to most of the men whom I have known.) Dusty's MMPI, for instance, and his psychological evaluations have shown marked improvement. He is aware now for the first time that he has value as a human being, and I believe this is true because of the unifying power of faith.

MARGIE

Margie is a bright, very seductive woman, a caring mother of 26, originally from a northern midwestern state. She served several years in prison for robbery. Her story begins from her account at age 2.

Her early life began by her being passed around from orphanage to orphanage and various foster homes. She has no memory of her biological parents and was adopted along with her brother at age four by alcoholic parents who were physically and psychologically abusive. While living with temporary foster parents prior to this, she was kicked down a flight of steps at age three into a basement for soiling her pants. She and her brother were spanked with ping pong paddles. Her adoptive mother later repeated this punishment with the full knowledge that this happened to Margie at the age of three. This is an entrenched and angry memory and still causes pain. While recounting this part of her life, Margie began to perspire profusely.

When asked about her earliest memories, she recalled at age two being thrown into a tub of water from some distance, fortunately without injuring herself. She was also introduced to sexual contact by a ten-year old girl who happened to be her foster parents' natural child. Her brother was also included in these sexual encounters. Margie and her brother were adopted by what she terms northerners and seems to stress the fact that it was a northern Catholic family. There were two stepbrothers in the family, and at approximately the time she entered the fourth grade Margie's own brother and her stepbrothers began sexually molesting her (forcing her to perform oral sex and giving her magazines such as *Playboy* and *Penthouse*). The sexual abuse continued until Margie ran away from home at age 15.

On one occasion her stepfather got drunk and got into bed with her and remained there until his wife ordered him to leave. By the age of 15, running away became a regular event. On another occasion she ran away with two boys and began stealing purses from women who were trying on clothes in clothing stores. She was jailed and her parents picked her up; no actual charges resulted. Later she ran away with a girlfriend and they were arrested, but not charged, for possession of marijuana. After having run away with a boyfriend, Margie was placed in a Catholic unwed mother's home by her parents even though she was not pregnant at the time.

To digress a bit, at the age of 14 she was taken to a psychiatrist who stated that she was abnormal because of the things she said in her poetry. He asked her why she was depressed and Margie recalls that she was afraid to speak of what really concerned her, namely, the sexual abuse by her brothers. She recalled how she had to fight to hold these feelings inside, afraid to reveal them out of guilt and shame.

At age 15, she left home finally for the last time and went to Myrtle Beach, South Carolina. She was totally rejected (disowned) by her parents. Within two weeks she had met a man 13 years older than she and moved in with him. For the next 2½ years she lived what she terms a normal, quiet life "because he protected me." She states further that he taught me "the facts of life," that is, "he told me about life." He apparently taught her the things a father would teach a young daughter. She was not making reference to sexual facts of life which Margie was already too well aware. They were going to get married the year that Margie turned 18 and then she "got curious about hippies and beach types." She had sex with "lots of people." While living with the older man, she met the man she would later rob. He (R) enticed her she said with his big Cadillac, smooth talk, and "he fed my ego like crazy." It was in fact this smooth talker who brought about the breakup of probably the longest relationship she had ever had, as fraught with obvious difficulties as it was, not to mention statutory rape. R flattered Margie and persuaded her to pose for semi-nude photographs. He had an extensive collection of other pictures showing numerous deviant acts. She reports that he kept her as a virtual prisoner miles from town. When she tried to leave, he chased her with a gun and threatened her life. She was able to get away and returned to her older boyfriend, but then finally she returned with two other men again to R's home to obtain the pictures which were made much earlier. One of the men had a gun and the final result was that Margie was charged with armed robbery.

Margie, at the age of 18, was approached by a young woman who introduced her to a local madam and she was lured into prostitution, a call girl service, because "the money was easy and fast." Rich businessmen were her clients, but she soon became tired of hearing them say, "What's a nice girl like you doing this for?" Margie seemed rather pleased, however, that on four separate occasions businessmen from Canada had proposed that she become their mistress. She very quickly got tired of, as she says, coming home *alone* after a night of prostitution and proceeded then to run off with the madam's young boyfriend. She hated the madam who had gotten her "hooked on speed to keep me working long hours."

It was the armed robbery charge that brought Margie to prison from which she quickly attempted to escape because of homosexual threats and harassment. She was at one point raped by another woman in the prison. She had one meaningful relationship during this period with a woman for whom she felt genuine affection. "She was like a mother in a way to me," Margie says. The woman was a practicing homosexual and Margie appears naive as to her real intentions because of her desperate need for affection. Later Margie became pregnant by another inmate and yet another dilemma began. She states that upon becoming pregnant she was "afraid of God's wrath for having sex, and did not want to have an illegitimate baby because God might deform the baby for having sinned." She recalled a passage from the Bible where sinful mothers would weep and wail (because of the punishment God brought on their children).

Immediately prior to becoming pregnant, Margie attended a prison crusade where she met a woman she describes as a "sweet lady.' This volunteer crusade member asked her if she would "like to ask Jesus into her heart." At first Margie responded affirmatively only because she felt, in her words, that she needed to be accepted by everyone else at the crusade by responding as they did. But then she goes on to state that the people in the crusade represented cleanness, wholeness, goodness, at a period when "I was really down." This is seen as a clear expression of remorse and guilt over her past life. A brief period of what she calls religious fanaticism set in. She constantly attended Bible study groups, gave testimonies to other residents, reporting that she honestly wanted to feel good, "like a good person." She then stated that "I still feel today that the only way to live a good life is to follow the teaching of Jesus." She continued by saying, "even today I don't contemplate much about Heaven or Hell, somewhere in your mind you have to decide yourself about how to live with the help of the Bible."

It is noteworthy that the nice lady of the crusade still writes to Margie and signs her letters Mother in Christ. Margie signs her letters Daughter in Christ. She had for the first time found a woman who represented goodness, who accepted the bad little girl that her parents had told her she was when she was a child and had offered a means of forgiveness. When the sexual molestation by the brothers was discovered, her parents had blamed Margie and told her that she was dirty. Margie felt forgiven at the crusade and as she put it "clean for the first time in my life." This feeling of forgiveness has been consistent since then, even though, as she says, "I have gone astray since my conversion." To this point Margie is not professing necessarily to be that "good person" that she wants to be, but a dramatic shift has taken place in her life. She is learning to put the trauma of her youth and young adult years behind her. The emotional scars are still quite present, but there is today a note of hope in her view of her world. She no longer feels totally alone, and she feels less and less like the victim who is justified in doing more or less what she wants because of what "they did to me."

Margie's subsequent marriage has been a growth experience, though not without some real difficulties. Her child is a very bright little boy whom she adores. Her motherhood represents the first time in her life where she is responsible for the welfare and nuture of another human being. She has handled this far better than might be expected, given her own lack of nurture and abuse as a child. The economic struggle alone has been most difficult and her survival is a testimony to her courage. Margie left prison before her husband and made her own way with the baby for some time. At present she runs a dental lab, is well thought of and does an excellent job.

Margie's views on organized religion are of interest. She joined a large metropolitan church but never really felt accepted because she did not have "the proper clothes." She went to the minister at one point for counseling and for other kinds of help. His response was to recommend that she be baptized and then he gave her $100. She reports that what she really wanted most of all was some kind of "Christian counseling." This actually meant to her that she wanted to feel accepted by the head of the church, to be encouraged by a kind of father figure. It has been a long time now since brother Sigmund Freud dwelt among us, but ministers would do quite well to recognize that they do represent a father image to many churchgoers, and they also still stand as a visible symbol of redemption. It is the minister's task, in my view, to help people work through these dependency needs more than it is to offer immediate and outward signs of faith such as baptism.

Margie further states that "the church wants you to come in, be baptized, smile, be happy, make no mistakes. But if you are poor, you can hang it up." She continues, "I was asked repeatedly by members to come to church, but because I had no church clothes, I felt embarrassed." On one occasion, Margie stood before the entire congregation of several thousand people with the minister who stated that this young woman had a baby and needed a job. It still infuriates Margie that no one came forward. Granted, this is a somewhat unusual procedure for the organized church today.

Margie and her husband both have good jobs and the economic struggle has been greatly relieved. The issue of inner growth and maturity continues. As far as the future is concerned, Margie says, "I will always have faith, I need to nurture it some more," and I take this to mean that she also needs to be nurtured so that she can live a more fulfilling life. She says, "I need more knowledge about the Bible and I need to belong to a church "by which I feel she means she needs to belong to a community. Part of her need to belong to a church stems in her mind from early parental messages that "you must go to church to be a good Catholic." Part of this comes from her need to be accepted by a group that represents decency and goodness. She needs this reinforcement and it is indeed sad, but I feel accurate, to say that much of the preaching in the southern U.S. stills concentrates on Heaven, Hell and punishment for sins. (Sins, I would stress, in a quantitative sense, not sins as a product of something). That is, sin is not seen by many southern preachers so much as a condition but as a group of individual acts. A healthier view would be to see sin as a condition which calls forth the prospect of personal growth in the sense that St. Paul spoke of missing the mark. This implies that one can do better, that one can move toward a more positive life style and toward a more holistic view of the self. Far too little of our effort goes into truly uplifting our brother as an expression of felt grace and a good deal of effort seems to be expended in condemning people.

There are thousands of young women like Margie who may remain marginally open to secular counseling. In Margie's case this is true, only in part, because of the condemning diagnosis that she still remembers all these years later (the diagnosis given by a psychiatrist who simply did not understand his patient's need and her desperate situation, the sexual abuse and the terrible guilt and shame involved).

Margie feels that her struggle for a more secure faith must continue. She needs to achieve a feeling of belongingness and to accept herself as a whole and creative person. All through her life the theme of punishment has been present. She has often punished herself out of a sense of feeling unworthy. She does not feel completely worthy of success and has shattered many relationships by being sexually permissive, whereby she either gets rejected or rejects the man involved. I believe that she has a sort of love-hate relationship with men as acted out in prostitution. As she says of prostitution, "I ditch them before they ditch me, after the money changes hands, they're all through." I believe that women enter prostitution for at least three main reasons and Margie is no exception: (1) for purely economic reasons; (2) out of a deepseated hatred for men; and (3) out of a desperate need for affection or attention which is never sated by sexual encounter alone, but is held onto as the promise of future fulfillment.

There is also the constant fear that she needs to control personal relationships or be hurt because of past experiences, and this goes far beyond the mere fear of intimacy as it is usually encountered. Prostitution, because it is not a true giving of the self, may be seen as a means of being physically close but remaining in control. Unfortunately, many marriages are lived out on this level of communication, the woman's body becoming a bargaining tool or an object that is used to obtain needs that should be simply asked for. The payoff is that true intimacy is avoided (which is risky) because it is a kind of self-giving that exposes our personhood, our deepest needs and fears.

Margie states that, "I wanted to give myself completely and I never felt really right about taking money for sex," she continued, "but I feel subordinate to my husband. I don't want to be subordinate to a man who thinks stupidly." Perhaps, this is a reflection of her feeling toward men in general. "I need to give in, but I can't," she says. It is interesting that Margie also has trouble with sexual orgasms. In fact she states that she has never had an actual orgasm which was not self-induced. "My husband is stupid," she says, but I feel that indeed the husband is not intellectually inadequate. She may be in some ways more imaginative than he, but certainly he is not all that inferior to her. It may well be that he does not, and I think many men would have difficulty doing so, offer her the emotional security she craves from a mate. She is afraid to trust her husband because of her own insecurity. It is interesting that he is the victim of the attentions of two very jealous women, his own mother and his stepmother, who are still in touch, and who still vie for his affection and attention. He felt smothered as a child and this need to control others, particularly women, in order to be safe continues. Margie's husband has had difficulty giving himself because he fears being smothered in a relationship with a woman. His first wife, for instance, was unfaithful and very "kindly" told him that she had been raped by another man. Upon hearing this, Margie's husband then went out and shot and killed the man. Later his wife confessed that she had not been raped at all. It is not difficult to see why this man may in some way have a trust problem with women.

Margie has said that in regard to the power issue or this need to control, "I need to give in completely to God but right now God is second to my husband. I need for God to be first. I know that Christ is asking me to give over my power to him, but when I think of this, I feel helpless. I guess it may be pride or something." I feel that here Margie has unwittingly come upon the dilemma of St. Augustine when he identified pride some centuries ago as the source of sin in the human condition. Margie needs to be able to give without feeling vulnerable. If faith could bring her this freedom, she would be happy and at peace. She has refused psychiatric help on several occasions and at one point I suggested this. I now feel that for her a continuing pastoral relationship may be a resource that she can both accept and from which she can profit. Finally, she sums up her situation in these words, "I need faith roots firmly planted where I can find acceptance finally through Jesus Christ."

PERSPECTIVE OF A CHRISTIAN IN PRISON:
Freedom in Prison (Jarvis)

A Christian is a follower of Jesus Christ and His teachings. In II Corinthians 5:17, it says if any man be in Christ he is a new creature; old things are passed away and a new life has begun. Going by the above verse, it is easy for me to be a Christian in prison. I'm not the same person who came to prison two years ago.

One thing I have found about being a Christian in prison is this. If you are not sincere about being a Christian, the men in the prison will know it. The men who live here expect a lot out of the Christians in the way they carry themselves. On the streets, when you go to Church, you only see other Christians for a comparatively short time. In here you are around the same people *all the time.* You pretty well get to know everyone. If you claim to be a Christian, then you smoke marijuana, drink buck (homemade liquor), take dope, etc., it shows very quickly that you are not sincere.

On the outside, if you go to church and claim to be a Christian, then you live your life the way you want, it is harder for people to know you aren't sincere. You can go to bars, x-rated movies, the pornography shops, drink, etc. While doing these things, you can completely get away from the people of the Church, but you can't get away from *self.*

I'm thankful for coming to prison because it has forced me to take a very long look at my life. What I saw made me sick and I wanted a new life. In order to do this, I asked Jesus to come into my life and to become my Lord and Savior. This change was not like snapping your fingers, but, it has been a growing process for me. I can see a big change in my life since becoming a Christian, yet I still see a need to keep on growing and striving to be like Jesus. By reading God's word, I found out this was possible. It is hard to be content all the time, but I have a peace in my heart now. This is the peace which passeth all understanding.

There are a lot of men in prison who try to use religion to help themselves. These men do not last long because they have made no real commitment to be a Christian.

Personally, it is easy to be a Christian in prison! The reason for this is I now have made a commitment to follow Jesus Christ. I am no longer playing Christian as I did before I came to prison. We can fool people by the things we do, but we cannot fool the Lord. He knows what is in our hearts.

My goal in life is to help other people in some way. I look forward to the day when I will be a free man in society again, but right now I possess a freedom which is the greatest freedom of all! There are many different kinds of prisons. A job can be just as confining as prison walls. An addiction to drugs, alcohol, lusting, etc., can be just as confining. There is only one way to escape any of the prisons and that is by being born again; to claim the new life which Jesus Christ gives us.

JARVIS' TESTIMONY

My life and attitudes before following Christ: I went to Church regularly, sang in the choir, did solos. But I hated to be called on to pray or read scripture. The solos were for my own glory. I had a home, family, good job, but there was something desperately missing in my life. (In trying to fill this emptiness, I bought a pool table, Atari game, always on the go playing sports, motorcycle riding, unacceptable behavior, etc.) Most important thing was to make self happy. I never could understand how I could love God more than my wife and children.

How I realized God was speaking to me: I was arrested on April 28, 1980, and I began my bargaining with God. (It had been a practice of mine that when things went wrong, I would always pray and promise God that I would change, and when things got better, I went back to my old ways.) *Give examples. I received a very long prison sentence of 80 years, and my life as I knew it began to change. My wife divorced me, friends deserted me, and I began to blame God for all this, and finally tried suicide as a way of escaping everything.

How I became a Christian: When I first came to prison, I prayed for God to change other people so they could accept me. One day I changed that prayer and asked God to *change me*. And the scriptures Proverbs 3:5 and 6 became to be a part of my life in a real and meaningful way. I was born again at this point in my life when I asked God to change me and I meant it. This change is not overnight!! It is a growing process. Your old nature will still try to control you. There are four important points I would like to mention here. (1) Sin controlled my life before I was born again. (2) The penalty from a sin-controlled life is separation from God. (3) Christ paid the penalty for all of our sins. (4) All we have to do is receive Christ as our Savior in order to be free from sin.

What being a Christian means to me: I now have a happiness which I never knew before, I realize that Jesus Christ is with me 24 hours a day, seven days a week. Since my life has changed, the hurts in my life seem to hurt more. I feel that is because I now see sin for its true worth. Sin destroys life. Things may look good on the outside, but sin has a way of slipping into our lives and completely destroying them. The sad thing is most of us don't even realize what is happening. My heavenly Father is always with me and when sin does begin to cause hurts in my life, My heavenly Father takes care of me. To me, being a Christian means that once we trust the Lord, no matter what happens in our lives, the Lord is working in all of them. He gives us the peace that passeth all understanding. Philippians 4:7.

AUTHOR'S COMMENTS

Jarvis recalls a tormented childhood. His father, an alcoholic who was always "cussing and fighting," would often beat his son. These beatings are described as "mean whoopings" followed by the injunction of don't cry, big boys and men don't ever cry. Jarvis feels today that he really was the victim of child abuse. He recalls in terms of his feelings just sucking it in, as he puts it, showing no emotion. As a youngster, Jarvis was forced to attend church. It is significant that he has virtually no memory of his mother during the early years of life. His earliest memory dates to his age of six. His two sisters and younger brother were at home alone. The iron turned over and a fire resulted. Jarvis rescued the family getting them all out safely. Then at age 8 he remembers "getting a shotgun after daddy" when he came home drunk one evening. When asked at the beginning of the interview about his childhood, his immediate reply was "I only remember bad things." By the age of 12, Jarvis had become a voyeur. He has no real idea of why he entered into this practice except, as he says, "I guess it was gratifying to sneak around at night and peak."

For a good many years, voyeurism was perhaps thought of as a relatively harmless crime. Certainly very few arrests were made. Some thought that this form of activity was a substitute for more sexually aggressive acts such as rape. It is now seen by many people working in this field, Dr. A. Nicholas Groth among others, as a forerunner to more serious sexual acting out. Exhibitionism and voyeurism are both forbidden activities which in and of themselves prove to be sexually arousing. They are both a form of rebellion.

Jarvis reports that the peeping intensified through the years from age 12 through age 30. He felt, however, that he could "control it and never hurt anybody." By the age of 29, he was, in his words, going out every night and the activity had now become a real compulsion.

Jarvis had married at age 17 during his last year of high school. His wife was six years older than he and his reason for marrying was to get away from home. He finished high school. His wife was also pregnant, I might mention, before marriage and this was also a motivation. They were together for 11½ years and had two other children. She miscarried with the first child. His wife divorced him upon entering prison.

Jarvis stated that all through his life he was never allowed to be who he wanted to be. In his words, "if you express who you are as a child you'll get your teeth knocked out." He was constantly restless and completely unfulfilled. The anger that he felt was not directly expressed and resulted from these blocked expressions of growth. He was literally not allowed to *become* and was constantly ridiculed by his father.

By the age of 29, he had attempted his first rape. The woman cried out and he ran away. Later, he raped a woman of 30 in the same neighborhood. He had peeped into her house prior to the attack. The assault was not planned and afterward he told the woman, "I don't care if you call the police or not." He looks back on this and says, "I guess that I wanted to be caught." He was given 80 years in prison which will make him eligible for parole in a total of ten years. He has now served 4¼ of those ten years.

In prison, Jarvis has participated in sex offender group therapy and has been very positively helped by the chaplain at his institution. He now says that "I talk about problems rather than suffering them in my gut and I let anger out a little bit at a time. This way you won't get in trouble." As he states in his testimony, he has become a Christian and it is this life stance that gives his life meaning. As he says "I now feel deep in my heart that life is good." He would like, when he makes parole, to work with men in prison. Looking back he says "all the pain I feel comes from the past. I pray to God the woman that I raped is alright today. It is wrong to hurt people. The past cannot be erased. I wish that it could be, but remembering the past makes me aware of what an awful thing I was. Maybe it shouldn't be erased, then, for me."

Shortly after entering prison, Jarvis attempted suicide, cutting deep into the main veins in both arms. He was very angry because his home church, he felt, had rejected him. He says "they (meaning the church) are supposed to forgive but maybe they just can't for rape." I feel that in many cases when a man realizes he has gone beyond the point of no return, a point where society totally rejects him, that he may throw himself upon the mercy of God. It is felt to be a final and desperate act of begging for acceptance as well as forgiveness.

Jarvis states that following the suicide attempt while in the prison psychiatric unit, he was "arguing with God about the way life turned out." And then he says "I asked Him not to change others as he had in the past so that they (people) could accept me, but to change me." This was seen, and is still seen, by Jarvis as a real turning point in his life. Further he states "I see myself and others in prison as lepers, but Jesus changes lepers. I can now relate to others who are down. I feel in control now." This is something that he has not felt throughout his whole life. He feels that "becoming a Christian is a life-long growth process. A person either gets worse or gets better. He never just stays the same."

Of his sexual assault, he says "I have ruined my victim's life, and I pray to God that she gets help. There is no restitution for what I have done. None of the abuse I knew as a child makes what I did okay. I want to make it up in some way to life for the things I have done."

Then he closed the interview by a quotation from the Bible "Sorrow is better than laughter. It may sadden your face but it shapes your understanding."

ZEB'S STATEMENT

Neither my Dad nor Mother went to church with us when we were small, but they were both members of the First Baptist Church in Brevard, North Carolina. All the members of my Dad's family were, though none of the grown people attended, just the children. What prompted this attitude I do not know, but it left me with the feeling that when I got big enough I would no longer have to go. It was a duty, never a pleasure.

My joining the church at age 11 was to keep me from getting a whipping I knew I truly deserved. I had misbehaved while Dad was working out of town during the week, and I saw the baptismal ceremony as a chance to avoid the whipping. I knew that Dad and Mother respected such church ceremonies, so I played to their sympathy. In Sunday School I had learned the stories about Jesus Christ, but that is all they meant to me, just stories.

Several incidences in my family in my early teens made me start hating my parents. But the greatest hurt was that I had lost my grandfather who I had been very close to. He was the one person who never expected me to be anyone except myself. The other things brought shame upon our family name, and my pride caused me to start hating my parents as well as my oldest sister. When my family most needed my love and support, all they got from me was rebellion and hatred. In these actions, I felt perfectly justified. I stayed away from home with people I knew they disapproved of just to hurt them. These things are clear now, but not then.

I had a couple of times of brief seeking the Lord during the next few years, but some incident would happen to make me more sure that Christians were phony. A girl I dated took me to church with her and when we were alone, she played the whore as if it were just fine to do immoral things as long as you went to church. Another time was, in 1966, after I had been in Federal prison for over nine years. My first marriage had ended in divorce after seven years of my incarceration, and I had started going with my childhood sweetheart. She had always been a Methodist, but changed her membership and was baptized into the members of Calvary Baptist Church where my letter had been moved with my Dad and Mother's change of churches. I went faithfully each time there was a service, for somehow I knew this was a step in the right direction. One week before we were to be married in the church, the pastor called her out to talk to her and told her he could not marry us because we have been divorced. That crushed me and all I could think of was how phony could you get. To profess that we could be members of the church but could not marry. I reacted violently and was going to shoot the minister, but my girlfriend made such an effort to stop me, I was able to calm down. That did not stop me from hating with a vengeance the pastor and all those phony people who said they loved. Anyone lame enough to go for that phony, sissy bull only deserved my hatred and contempt.

With this attitude, I started pulling armed robberies again and was very sure I was justified in doing so. Three months after we were married, I shot a man in a robbery in Greenville and was caught. By then, I had grown so hard I would not confess to anything and even convinced my wife, Dad and Mother that I was innocent. I built upon that lie a life of justifying myself no matter what I did. I was always the victim, the one picked on, and it was always everyone else's fault, never mine. I built upon lie after lie a life of self-justification.

In prison in South Carolina, my reputation of being cold-blooded made me a person to be feared and respected. I gloried and gloated my ego off other's fear. My wife and young child grew afraid of me though they were faithful to come visit me at every opportunity. When our daughter ever mentioned going to church, I tried to dissuade her and imposed my feelings about there being nothing good that could come from depending on phony stuff like Christianity.

That attitude went on and worsened over the years until I could tell my mother not to write if that was all she could talk about. She had really committed her life to the Lord after I got into trouble. And she never failed to let me know that she loved me and was sure that some day I would turn to the Lord.

In 1975 (December), I was in a fight with several blacks and lost the first fight that I could ever remember. My face crushed, one eye gouged out, and my tongue bitten completely in two kept me in the hospital for six months. One month out, another fight, this time with just one man; my nose was bitten completely off. All this time, I kept storing up more hatred until I was a time bomb ready to explode on anyone who got in my way. Prisoners and guards were afraid of me and the disfigured face did nothing to make me more pleasing in their sight. I dealt drugs, gambled, set up robberies outside, bought and sold homosexuals all with the excuse that I was justified because really I was a good person. (One who did not participate in homosexual acts, and one who did little things to make myself feel good about doing good deeds for others like keeping a young boy from being raped when he came into the prison).

My wife had a heart attack in 1975; I could feel no compassion for her, just sorry one of my possessions was not up to par. I selfishly gobbled up other people's love and affection, but could never let myself feel affection for them because it might make me weak and an easy target to be hurt. I was too much of a man to feel hurt.

In 1977, I was caught with a knife and for fighting and was given a six-month sentence in solitary confinement. All this right after I had been busted with a load of drugs and was being charged in street court on a contraband charge that could get me another ten years. I lay in the solitary cell wallowing in self-pity and being consumed with hatred and anger. I was very sure I was going to get even with those I blamed for what had happened to me. I had already gotten revenge on a couple of men who had been in the fight where my face was crushed and I planned to get the man who bit my nose off. I never took the blame for anything, it was always some else's fault, not mine.

My mother had written me on my birthday, April 22, that she was happy for something good was going to happen to me. I told my wife she must have gone crazy. God had revealed to her after years of praying that I was going to be saved. This was not revealed to me until after I was saved. Besides, I could see nothing good about being in solitary confinement and being charged with a murder and another charge in street court. I had been charged with a murder and armed robberies and first degree burglary in Anderson County and these charges were still pending, with sure conviction almost certain. This added more fuel to the fires of my hatred.

Some way the book, "Run Baby Run," written by Nicky Cruz with Jamie Buckingham got into the cell with me and the tough looking dude on the front cover appealed to my self image of being a tough dude. As I read the book about a young boy who started running from responsibilities, my own life started being revealed and for the first time I faced the fact that I was not a bad dude, but a craven coward who had never stood up to even one responsibility. And with this came the realization that I was not a good person, but a terrible sinner. The book told about a little preacher who had told a dude like me that "God loves you!" Then to know he was smacked by this dude and the little preacher just stood there and said, "I love you," scared me to death. I remember my mother and others who had tried to tell me about his love and the love some Christian brothers and sisters had tried to share with me. Then I saw what a man or a woman really was. It was someone who could say, "I love you," and really mean it because of what Jesus Christ had done in their life. Not someone who could rob and steal and kill and take what they wanted from life. The book told me about Jesus Christ dying for my sins and that He had paid the price for them all at one time. I got down on my knees and asked Him to forgive me of my sins and to please be my Lord and Savior, to please teach me how to love instead of hate, and praise God He did do all these things for me. He showed me that a real man was one that could follow Him and stand up to the rejection and suffering and yet love those who were doing these things to Him. He revealed Himself as the Son of the Living God and that He had come to save lost souls such as mine. For the first time in my life, I knew what love is and who is the source of love. Jesus Christ set me free right then and there and I cried for days and days. I hadn't cried since I was a small child, for I was sure you weren't a man if you cried. The door of the cell didn't fly open, but my heart and soul were free, never to be in prison again, praise God!

Jesus Christ gave me the strength and hunger to study about Him and find out more about this Savior I had committed my life to. This Jesus Christ who loved me so much, He had died to set me free. He gave me the love to start looking at people, who all my life had been objects to use or not to use, and seeing them for the first time as people who hurt, cried, who needed to know this wonderful Savior who is alive and well, who is healing and ministering today through His people. It was a whole new world to me. The first feeble attempts to reach out were childish and uncertain. But God gave me the strength and boldness to keep on. I found out real quick that when you love with His love you suffer because of it, but the joy of knowing His love overcomes all the suffering and lets me realize more fully His presence in my life.

My wife committed her life to Jesus Christ after I did, then my oldest daughter, Debbie, then the next daughter, Diane and her husband Ralph (who starts school this year for the ministry, praise God). Then my wife was privileged to lead our daughter, Tammy, to the saving knowledge of our Lord Jesus Christ. Acts 16:31 is a promise from God that I rejoice and stand on in faith, this faith is His gift to me. Debbie, as you read this, is having a real struggle in her walk with the Lord and I humbly ask for your prayers. My Dad committed his life to the Lord and I got to be assured of this while still at Kirkland Correctional Institution. He is growing in the grace of our Lord daily, praise God.

Before I realized it, our Lord opened the doors for me to go into schools and share with the children there. Then to work with the youth incarcerated at Youth Services Department. From there, after many more miracles of softening hearts and opening doors, God made the way for a reluctant disciple to be accepted at Erskine Theological Seminary. Dr. Randall Ruble used daring Christian witness to help through what seemed like an impossible task. The whole school and community opened their hearts and arms in Christian love to share Jesus Christ with me in a way that books do not fully give credit to. The load is heavy, but it is made sweet by the love and fellowship all the professors and students enjoy together. God has done all this and His is the glory, the mercy, and love. He even lead Dr. Ruble to a man who is paying for all three years schooling, against all our doubts, fears, and unbeliefs. These are all gifts from God's grace and it is a pleasure to learn and grow in His life with those who do not hesitate to share one with another.

The decision to enter the ministry was really not one I could walk away from. Sometimes, it seems as if it were forced upon me. But then our Lord reveals that it is just my cowardly nature that makes my feet drag and reluctance comes from my lack of confidence in Him. Just as He brought forth Dr. Ruble and Mr. Bowie, He has met every need in such inspiring ways I can but stand in wonder at His love and power. The ministry is a responsibility I had rather run from, but God gives me the courage to stand firm. It is His ministry and I humbly thank him for letting me share a small part of what He offers.

Career goals for me will always have to be taken one step at a time. The heavy burdens in my life are for the youth incarcerated, for other prisoners both inside and outside prisons, and for the people locked in mental shells. The gospel of Jesus Christ seeks to set these people free, if they hear, and how can they hear unless someone cares enough to tell them what the Lord has done and can do for them. The next step seems to be a prison ministry work-ing with both the children, the prisoners, and their families as God ordains and opens doors. My wish and hope is that every child, prisoner, and family will be served the gospel of a loving Jesus Christ in a way that they will see the light of true life come into their lives and we can stop crime and people committing them for the glory of our Lord, and the sake of His Kingdom.

AUTHOR'S COMMENTS

One of the keys in understanding Zeb's flight into crime is found in his youth as is so often the case. A good deal of street crime begins as juvenile delinquency that has its origins in unresolved inter/intrapersonal conflicts. Zeb felt uncared for as a youngster by a rather cold, detached and yet demanding father. I believe he felt forced to be something he was not in a rather non-specific sense. Feelings of ambivalence were present. This caused him to grow up with a feeling that he was not acceptable in some important way. He is short and has told the writer that he was very much aware of this as a youth. His stature seemed to confirm his inner feelings. Zeb is not specific about the incidents in his early teens which "made me start to hate my parents." So often these events that are remembered serve to confirm feelings that began much earlier, and I suspect this is true in Zeb's case. It is of importance that he comments, "The greatest hurt was that I had lost my grandfather with whom I had been very close. He was the one person who never expected me to be anyone except myself." Zeb then had lost, through his grandfather's death, the only significant other person in his life—a man who confirmed his worth.

Zeb became an outstanding football player and was offered three schol-arships to college by the time of his senior year in high school. He was also granted an appointment to West Point through a prominent senator who is related to the family. He rejected these honors, again in rebellion against being pushed, I believe, into a course that was chosen by the parents and not by Zeb. He joined the Marine Corps at the age of 17 and the rebellion intensified. One evening after staying out rather late, he returned to his duty station at a naval hospital. After being questioned about the late hour he became angry. A fight ensued and before it was over $150,000 worth of damage had been done to the hospital ward with water from fire hoses. In addition, several MP's had been locked in ward rooms. It was felt by the Marine Corps that perhaps Zeb could not adjust to military discipline and he was dishonorably discharged. This incident confirmed that Zeb was tough, as big as the Marine Corps, invincible, a man who needed nothing from others, a man who could defiantly reject the world and live life on his own terms. He could also avoid facing or recalling the early memories of rejection and unacceptability. He was confirmed, then, in his flight away from himself. Zeb describes his life from his teens on as self-justified. It is this stance when deeply entrenched that is of course seen by many psychiatrists as the main trait of the anti-social personality. A judge later called Zeb a menace to society and there was much additional evidence to support this view.

The punishment by prison officials, including numerous shock treatments, merely served to further substantiate in Zeb's mind that (1) he was the toughest con around, and (2) that rejection is the way of all authority figures. The punitive actions of authority were seen as a challenge and further justified his vitriolic anger and retaliation.

The book that Zeb mentions served as the beginning point of his return from what could be called a self-imposed hell. He identified with the author, whose life resembled Zeb's, beginning with running from responsibilities as a boy. His moral values were transvaluated, I believe, in what could be seen as an almost miraculous moment. This is not to say that all of these values came about overnight or in the flash of an eye. I believe that this was a moment in Zeb's life where all of the many scripts of the past were brought before his eyes in a kind of capsule form. Then, it suddenly struck him—he needed to change. This is much akin to William James' idea of the conversion experience, his contention being that it does not totally occur in one instant, but there is an important moment whereby many past experiences are brought together, and there is some real moral or religious meaning produced. I believe this is what happened to Zeb. Many, of course, saw the change in Zeb as "jailhouse religion." Many of us who know and love Zeb held our breath, but his seminary experience further broadened his views and helped to mature him in his faith. Now, on federal probation and in essence a free man, he is back in prison as an ordained minister working with many of the same men who remember a far different man.

I believe that Zeb's life began with the feeling of inferiority and rejection—a total, unsettled kind of feeling which was dominant and remained with him for a long time. The early rejection was felt because love and acceptance always seemed to have a price tag; that is, love and acceptance were conditional. This led to delinquency, then to more serious crime as a response first of all to these feelings; then the behavior became habit and an entrenched lifestance. The Christ event broke through as unconditional love, whereby Zeb could face his own terrible failures without fear. Forgiveness of himself and others continued to bring a new inner freedom and allowed him to pick up and to go forward. The feeling which was created was one of gratitude for this release from bondage, which was indeed a severely entrenched anger toward the world. The feeling, then, results in a need to give oneself to others.

Chapter 9

A Perspective on Crime, Values, and Religion

Richard J. Skoog

**Reformed Church in America and
Westchester County Department of Corrections
Valhalla, New York**

A CURRENT EXPRESSION. This is one person's expression on the subject of Crime and Religious Values. Confessed is an adaptation as a social worker, pastor, police chaplain, teacher, and coordinator of programs in a correctional facility.

A WAY OF LIFE. Presented is a point of view, an attitude, a spirit of approach, a Way of Life. This is more than a statement of religious belief resulting in religious values. It reflects the experience of being effected by the human problem of courage to live, contrasted with survival response in a world of relative values. Responsible people hold different, individual and often contradictory views. Their intent is to act in the best way they know. We approach life by different avenues—social, religious, political, economic, etc. Each person is to be treated with dignity and respect. What we do, however, springs from what we believe. Acts follow from what we believe. Thus, the approach here expressed reflects beliefs put into action, always coming under the test of results, current and ultimate, and illustrated by the New Testament, not as proof nor to present The 'only' truth, but to examine a viewpoint integral with life.

WHAT IS NOT SAID. No attempt is made to dignify numbers as statistics to prove the Way. 'Whole' people are beyond each thought. Mention of any person is not a violation of privacy but a composite picture. Human dignity and respect for the individual is accorded. Nor is any attempt made to correct individuals, church or political institutions. Whatever truth there is carries its own authority. Nothing offered is really new, but a lively reaction is felt among persons meeting which makes things "new".

IMPOSSIBLE WITHOUT HIS SPIRIT. What *is* offered is a growing belief, associated with a response on my part, that the accepted and ideal ethic to "love your neighbor as yourself" (Matthew 19:19) is *impossible to live without God's help and Presence.* Life is personal response. In keeping with the Old Testament, the New Testament (Covenant) stresses that without God's help, through Jesus, the Christ, as the Word on earth, there is no hope of attaining the Will of God. Life is receiving God's personal Love, responding by accepting one's whole self, as is, just as we are, *depending on HIS Presence to become what we are.* A consequence is to treat others with dignity, as we are to accept and treat ourselves. For each person this decision is *unique.* Seemingly impossible for us, such life *is* possible with God (Matthew 19:26). Our personal life style is confronted by a choice between treasures on earth *or* treasures *within.* Such treasures within last forever while treasures here on earth may or may not be included. Yet, to be free to live the ideal ethic depends on making the right decision of action with God's Presence.

A DECISION IS NEEDED TO PUT GOD FIRST. Confrontation with the Good News demands a decision on our part to put His Kingdom, His Way, first, or to go our own way without the guidance of His Presence primarily. While the ideal law is fulfilled in loving (Lev. 19:18), life is *not* a matter of law. Law ends in self-centeredness. Life in the Spirit ends in godcenteredness. Life is a fruit of the Spirit, freely given by God, of love, joy, peace, patience, kindness, goodness, faithfulness, gentleness, self-control; against such there is no law (Gal. 5:22). Freedom comes in deciding.

BIBLICAL LAW OF RELIGIOUS VALUES IS SUMMARIZED IN THE "SUMMARY OF THE LAW." The familiar story of the meeting of the lawyer and Jesus is about values in religion relating to life situations. When the lawyer asked, "Teacher, which is the great commandment of the law?" The teacher replied, "You shall love the Lord your God with all your heart and with all your soul and with all your mind. This is the great and first commandment. And the second is like it, You shall love your neighbor as yourself. On these two commandments depend all the law and the prophets" (Matthew 22:37–40).

CREATIVE PERSONAL ENCOUNTERS RAISE VALUES IN A LIFE OF GROWTH. The confrontation relates to crime and religious values. Whatever caused the lawyer to ask the question, the reply was a personal conviction—a confession of faith and a belief in the reality of the relation human people experience on earth with God. Human beings need *values*— personal qualities of worth expressed through mature people. *Crime* may be a violation of a law or custom. *Value,* however, carries a personal conviction—a discovery through one person and another. Genuine feelings, freely developed, reveal themselves through a capacity to live. The lawyer's question was to a person. And the answer set the world stage for higher religious values. Those values are expressed by people in various ways through aesthetic, moral and spiritual avenues. Art, law, and the inner spirits of people exhibit a growing appreciation of this human struggle toward growth and integration through human encounters reflecting holiness within individuals.

JESUS' LIFE IS CENTERED IN THE KINGDOM OF GOD. Jesus' Life, as His values, is centered in the Kingdom of God. For Him, people have supreme worth to God. Without using the words and phrases so overused today, such as dignity, self-awareness, being your own man or woman, getting-it-together, Jesus demonstrated God-centeredness, contrasted to being self-centered, ego-centered, idea-centered, crime or law centered. His values on earth are His values both here and here-after, human and heavenly. His theology and ethics are one. There is no distance between His life and His religion. What it looks like, it is. Reality and facts go together. We can trust His word. Ultimate meaning is related to God. The result is a command of God, a demand for the actual to be completely related to the ideal in living. Jesus showed in everyday living and by His Death the love of God, enlarging the depth and meaning of God's love for every human anywhere and anytime. His relation with God demonstrated a new demand upon each of us-a *response* once we are confronted with the Good News called 'faith'. This act of faith is from within and evidences itself in acts. Our faith is outwardly seen in trust, confidence in living because we feel right with God, loyalty in pursuing life with Him, forgiveness of self as we forgive others, and a new sense of being free. To love God means to help somebody, to obey God, to love oneself, to be oneself in a natural and relaxed way, without hypocrisy. Because Jesus values us, because of His Life and Death, God's Kingdom becomes central.

DEATH OR LIFE. Jesus's approach is twofold. He saw human sin result in death, lies, falseness, compromise, crime, violence, and more basically, broken human relations and ties, with all the hurt. He also believed a person can be renewed, change attitude(s), change, be different, *inspite* of knowing all about oneself and one's environment. His center, being in God, changed the meaning of death into life. That inward reality works not only through facts of each of our lives, but *inspite* of knowing about human psychology and human institutions. Death or life is the choice we are freed to make. "Rehabilitation" is possible.

A COMPOSITE PICTURE OF A "CRIMINAL." An inmate asked to leave the prison on a program. Many ask. Some are "ready". Afterall, most sentenced persons will eventually re-enter the community. The sooner a workable relation is established with the community the better. But how "ready" must a convicted person be? Does he or she have too many characteristics unacceptable to the community? Can the privilege be given without the capability of handling the freedom? A composite picture of a program applicant in criminal justice might show the following traits:

Street-wise, poor work habits and behavior illustrating lack of good judgment are evident. Claiming not to be lazy with a combined declaration that a job is needed to "straighten everything out" is supported only by evidence that past employment was lost for not being at work on time. Association with friends of similar life-styles, who also work-off-the-books and spend more money than others who save and invest for the future is common. A denial of drug or alcohol abuse is often mentioned when further investigation reveals the person left one or more programs in the past to overcome such abuse. Yes, the arrest had taken place while under the influence of alcohol or drugs. Tendency toward impulsive and immediate gratification reveal themselves in wanting an answer without taking responsibility. Feelings of anxiety, hypochondriasis, "family problems", a probable seventh grade level of education, poor writing habits, "cocky" attitude, possible homosexuality, shallow emotional life, apparent inability to change and failing to profit from experience are traits often evident. As time passes there often develops an anxiety within the applicant to return to the street. Discipline problems within the institution appear, pointing to a way of handling problems in a negative manner, lacking direction, without remorse. A manipulative, dependent, "gaming" attitude, mingled with lies and blaming problems on others is used to support a devious and immature person.

RISK. From a security viewpoint such a person is a risk. He or she must deal constructively with personal shortcomings to be given the privilege of re-entering the community. From an ethical basis the individual may be viewed as a *human person, inspite* of negative traits which make him or her inappropriate as a person for release to the community. The choice of leaving the institution on a program depends on both the applicant and those legally responsible for security. Remembering that there is always a risk, even with the "best" of applicants, the choice remains two-fold. Work, however, from the value system (if it can be called such) of the New Testament is not given because a person is good, but as an expression of living a life of faith, loyalty and trust. We *can* change. Will the motivation be sufficient to overcome the actual risk of being free to return to the 'street'?

VALUES OF AN INSTITUTION NEED CONTINUAL RE-EVALUATION THROUGH RELIGIOUS VALUES AND HOPE OF RE-HABILITATION. Values within an institution must be continually questioned by a culture which adapts itself to the present. As a social worker recognizes the effect of past social experience on a person and the psychologist aims to help the person gain self-awareness, so those working within the criminal justice system are effected. Such experiences may encourage or discourage growth in a healthy manner. This pertains to the criminal, police, lawyers, judges, social workers, probation and parole officers, correction officers, psychiatrists, psychologists, physicians, and chaplains. It is here where those convicted of breaking the law or custom (crime) are placed to live in a *limited* freedom. Even the best correction institutions house the severe with the less serious "cases". Past crimes, "knee jerk" responses of politicians, emptying of mental hospitals, political pressures on police, popular opinion, all generate a growing prison population and increased staffing. As institutions of education and police are erroneously expected to correct inadequacies of home life and community misbehavior, so correction institutions are expected to change people who will, one day, re-enter the community. But the system responds with human people. And since its nature produces a de-humanization, attempts are made to meet the challenge only to be frustrated by negative-lip-serving support of a society uninterested in what happens therein as long as the streets are safe. Agencies fighting for limited funds also tend to write glowing reports which consume time. Coping with a great need of communication answered by modern management techniques falling short of seeing people as people, knowing inmates need promises kept, even if no help can be given, those actively participating in the system are forced into being a caretaking system short of offering rehabilitation beyond personal contact.

A NEED TO GO BEYOND FINALITY IN A PRISON. The "civil servant" name saving reputation contrasted with the active approach of helping people help themselves until we become 'useless' to them is a temptation in the criminal justice system. The obvious need to maintain a clear chain of command without losing people in committees is a problem for those working with inmates as well as for inmates. Respect for those responsible for security and for "mere social workers" may differ. But people, contrasted with a mechanical view of "cases" or "patients" are not robots to be programmed by behavior therapy or the latest psychology fad to become good or mature. Delegation of authority is not an easy matter when the "boss" is constantly aware of being watched by legislators soliciting votes and executives who have grown to become more aware of images than of reality. Creative imagination and work with an inmate can be limited for an inmate, staff member and administration because of having to meet 'numbers' and appearance rather than effective programming. As the charge of 'hypocrisy' is mentioned for not attending church by people, so a parallel is found in the criminal justice system. The person making the accusation may fail to see that a genuine relation does exist with God and man for some inmates and employees are effectuating change. The Spirit is needed to offset these facts. This Spirit, Jesus with us, integrating life, through the realistic and creative power of Love, is a value not to be overlooked in effect. We need to go beyond facts of this world into reality. Love and meaning-well do not replace the necessities of helping a person realize self-affirmation, self-assertion and self-awareness through counsel and education. If the source of such personality "traits" is the value of love, however, such traits are formed within the person freely through the Spirit in a System which does not view itself with finality and rigidity. Such a Spirit is *centered* beyond the apparent finality of a prison.

LAW'S MERCY: READY. An attorney inquires if a client may be released daily to work or attend school outside the institution. The client's employer or school knows the reason for incarceration. He is wanted on the job. Many agree that greater good will come about for the family, inmate or employer instead of "wasting away". The convicting judge assures the facility of a willingness on the judicial side. The arresting police agree. Correction officers and staff offer their view of the inmate's institutional behavior. Legal records, probation and parole reports indicate the direction of crimes. A common thread usually weaves itself through the replies. Divergent views appear, except in the most obvious threats to society, about how "risk free" an applicant is. There is always a risk—humans are human. The more subtle character traits of a person's values and life style call for scrutiny of the psychologist, social worker, psychiatrist. Rules are interpreted with mercy. "When can the client be released?" The reply, "When he/she is ready!" The three "r's"—ready, reply, rely.

READY. Obviously, the privilege of allowing an incarcerated person to leave and return daily on a release program is to be given to those whose ability, motivation, personal values evidence readiness. A direct and honest approach is to ask the applicant, "Are you ready?" But ask intelligently. That is, the psychologist will enable the applicant to ask himself or herself, 'Who am I?', 'What am I doing?', 'Where am I?', 'When am I doing it?', 'To whom am I doing it?' The replies reveal much as to whether or not the applicant can be relied upon and is ready. These questions deal with values! From the view of personality growth, answers to the questions are helpful to determine how reliable a person may be, providing that they are accurate. The teacher helps determine what school level the person has reached and what type of work may be most appropriate. By understanding the way in which the applicant sees the world, a step is made toward readiness. True, to explain a person's viewpoint does not excuse criminal behavior but it is another step toward readiness. Confrontation of the bigot and the delinquent may be necessary. An acceptable quality of life must be worth having. As the applicant answers personally, improvement is closer.

THROUGH LOVE THE RECOGNITION OF PERSONALITY IN OTHERS OPENS THE MIND, DEMANDING DECISION. The questions above suggest the "composite picture" of an inmate also describe a person *loved by God.* Something happened to the human view of God once Jesus died on the Cross. As the Old Testament prophets effected their contemporaries so a re-evaluation followed Jesus' giving His life. The value of both people and God changed. The "composite person" above is guilty of a crime, or is judged so. He or she is also the person for whom Jesus died, thereby changing religious values. There is no room for hypocrisy while working with the convicted, no apparent worth distinguished from real worth, no room for broken promises. Fact is fact. As the convicted person is confined, so, whether we accept or reject Jesus' values, Jesus lived and died as a convicted person for all of us. We are all, therefore, accepted *as is* —whether we admit guilt or complain of being falsely convicted. In a society prone toward legal conviction for lack of money to defend ourselves legally—for money is power—Jesus' view of supreme worth of a person in the 'eyes' of God questions such active fact. Without treating a person with any less or more dignity than another and *inspite* of good or bad personality characteristics, Jesus demonstrated the supreme worth of a person to God. This spirit, attitude, approach can be and is transmitted in the criminal justice system by people who believe. This does not imply those "outside of the church" are not influenced. In fact, without open confession of religious values and faith, without talking about how religious they are, some people evidence Jesus' values in the system. The recognition of personality in others opens the mind.

SIN IS AS REAL AS A COMMITTED CRIME. Do not mistake me. Crime is factual. Values of people are different. People are to be respected. But, as a human judge empowered to convict a person of a crime may give recognition to the possibility for that person to begin life anew, using "shock probation", so Jesus forgives sin, freeing a person to resume life with the admonition to sin no more. Jesus' view of sin goes straight to the problem most basic to mankind. His view of sin, however, has no meaning apart from a present, living God Who cares for us. Sin (a broken relation with God resulting in moral problems among people) troubles Him deeply to the cost of His earthly life. A high price. His view is evidenced in hardness of heart and mind where a person fails to even see human need. His view is illustrated in one's lying to oneself and God and others where he may say one thing and do another. It is enjoying thoughts which reduce life's better meanings while pretending to be good. And, also, in the failure to dare to do the deed thought of. Finally, His view of sin is illustrated by the failure to make a decision before it is too late—where we run the danger of not making up our minds. These four practical illustrations of seeing 'sin' bring the religious view of sin down to earth. The actuality of sin is, for Him, more basic and as real and factual as committed crime. Crime being a result. Conviction does not end the problem for criminal justice anymore than conviction ends religion. It is one thing for a person to discover that "the system does not work" and another to answer how it can work. So Jesus' values must become part of the condemnation of a person's act to complete the news that there is an answer in being able to live again through the door of forgiveness. More, in keeping with the thesis of this paper, He, Himself, must be accepted as part of the experience of conviction. To begin life again, information or acceptance of His values alone is not enough. Person to person. As the criminal's convictions remain on record, so the results of sin remain on the personality. Their 'expulsion' is now accomplished by law change—legal and law of love paid for at a Price. But Love has a creative work in lives of people. And all things become new through Him Who is Present.

THE HISTORICAL JESUS PROVIDES THE MEANS. The historical Life, Death and Resurrection of Jesus provides the effective means for God in Christ to enter our everyday lives. He opens our capacity to recognize values of worth. His Presence enables us to both know and do the Will of God. Resurrection, God's Act, enables Jesus to come back and enter our lives. He returns through the Holy Spirit. The Spirit within us is the continuation of Jesus in today's world. Often called a "religious value", Christian faith is, rather, a *Way of Life.* A person experiences a relation with an all-embracing reality of the universe in a personal way. If Jesus is present with us, He is God in us, His nature is realized in practical results and facts. His effectiveness enables us to realize true values in a world of relative values. Such is a free gift. Life is viewed as a forgiven person, able to overcome the 'block' which prevents us from being good. We view ourselves as a person for whom Jesus lived and died and Rose that we may live as God created us to be. Going beyond legalism, where we may see ourselves falsely as in the center, there is a restored relation in a world of Grace (God's love in action), with the center of living and the treasure of our life in God. God-centered. Effective daily living, recognizing ultimate responsibility rests in God's continuous grace, relevant to personal decisions, in faith, is the Way. He provides the means.

A COMPOSITE PICTURE OF A PERSON WITH "RELIGIOUS VALUES." The characteristics valued by Jesus are given in His Beatitudes. (Matthew 5:1–13). They describe "happiness" for citizens in the Kingdom of God. He no longer calls His followers servants, clients, inmates, patients, staff, students, teachers, managers. He calls us friend. The human soul is to be related to God, as friends, where we may both glorify and enjoy God. Final allegiance moves beyond culture. Ambiguities and uncertainties bow before Love—personally. No longer is there merely a display and fear and respect for power, for actual authority is discovered in Character.

Characteristic values of a person in the Kingdom Jesus describes are those evolving spontaneously, without compulsion, without severe ethics, nor is fear of punishment sufficient restraint. Life is offered free. It is a special kind of Joy—where satisfaction is in who we are, related to others, in a healthy way, inseparable from God.

Such people recognize their imperfection. They are not God. But they (1) trust enough to learn something new about God and God's influence in living. (2) People who are truly sorry for their past mistakes and sins, for hurt of others, who recognize their error(s), find comfort. Able to do better in the future they accept forgiveness. A mistake is not the end. (3) Self-controlled and self-disciplined people find their authority from within. Fear of police, law, security lapses, life on the outside is overcome in Jesus's view of a so-called "meek" person. Happy to decide issues which come before them they are aware of their control. (4) People with a passion to learn and do what is right are satisfied people. They have their reward. Life is a gift to experience with God's friends. (5) Merciful people are kind to both those they like and those they do not like. And, possibly, with a touch of humor, because the world of human relations is as it is, Jesus insists that there is no exception to this rule. Others will be kind in return. Religion has to do with emotions, intellect and will—all of a person. So, (6) those with a pure heart reach beyond the classroom, management, and institutions. Intelligence is not the key to answering the world's problems. Shrewdness is one thing, wholeness of a person is more. According to Jesus, a whole person must want only one thing, namely, the 'right thing!' We must strive to be like God. To see God is to take on the Character of God, His personality. Rather than our innocence being seen as a weakness, it will burn away false views. Values must be clear—for happy people want one thing, God's 'thing'. Ultimately, good depends not on intelligence, but on power of God. (7) Such people work for peace, continually, without letting up. Creatively, artfully, refreshingly, God, Life, Love, friendship, the universe, self-awareness move us from a need for salvation into the presence of communion. The whole and the parts are one. The earth, universe, inner life are part of a whole. There is oneness in diversity. Rapport. The greatest aims of the psychologist are attained in their mature form in the religious value of Jesus's Peace. (8) The final picture Jesus offers in His declaration of happiness is that of persecution. To be part of the criminal justice system may mean persecution in that some person caught and sentenced may find punishment. So in the world Jesus pictures. To be good enough to impress people who differ can bring a negative and unreceptive reaction. When we attack evil we may suffer. But life is able to overcome evil with good—at a price. This is demonstrated on the Cross.

THE WISDOM AND POWER OF GOD. Suffering may be evidence not of defeat but of success. Life overcomes death. And a person who follows this Way may have trouble with even so-called nice people. A person may be incarcerated, convicted, analyzed, behavior modified, pressured to conform to what society views peace and good to be. But Love is stronger than death and can act in suffering, even in Joy, as many testify by their lives. As God's enemies see to it that a believer may be persecuted, Jesus is with that person. In this, the criminal and the convicted person of faith share an experience. In spite of life's experiences, however, the "composite person" Jesus describes as "blessed" or "happy" realizes he or she has found something new about God. As in the First Beatitude, that person has a present gift of strength and direction. For the Cross means both Death and Life. It is the Wisdom and Power of God.

CONCLUSION. By definition this means we must clarify the meaning of words such as evil, wrong, crime, sin, love. By relating to the actual situations of crime and religious values, whatever the religion or crime, we may begin to see actual authority uppermost in the meeting of Jesus and the lawyer is not so much the display of power but Character. Final allegiance moves beyond culture and conditions of one's life to One Who is not just powerful but Holy. All ambiguities and uncertainities bow before such Love. Against such there is no law beyond the Law of Love demonstrated, offered and present in Jesus, the Christ, a Friend.

Chapter 10

Methods, Morals, and Meanings: On Psychology, Religion, and Effects

James M. Day

**Program in Professional Psychology
Graduate School of Education
University of Pennsylvania**

For some years I have been concerned by the apparent lack of integrative research among scholars who have studied the relationship between religion and explanatory theories of criminal behavior. In particular it is disturbing that psychologists have ignored substantial evidence from within the discipline of religious studies concerning the "moral dimension" in religious experience. Theories of moral development, and attempts by moral philosophers and psychologists to make sense of criminal behavior have great promise, but their failure to fully explore religiosity, or more significant dimensions of religious experience, is a profound and critical error.

This chapter considers the relationships among religion, moral development, and behavior. It will outline some specific problems in psychology that have prevented a comprehensive psychological study of religion and its effects on behavior; especially criminal behavior.

To begin, I offer a brief description of context— a little picture of the historical antecedents that may account, in part, for the current predicament.

Next, some perspectives that explicitly consider the relationships among religion, moral development, and behavior will be described. The first among these perspectives may be familiar to the reader while the remainder are probably less so. In consideration of the latter, the chapter will explore claims by scholars from several religious traditions about the inherently moral dimension of religious experience.

Based in part on these claims the chapter will also address several problems in the analysis of religion by psychology, problems that have led to an incomplete picture of religion and that have, in turn, resulted in inadequate references to the psychology of religion in psychologists' discussions of religion and crime.

Finally, I will pose some research questions that will hopefully stimulate a rethinking of religion in both psychology and mainstream criminology.

DESCRIPTION OF CONTEXT

Psychology and religion have for more than a century endured an uneasy, and sometimes hostile relationship that has had detrimental consequences for understanding behavior. Since the rise of modern Continental philosophy, psychology and religion have, with rare exception, gone different ways.

Despite Argyle's (1958) claim that a fundamental distinction should be made between those who are 'conventionally' religious and those who are 'genuinely devout,' psychology has mostly neglected the factor of religious experience and claims about its meaning.

This neglect has taken three principal forms. The first is theory, where psychologists have spoken of religion as a desparate endeavor to answer basic questions about the meaning of human life and the mystery of its relation to the cosmos (Freud, 1927). Such theory ignores the claims of religious individuals, groups, and scholars of religious traditions, that religion begins with an experience in which meaning is already present.

Second, religious belief has been construed to mean (1) belief as a noun, indicating what one believes (2) belief as assent, accepting a proposition as correct; and (3) belief as commitment to some particular issue (Spinks, 1960; Scobie, 1975). In turn, psychologists have reduced religion to a set of propositions or persuasions to be endorsed or rejected on questionnaires, without regard for the place of religious experience in their formation or effects in subjects.

Third, where religious experience has been considered, it has been construed as pathological (Scobie, 1971) or interpreted without attention to one of its crucial and distinguishing features (James, 1902). Psychologists such as Allport, Jung, and Frankl whose work has suggested otherwise, have been ignored.

Religion hasn't helped matters much. Many representatives of religious sects have ignorantly described their beliefs, institutions, and programs as the whole or only truth about religion, and others have made preposterous attacks on psychology as if psychology were responsible for declines in religious hegemony over the loyalties and persuasions of modern people. Scholars of religion have balked at the presumptuous incursions of psychology into constructions of theory about religion that tend to ignore the massive evidence within religious traditions regarding the etiology of religion, and the meaning and effects of religious experience. The same scholars have rarely directed their comments in the form of constructive criticism toward makers of theory in psychology.

The result has been a deficit of understanding that may have impeded efforts by members of each discipline to translate theory into practice.

WHY MORAL DEVELOPMENT?

To neglect moral development in the crime-religion relationship would amount to pure folly. It is moral development that is most often thought to mediate functioning with regard to prosocial or antisocial behavior and is the feature of crime-religion relations most often discussed in places of worship, schools, and courts of law. Whether criminals are regarded as "just plain bad" or as candidates for moral improvement, "immoral" has come to be equated with "antisocial." Unfortunately, as has already been observed, the whole matter of crime, values, and religion has suffered from considerable neglect of social-scientific scrutiny.

PERSPECTIVES ON RELIGION, MORAL DEVELOPMENT, AND CRIME

To date, three major theories have elicited and sustained much attention in the public domain.

The Evangelical Position

Perhaps the most prominent position in our day is that advanced by the Reverend Jerry Falwell and Cal Thomas of "The Moral Majority." Their views command a large following and have found their way into the language of policy. In brief, they suppose that crime results from and has increased because of a kind of moral chaos. This moral chaos, they believe, is the inevitable consequence of an erosion of religious, and specifically, Christian consensus in America. Dissolution of common Christian belief simply results in moral decline. The prescription, then, is to resurrect for, and failing that, impose upon all members of society, this belief. The majority of citizens then, having come by virtue of belief, into a right relationship with God, will prevail upon themselves and upon others to behave

in such fashion as will be pleasing to God, holding fast to God's commandments, and making unlikely the commission of crime.

Such arguments appeal to the faithful and offer clear guidelines as to
what and whom will be considered good and bad, but sometimes seem to
lack grounding in either history or reason. The number of Christian believers who have at one time or another behaved immorally and/or crimi-
nally are so great as to defy summation, and there is no logic that would
lead one to assent to the notion that uniformity of belief will lead to invari-
ate, let alone, noble action. Such simple equations of belief and action
may in fact lead to a suppression of other points of view that may itself be
considered immoral.

Falwell, Thomas, and others who are party to their assertions do make
an important point about the human need for symbolic sources of illumi-
nation that will help us find our bearings in the world. Undirected by culture patterns—patterns of organized and significant symbols—human
behavior would be virtually ungovernable, ". . . a mere chaos of pointless
acts and exploding emotions [his] experience virtually shapeless. Culture,
the accumulated totality of such patterns, is not just an ornament of human existence but—the principal basis of its specificity—an essential condition for it" (Geertz, 1973).

Falwell and Thomas make the common, but profound error of viewing
culture and social system as identical rather than as independently variable, but mutually independent factors. In reality culture ought to be seen
as an ordered system of meaning and symbols, in terms of which social
interaction takes place, while the social system should be viewed as the
pattern of interaction, itself (see Parsons & Shils, 1951). Culture is the
fabric of meaning wherein human beings interpret their existence and
guide their action; social structure is the form that action takes, the actually existing network of social relations (Geertz, 1973).

Geertz (1973) has insightfully observed that the distinction between
culture and social system is revealed more clearly when one considers the
contrasting sorts of integration characteristic of each form. He follows
Sorokin (1937) in noting that it is a contrast between 'logico-meaningful
integration' and what he has called 'causal-functional integration.' The
former is the sort one finds in a Bach fugue, in Catholic dogma, or in the
general theory of relativity; a unity of style, of logical implication, of
meaning and value. The latter, characteristic of the social system, refers to
the kind of integration one finds in an organism, where all the parts are
united in a single causal web, each part an element in that which keeps the
organism going. Geertz makes the crucial point that because these two
types of integration are not identical, because the particular form of one
does not imply the form the other will take, there is an inherent incon-
gruity and tension between the two and between both of them and a third

element which is the pattern of motivational integration within the individual usually called personality structure.

The Social Justice Position

A second position focuses more upon justice than on belief. It derives from a vision of God's domain in which right action is just action, which vision, issuing from centuries of Judeo-Christian precedent, has widely informed our Western common life. Our notions of law, rights, and duties, have their foundation in this vision. Presently the position of its adherents appears to be that crime results from injustice: inequality of opportunity for access to material and social goods, subjection to inadequate or inappropriate environments, etc. The emphasis is on bringing about and managing a just system of social life, and on fair treatment of those, including criminals, who have not been privy to justice before now. Such a position is advanced from the halls of the liberal religious establishment in our society, in concert with numerous social scientists and critics of the social order. It may hold in large measure as a macrosociological assessment, and it has value as a broadly conceived institutional moral admonition to fair treatment, but it fails to illumine the relation of religious belief or religious experience to personality and crime, cannot answer the haunting questions posed by the varieties of crimes and criminals, and it offers no explanation for why some individuals who are subjected to the worst of injustices and afforded the fewest opportunities for access to material and social goods resist and do not commit immoral or criminal acts. In short, it fails at the level of individual description, analysis, and explanation. At the individual level there are too many exceptions to the rules for the theory to be very enlightening.

The Faith-Developmental Position

Many of those religious and in religious authority have looked with interest, if sometimes because of their perception of threat, upon the work of Lawrence Kohlberg. Kohlberg has for some decades devoted himself to the study of moral development and has formulated a controversial, yet highly respected, theory of its nature and processes.

Kohlberg's moral-development theory is, in its current form, based on Piaget's (1932) work and Kohlberg's (1958) own formulations (Jennings, Kilkenny, & Kohlberg, 1983, in Laufer & Day, 1983). His principal concern is with moral judgment development which, according to Kohlberg (1976) and Colby and Kohlberg (1981) centers on qualitative form and developmental changes in moral reasoning. The theory endeavors to describe general organizational or structural elements of moral judgment that can be demonstrated to develop in a regular sequence of stages (Jennings, Kilkenny, & Kohlberg, 1983).

According to Jennings et al. (1983) the concept of structure implies that a consistent logic or form of reasoning can be abstracted from the content of an individual's responses to a variety of situations. Thus, they note, moral development may be defined in terms of the qualitative reorganization of the individual's pattern of thought rather than the learning of novel content. Each new reorganization integrates within a broader perspective the insights which were achieved at lower stages, according to this point of view. Jennings et. al. assert that in this sense, each stage presupposes the understanding gained at previous stages, and each provides a more adequate way of making and justifying moral judgments. They conclude that the order in which stages develop is the same in each individual not because the stages are innate, but because the underlying logic of the sequence is such that each stage subsumes the logical structures of its predecessor.

There are three major levels of moral judgment development in Kohlberg's scheme: preconventional, conventional, and postconventional.

The first level is one in which the moral rules and values of society are understood as "do's" and "don't"s, safeguarded and obeyed because of adverse consequences in the form of punishment that follow upon violation. This level is characteristic of children ages 9–11 and of many adolescent and adult criminal offenders (Jennings et al., 1983).

The second level is one in which the reasoning subject understands, accepts, or endeavors to maintain and uphold the values and regulations of the social group. Characteristic of the average adolescent and adult in our society and in others (Jennings et. al. 1983) the stage is one in which the individual identifies with or has internalized the rules and expectations of others, particularly those of authoritative persons and institutions.

At the third level individuals consider social rules and values from the point of view of universal rights, duties, and principles. The subject is capable of abstraction from the particular moment in the particular group in the particular value context and seeks to act in a way that conforms by reason to moral principles applicable in all situations, respectful of everyone's rights. The postconventional person describes values as internal to the self and as possessing worth because of their inviolable and universal nature.

Jennings et al. (1983) claim that within each level there are two stages of moral reasoning, each a better version of the general perspective of each major level. Each stage also contains a unique social perspective, characterized by where the person stands in society when she/he makes an ought judgment.

Kohlberg also believes that there can be isolated within each stage four varieties of moral orientation. He and his colleagues say (1983) that some people orient to (1) the rules and roles of the social moral order, (2) the good and bad welfare consequences, (3) relations of equality or reciprocity, or (4) the virtue or goodness of a person. The first two constitute one substage, the second two another, of which the latter is more predictive of just action in real-life situations (Jennings et. al. 1983).

Recently (1981, 1983) Kohlberg and colleagues have vigorously restated their claim (1969) that moral-developmental levels and stages constitute stages in the strict Piagetian sense. That is, they are universal, they are hierarchial, and they make structural wholes. Furthermore Kohlberg (1976, 1983) and colleagues say that the ideas about which the stages are organized are neither arbitrary nor convenient simply for the purpose of theory-making in psychology but, rather, apparent in the reasoning of subjects from all parts of the world. The position that people's moral ideas cohere in a stagelike way and that they are always upwardly inclined has been substantiated by studies demonstrating high test-retest reliability, a high Cronbach's alpha, and the results of factor analyses of issue scores (Jennings et. al. 1983). Internal consistency has been further substantiated by analysis of distributions, by subject, of proportions of reasoning scored at each of five stages (Jennings et al. 1983).

Religious leaders and congregants have sometimes found Kohlberg frightening because of their sense that in Kohlberg's scheme of moral development, and its applications in settings of moral education, there lies some world view rival to their own, and their belief that if Kohlberg's point of view is adopted some moral doctrine foreign to their own will be transmitted and given legitimacy by the state. Kohlberg responds that the problem disappears if the proper content of moral education is recognized to be the values of justice, which themselves prohibit the imposition of beliefs of one group or another (Kohlberg, 1981).

Kohlberg has considered religion in his scheme of moral development and his explorations into its place have chiefly taken him down three paths. One is that charted by James Fowler, a theologian who has engaged in empirical efforts to study religion and morality. For the most part, Fowler focuses on faith, which he defines as people's orientation to the ultimate environment in terms of what they value as being most relevant and important to their entire lives (Fowler, 1976, 1978). In Judeo-Christian thought, the ultimate environment is defined as a personal God and his (sic) kingdom, which is the end point of human history. However, the ultimate environment need not be linked to a personal God and his (sic) kingdom—it is also reflected on in pantheistic and atheistic thought (Kohlberg, 1981). Kohlberg and Fowler see faith as a largely tacit, universal quality of knowing and relating, religion as a particular expression of faith in which concerns about the ultimate environment are made explicit.

One can hardly be surprised by Kohlberg's sympathetic treatment of Fowler, for Fowler (1976) makes explicit his own model for understanding faith as one reliant upon Kohlberg's developmental scheme. In turn,

Kohlberg has demonstrated a significant empirical correlation between the two models (Power & Kohlberg, 1980). In Kohlberg's view religion is a conscious response to, and an expression of, the quest for an ultimate meaning for moral judging and acting. As such the main function of religion is not to supply moral prescriptions but to support moral judgment and action as purposeful human activities. His claim implies that a given stage of solutions to moral problems is necessary but not sufficient for a parallel stage of solutions to religious problems (Kohlberg, 1981).

Kohlberg has also discussed religion in his consideration of the possibility of a seventh moral stage, a stage in which integrity is found and despair ultimately confronted (Kohlberg, 1981). In this stage, as in others, there must be some solution to the question "Why be moral?", and at the seventh level this question entails the question "Why face death?" Ultimate moral maturity requires a mature solution to the question of the meaning of life, a question as much religious as it is moral (Kohlberg, 1981).

Kohlberg's explorations into the world of relations between religion and morality are important ones. They are, though, full of problems. For one, his claims about religion seem sometimes to amount to little more than rehearsals of his own philosophy of moral development. Those who are religiously mature are necessarily those who are morally mature, and religious development is predicated upon the need for making larger meaning of moral insight or reasoning. There is no room for the person who falls short on Kohlberg's moral scale but who is moved up the scale of moral reasoning by virtue of some major religious experience that affects reasoning, or for the person who is similarly affected by the accumulation of limited religious insights. Then we get to stage seven, and Kohlberg illustrates with talk of "Andrea Simpson," the alias for an exemplary religious and moral character. Kohlberg (1981) admits in her case that moral reasoning, and action, followed religious 'openings' (p. 349). What then, of moral reasoning and religious experience, moral reasoning and moral action, and the fixed sequence of moral and religious stages? Finally, what about the realms of life apart from reason? Surely religion and morality have as much to do with guilt, hope, fear, trust, anxiety, love, hate, the desire for unity and reparation, at a constantly primitive, emotional level, as they do with an ever ascending, fixed set of stages of reason.

AN EXISTENTIAL-TELEOLOGICAL RELIGIOUS PERSPECTIVE

Another writer whose work merits attention is Paul Tillich. His work addresses theology, philosophy, and the social sciences, and is deeply concerned with morality.

Tillich speaks to the modern audience of thinkers who are as compulsive in their reaction to religion on the scientific side as they are on the religious side (Tillich, 1963). Tillich asserts that religion is a dimension in the spiritual life of humanity and wrestles with those from both sides who dispute his claim.

Religious compulsives dispute his notion on the grounds that the meaning of religion is that humanity received something which does not come from it, which is given to it, and may stand against it.

Scientific compulsives emphasize the diversity of religious ideas and practices and the mythological character of all religious concepts. They claim that religion is characteristic for a special stage of human development. Religion, to such compulsives, is a transitory creation of the human spirit but certainly not an essential quality of it.

Tillich demonstrates that these two seemingly opposed sets of criticisms have something definite in common. Both define religion as humanity's relation to divine beings whose existence the theological critics assert and the scientific critics deny. But, Tillich says, it is just this idea of religion that makes any understanding of religion impossible:

> If you start with the question whether God does or does not exist, you can never reach Him; and if you assert that He does exist, you can reach Him even less than if you assert that He does not exist. A God about whose existence or non-existence you can argue is a thing beside others within a universe of existing things. And the question is quite justified whether such a thing does exist, and the answer is equally justified that it does not exist. (Tillich, 1964)

Actually, those who have refuted the existence of such a thing have done religion a service, according to Tillich, for they have forced religion to reconsider the meaning of the term "God."

Against both groups of critics Tillich affirms that if one looks at the human situation from this point of view it presents itself as being religious, by which Tillich means to say that religion is the substance, ground, and depth of human spiritual life; the dimension of ultimate concern.

In knowledge it is expressed as the passionate longing for ultimate reality, in aesthetics as the infinite desire to express ultimate meaning, in the moral sphere as the unconditional seriousness of the moral demand. All of this is ultimate concern.

Inevitably the question arises why, in view of Tillich's assertion, humankind has developed religion as a special sphere among other spheres, in myth, cult, devotion, and ecclesiastical institutions. Tillich answers that this is due to the tragic estrangement of human spiritual life from its own ground and depth. This estrangement is accounted for by all of the world's major religions and each of those religions anticipates a time when that from which humanity is estranged will be all in all. There will be no secular realm and for the same reason no religious realm in such an anticipated state.

Tillich observes that being precedes action in everything that is, including humanity, though in humanity, as the bearer of freedom, previous action also determines present being. This stands in opposition to both moral legalism and amoral lawlessness. It affirms morality and points beyond it to its religious foundations (Tillich, 1963).

Tillich's claim for the religious foundation of the moral demands, the religious dimension of the moral imperative, and the religious element in moral motivation belongs with his insistence that being has an essentially absolute and purposive character in the light of which all experience must ultimately be understood. His is a teleological ontology in which the roots of human morality are given in the very structures of being that design and constrain human existence.

Out of this ontology grows Tillich's assertion that the moral imperative is the demand to become actually what one is, the demand that one's true being shall become one's actual being, a being in relation to other beings, a person in a community of persons (Tillich, 1963). A moral act, then, is not an act of obedience to an external law, human or divine. It is the inner law of one's own true being, of one's essential nature, which demands that one actualize what follows from it. An antimoral act is not the transgression of one or several precisely circumscribed commands, but an act that contradicts the self-realization of the person as a person and drives the person toward disintegration. It disrupts the centeredness of the person by giving predominance to partial trends, passions, desires, fears, and anxieties (Tillich, 1963). The central control in such cases is weakened and the "will" becomes slave to conflicting demands that determine personal action and distort experience in what it means to be in relation to another or to the human community at large.

Tillich agrees with his critics that there are many cases in which conditional imperatives have some bearing on an unconditional imperative, and there are cases in which several imperatives compete for supreme allegiance, and in which any decision is a moral risk. But, he defends, the doubt concerning the justice of a moral act when a risk has been taken does not contradict its ultimate seriousness (Tillich, 1963). Rather, it serves as a reminder of the unconditional imperative that is constantly asserting itself in the experience of the actor.

For Tillich it is not a strange law that demands our obedience but the 'silent voice' of our own nature as persons. It is our awareness of our belonging to a dimension that transcends our own finite freedom and our ability to affirm or negate ourselves. Being precedes value, but value fulfills being (Tillich, 1963).

Tillich is important in the development of modern religious thought for some of the same reasons that he is important to the enterprise of this book. First, he seeks to describe religion in terms that are comprehensible in the modern situation, and that cannot be easily dismissed by theologians or social scientists. Second, he speaks in a language that takes discussion of religion beyond the bounds of any particular religious tradition. Third, while maintaining philosophical rigor, Tillich addresses his readers in a language that is accessible to psychologists. One gets both ontology and psychology in Tillich without a devaluation of theology or of scientific criticisms of religion.

What of moral development and religion? Tillich's assertions imply a view that moral development may consist in one or both of two movements. One is a systematic movement toward an opening to religious re-definition of moral perspective. The other is development that occurs as a function of religious experience which establishes the ground for moral action.

In the first case moral development is a sort of education for moral awareness, a step-by-step graduation toward an occasion of insight that transcends moral categories and that places them in the context of their participation in something that gives them meaning and is their source. In the second case, the moral awareness and activity of the person derives from an experience of the kind just described; he or she is "convicted" by way of an experience of ultimate meaning that includes moral judgment, and that inclines him or her to an increase of moral sensitivity and con-gruence of moral action.

Tillich calls this condition of moral existence that proceeds from reli-gious conviction and awakening "transmorality." The person whose life becomes this condition is defined by a transmoral conscience that experi-ences not only the moral dimensions of all actions but also the religious character of them, so that he or she perceives not only the moral claim and imperative that cuts across all activity but also the reason for its being so.

This description is consistent with the claim of all religions that, in ulti-mate terms, being and value are one. It is also consistent with the teaching of all religions that humanity bears within itself the possibility of direct apprehension, in experience, that this is so. Finally, Tillich's claims are consistent with the teaching of religion that such experience of ultimate truth has direct consequences not only for emotional sentiment and iden-tity, but for action as well. Just as the ground of morality is religious, so it is that religious experience necessarily includes moral consequences.

There are many examples of religious writers from several of the world's principal religious traditions who explicitly address the relationship of morality and moral development to religious experience and what, in common, they would call "the spiritual life." They generally write in psychological language and may be of special interest to psychologists who wish to examine their claims.

RELIGIOUS-PSYCHOLOGICAL CLAIMS

Soren Kierkegaard is perhaps the most brilliant writer in the Western Protestant tradition about the psychological nature of religious claims. Each of his books examines the question of human purpose, religious authority, and the psychological experience of all pertinent emotions. It is in *Fear and Trembling, The Sickness unto Death,* and *Purity of Heart is to Will One Thing* that he most powerfully describes the contrast between ethical and religious existence. The works are great not only by reason of their challenging consideration of the matter in experiential terms, but also in philosophical ones, for Kierkegaard is at once deeply personal in his psychological renderings and tremendously broad in his criticism of Kant and Hegel, the preeminent philosophical writers of his time.

For Kant and Hegel the particular individual is the individual who has his telos in the universal, and his ethical task is to express himself constantly in it, to abolish his particularity in order to become the universal. As soon as the individual would assert himself in his particularity over and against the universal he sins, and only by recognizing this can he again reconcile himself or herself with the universal. Whenever the individual after he or she has intered the universal feels an impulse to assert himself or herself as the particular, she/he is in temptation (Kierkegaard, 1843). Hegel says in "The Good and the Conscience" that human character, as it presents itself in the individual, is the particular, and that this is a "moral form of evil" which is to be annulled in the teleology of the moral, so that the individual who remains in the particular is either sinning or subjected to temptation.

Kierkegaard protests that this is not so, and that faith consists precisely in the paradox that the particular is higher than the universal—yet in such a way that the movement repeats itself, and that consequently the individual, after having been in the universal, now as the particular isolates himself or herself as being higher than the universal (Kierkegaard, 1843). This happens because the individual, after having been subjected to the universal, moves through and beyond the universal, and, by virtue of this movement, comes into "absolute relation to the absolute," which absolute is the ground and the possibility of the "universal" life of morals. For Kierkegaard the truly religious person must will to embark on this road through the universal to the absolute, and any other life remains subject to, actually exists, despair. Without this "teleological suspension of the ethical" there is no religious life, and failing such a life, the moral life is nothing more than an extinction of the individual in obedience to the law of the crowd. The truly moral life grows out of an absolute experience of its absolute foundation. As Tillich states, religious experience discloses not only the universal moral strain running through all of life but, also, its ground, its reason for being.

If we turn to Roman Catholicism we find in our own century an eloquent spokesman for the spiritual life and its moral dimension in the Trappist, Thomas Merton. He offers a profound discussion of religious experience and its implications for the moral life. His writings on this subject may be found in several of the many volumes he authored, but one of the best for the purposes of this chapter is probably his reflective and very personal *New Seeds of Contemplation*. This work is especially pertinent because of its discussion of contemplation, its contrasts and comparisons between contemplation and other experiences, and the implications of contemplation for day to day living, for decisionmaking, and for acting in relation to other persons.

Merton, like Tillich, argues that proper talk about religion and religious experience must dispense with reference to God as a thing. The "object" of religious experience is not a "what" or a "thing." That is precisely one of the essential characteristics of contemplative experience, the awesome recognition of this no-thingness (Merton, 1961). Merton observes that there are many respectable and even conventionally moral people for whom there is little or no recognition of the experience he describes as contemplation. Merton does not so much disparage such people as he does admonish them to aspire to fulfillment of their greatest possibilities. He asks that they look beyond the life of self-deception and illusion that consents to know itself only within the limits circumscribed by the finite ego and the bounds of the five senses.

It is Merton's claim, as it is of the other great religious writers, that true morality grows, by way of religious experience, out of that increasingly refined possibility within every person for pure compassion and wisdom deriving from conformation to the divine and one true principle of life that transcends distinctions of being and value and weaves them together into one.

Within Judaism this point of view is best expressed by Martin Buber. His remarkable book, *I and Thou* details the aspect of religious experience that is known by the subject as a confrontation with a radically other but intimately related "Thou," at once beyond the subject's capacity for capturing or definitively discussion it, and at the same time powerfully alive and subsequently determining of the subject's ongoing experience.

For Buber, the heart of religion is the fundamental truth of relationality. In the beginning there is the relation (Buber, 1970). For the religious person the reality of life proceeds from the awareness of relation that is disclosed in advents of eternal presence. Such experience has inevitable moral consequences. Buber observes that:

> He must go forth with his whole being; that he knows. It will not turn out the way his resolve intended it; but what wants to come will come only if he resolves to do that which he can will. He must sacrifice his little will, which is unfree and ruled by things and drives, to his great will that moves away from being determined to find destiny. Now he no longer interferes, nor does he merely allow things to happen. He listens to that which grows, to the way of Being in the world, not in order to be carried along by it but rather in order to actualize it in the way in which it, needing him, wants to be actualized by him —with human spirit and human deed, with human life and human death. This is to say, he believes. . .; but this implies: he encounters. (Buber, 1971)

Buber claims that "Man receives, and what he receives is not a content but a presence, a presence as strength. This presence and strength includes three elements that are not separate but may nevertheless be contemplated as three. First, the whole abundance of actual reciprocity, of being admitted, of being associated while one is altogether unable to indicate what that is like with which one is associate." Like other religious writers, Buber notes that this reciprocity does not make life any easier for us. On the contrary ". . . it makes life heavier but heavy with meaning" (Buber, 1971). The second element of this presence and strength is what Buber calls "the inexpressable confirmation meaning. It is guaranteed. Nothing, nothing can henceforth be meaningless" (Buber, 1971). The third is that this all has to do with this world. The guarantee of meaning does not wish to remain shut up within the receiver but wants to be born into the world by that receiver. "This is what needs to be known, this is what needs to be done. We can only go and put it into the proof of action. And even this is not what we 'ought to do': rather we can—we cannot do otherwise" (Buber, 1971).

Buber, like Tillich, Kierkegaard, and Merton, stresses the centrality of religious experience for the moral life, and emphasizes the point that one "claimed" by such an experience will have to relate to the world morally; will have to face the world as a series of "thous," in light of the "thouness" of life which has been revealed in the religious experience.

Perhaps no tradition is more rich in its possibilities for examining the relationship of experience to behavior than the tradition of Buddhism. Though divergent in emphasis and ritual practice the several strands of Buddhism have in common their beginning in the buddha's enlightenment experience, and discussions of it remain central to the aspirations of individual Buddhists and Buddhist institutions.

Buddhism makes clear the assertion that moral training and development exist for the purpose of moving the individual person toward a state of awareness that, once known and consolidated, becomes the wellspring for purely moral action. For the Buddhist, "selfless" action can only arise from an experience of selflessness which becomes one's dominant mode of consciousness. The theme, already addressed by way of reference to Soren Kierkegaard, of movement beyond the "merely" ethical to the dimension of absolute conformation with the absolute, is advanced and described in some detail by the Buddhists. If it can be said that Kierkegaard's ideal person is imbued by the absolute, so that the presence of the absolute is in all that is later known by the subject, then it is proper to say that the Buddhist saint is absorbed in the absolute, so that no distinction remains between the nature and action of the subject and the nature of the absolute, itself. Having become what she or he truly is, the selfless Buddhist, at one with the consciousness of selflessness, manifests behavior that arises from a clear and absolute recognition of whatever need is dictated by the moment of present interaction with other appearances, instances, occasions of the absolute.

Philip Kapleau, one of the West's most brilliant commentators on Zen Buddhism observes in this vein that the Japanese zen masters have always placed greater reliance on zazen, the meditative discipline, to foster moral conduct in their disciples than upon the mere imposition of the moral precepts of the Buddha's teaching, from outside the disciple. Kapleau states that while zazen practice and the precepts are mutually reinforcing, even the strongest resolution to keep the precepts will only be now and then successful if not supported by the deepening of awareness that comes with zazen. He notes that Japanese and Chinese masters of zen insist that one can truly know good and evil only upon full enlightenment (Kapleau, 1980). Only then does pure goodness occur in one's everyday actions.

Buddhism's contribution is significant here because it makes the point, for this chapter, that there is a generic quality in descriptions of religious experience despite significant differences among religious traditions. In this case the point is especially interesting in light of the marked difference between theistic and nontheistic traditions.

The further point is that this generic quality not only pertains to the immediate psychological event but to its effects, as well. In the event of religious experience lines separating being and value converge in the perception of the subject, and in effect, the subject's world necessarily takes on a moral dimension, the subject's perception a moral character. Alan Watts, a Westerner writing in the manner of the Taoists, puts it this way:

> Where there is to be creative action, it is quite beside the point to discuss what we should or should not do in order to be right or good. A mind that is single and sincere is not interested in being good, in conducting relations with other people so as to live up to a rule. Nor, on the other hand, is it interested in being

free, in acting perversely just to prove its independence. Its interest is not in itself, but in the people and problems of which it is aware; these are "itself." It acts, not according to the rules, but according to the circumstances of the moment, and the "well" it wishes to others is not security but liberty. (Watts, 1951)

The liberty that derives from an absolute relationship with the absolute and which includes moral consciousness.

PSYCHOLOGY AND RELIGION

The psychologist who wishes to consider the matter of relationship between religion and behavior, and especially the relationship of religion to moral development and/or criminal behavior, must consider the element of religious experience in the formula of correlation and causality. If the psychologist is to reckon with these matters comprehensively, some recognition must be given to scholars of religion like those discussed in preceding pages, who claim that religious experience is, by nature, experience that influences the moral attitudes and action of the subject. Such scholars not only draw attention to an important point about the nature and importance of religion in the moral domain, they speak with a voice that is representative of religion, itself. To ignore them is to mock not only religion but good scholarship, itself, and will result in conclusions that are at once unfounded and unfair.

For the most part, those psychologists who have focused on the matter of religious experience have not done as much as they could have done to consider or accurately represent the testimony of religious persons about their own experiences, and that has carried over into their lack of attention to the evidence from those within the field of religious studies, such as scholars mentioned in this chapter, who have documented those experiences generically, across religious traditions.

William James's work remains the most comprehensive in the field of psychology concerning religious experience. His *Varieties of Religious Experience* attends to the relationship between types of personalities and types of religious experiences, and it addresses a tremendous number of questions, but it is lacking in one important respect. That lack, in conjunction with errors of omission, ignorance, and prejudice committed by psychologists who have come after him, must be rectified if psychology is to have anything of importance to contribute to the understanding of religion and its relation to moral development and criminal behavior.

James's failing is that despite his massive catalog of citations and his concern with precise attention to substance, he omits the moral dimension from the experiences he considers. My views are consistent with James's assertion that "One may truly say. . . that personal religious experience has its root and centre in mystical states of consciousness; so for us, who are treating personal experience as the. . . subject of our study, such states of consciousness ought to form the vital chapter from which the other chapters get their light" (James, 1902, p. 292). I cannot, however, agree with his assignment of definitive characteristics. James cites ineffability, noetic quality, transiency, and passivity as marks of mystical personal religious experience, but he would have done well to include the convergence of being and value that also occurs. In the whole of James's "central chapter" he makes only fleeting reference to the matter of moral features of religious experience.

One problem with this orientation toward religious experience is that it ignores two central claims of the phenomenon it sets out to investigate. The first of these claims is that religious experience provides an immediate experience of meaning. Moreover, the claim is that this experience of meaning is one of ultimate meaning. No other meaning compares to or can surpass the meaning known in the immediate moment of religious experience. Second, no other experience of meaning can compare with the implications of this meaning for the whole experience of life. Religious experience renders being, qua being, meaningful, and it renders being in relation all other beings, and the larger scheme of Being of which they are all part, meaningful. Thus the philosopher Whitehead provides a psychological description of religious experience as consisting in three recognitions, all occurring concurrently; (1) the value of an individual for itself, (2) the value of the diverse individuals of the world for each other, and (3) the value of the objective world which is a community derivative from the interrelations of its component individuals, and also necessary for the existence of each of these individuals (Whitehead, 1960).

This error by James and those who have followed him, has been made worse in psychology by the accompaniment of two errors of commission.

One error of commission has been psychologists' over-emphasis on the place of religion in psychopathology. The fact that so many researchers have concerned themselves with the religious content of expressions in psychopathological personalities, instead of focusing on the role of religion in the development of healthy personalities says more about the anti-religious bias of psychologists and the lack of attention within psychology to normal development, as well as saying something about the times we are living in than it does about the nature of religion in the life of human beings.

From this first error of commission we move to a second, by which I mean the sloppy formulation of psychologists regarding the place of religious belief in the moral and criminological formula. Aside from methodological problems inherent in much of psychological research regarding the direction of explanation or causation in such matters there is the almost facile notion that religious belief, per se, will or will not inhibit immoral or criminal behavior, without concern for experience. While people may say things such as "I believe in God and so I will not murder my neighbor" it is also true that they probably mean something more akin to "I believe in God, and I have had an experience that leads me to feel that my neighbor and I are responsible to one another as God's creations, and so, rather than violate this essential compact, which would at the same time violate the integrity of my soul in light of my experience of ultimate meaning in God's care, I will refrain from harming my neighbor." The crucial variable is the fact of an experience that mediates the belief in its relation to action.

Psychologists have avoided this element in the formula of religion and its effects. They have preferred to reduce religion to a crude set of endorsements and refusals of association with certain elementary statements. While there is no doubt an important place in psychology for the study of people who make such endorsements or refusals, and of their involvements with religious institutions, political causes, other beliefs and practices, and of their everyday behavior, psychology should also range more broadly across the territory of religion as it is lived by its adherents and known by its scholars before making sweeping pronouncements about the place of religion in the whole scheme of behavior. This is especially true when the matter at hand is something so profound and so complex as moral development and criminal behavior.

WHAT REMAINS TO BE DONE: A CHALLENGE FOR PSYCHOLOGY

The psychology of religion is still left with the claim of religion that one or a series of experiences can transform, deepen, or otherwise affect individuals such that they will more likely behave morally. I have cited several scholars of religion who make such claims, in this paper. If true, then not only the discipline of psychology, but indeed society, has an interest in understanding what happens, under what conditions, and why. If it is also true, as has been asserted here, that religious experience has a generic quality and effect independent of situation in a particular religious group or belief system, then it would be valuable for both psychology and society to know how to promote such experience.

At very least, it would be wise to promote research that considers the claim of religion in the place of moral and criminal psychology. Several questions come to mind in this regard, though they are only a few of the many worth asking: What percentage of criminals claim to have had religious experience? What kinds of correlations exist between when, and how often, criminals report having had religious experiences, and the frequency, type, and point in time of crimes they report having committed? What is the record of criminals who report having had religious experiences after the time when they committed crime, and after their having been apprehended by legal authorities? Are the parole records of such criminals, their self-reports of criminal behavior, or their rates of recitivism different from those who do not report having had such experiences? What about the self-reports of those who have not been apprehended or committed to penal institutions, but who say they have committed crimes, or that they have not, and their associations with religious experience? Can they be distinguished from those who have not reported their having had religious experiences? What role does religious experience seem to have in individuals' hypotheses about how they would act in a given situation of moral decision-making? Are people who claim to have had religious experiences viewed as morally superior by their peers, or in ratings given them by independent observers? What does incidence of claim to religious experience have to do with gender, class, age, and other demographic variables? How do those together relate to findings in the study of personality, social psychology, moral development, and crime?

Until religious experience, as a factor distinct from religious belief, is considered in the formula of correlation and causation with the behavioral phenomena psychologists consider to measure moral development and crime, psychologists will miss a crucial link in the process of formulating solid theory. There is plenty of evidence, as has been demonstrated here, to suggest that psychology can learn from religion, apply its own methodological rigor, and, in turn, better inform the disciplines and efforts of moral development and criminology, which are its natural allies.

CONCLUSION

Psychology and religion have a great deal to do with, say to, and learn from one another. To date their cross-fertilization has been impeded by prejudice and misconception. In addition, psychologists have made a critical error in their investigations and analyses of religious experience that has impoverished efforts to apply knowledge of religion to discussion of moral development and criminal behavior.

The moral dimension in religious experience, specifically, has been overlooked and should be included if psychologists are to speak of it intelligently.

I believe that a psychological reckoning with the moral dimension of religious experience can yield not only an enriched psychological knowledge and critical discipline, but suggest avenues that might more profitably be pursued by psychologists interested in moral development, criminal behavior, and links between the two. It is my hope that this chapter, and this book, will contribute to that development.

REFERENCES

Argyle, M. (1958). *Religious behavior*. London: Routledge and Kegan Paul.

Buber, N. (1970). *I and Thou*. New York: Charles Scribner's Sons.

Colby, A. and Kohlberg, L. (1981). *Invariant sequence and internal consistency in moral judgment stages*. Paper presented at Florida International University Conference. (see Jennings, Kilkenny, and Kohlberg, 1983, for a discussion).

Fowler, J. (1978). Mapping faith's structures: A developmental view. In J. Fowler, and S. Keen, (Eds.), *Life maps: Conversations on the journey of faith*. Waco, Texas: Word Books.

Fowler, J. (1976). Stages in faith: The structural developmental approach. In T. Hennessey, (Ed.), *Values and moral development* New York: Paulist Press.

Freud, S. (1927). *The future of an illusion*. London: Hogarth Press.

Geertz, C. (1973). *The interpretation of cultures*. New York. Basic Books.

James, W. (1902). *The varieties of religious experience*. New York. Mentor Books.

Jennings, W., Kilkenny, W., and Kohlberg, L. (1983). Moral-development theory and practice for youthful and adult offenders, In W. Laufer, and J. Day, *Personality theory, moral development, and criminal behavior*. Lexington, Ma: Lexington Books.

Kapleau, P. (1980). *The three pillars of Zen*. Garden City, NY: Anchor Press.

Kierkegaard, S. (1843). *Fear and trembling*. (1953 Translation by W. Lowrie) Princeton, NJ: Princeton University Press.

Kohlberg, L. (1981). *The philosophy of moral development*, V.I. San Francisco: Harper and Row.

Kohlberg, L. (1976). Moral stages and moralization: The cognitive-developmental approach. In T. Lickona, (Ed.), *Moral development and behavior: Theory, research, and social issues*. New York: Holt, Rinehart, and Winston.

Kohlberg, L. (1969). Stage and sequence: The cognitive-developmental approach to socialization. In D. Goslin, (Ed.), *Handbook of socialization theory and research*. New York. Rand MacNally.

Merton, T. (1961). *New seeds of contempltation*. New York. New Directions Press.

Parsons, T. and Shils, E. (1951). *Toward a general theory of action*. Cambridge, Ma: Harvard University Press.

Piaget, J. (1932). *The Moral judgment of the child*. New York: Free Press of Glencoe.

Power, C. and Kohlberg, L. (1980). Religion, morality, and ego development. In J. Fowler, and A. Vergote, (Eds.), *Toward moral and religious maturity*. Morristown, NJ: Silver Burdett.

Scobie, G. (1975). *Psychology of religion*. New York. John Wiley.

Sorokin, P. (1937). *Social and cultural dynamics*. (3 vols.). New York.

Spinks, G. (1960). *Fundamentals of religious belief*. New York: Hodder & Stoughton.

Tillich, P. (1963). *Morality and beyond*. New York: Harper & Row.

Watts, A. (1951). *The wisdom of insecurity*. New York. Vintage Books.

Whitehead, A.N. (1960). *Religion in the making*. New York: Meridian Books.

Author Index

A

Abdul-Rauf, M., 59, *108*
Acquinas, St. T., 187, *188*
Ahlstrom, S., 122, *131*
Albrecht, G.L., 112, *119*
Albrecht, S.L., 112, *119*, 193, *208*
Alcorn, D.S., 112, *119*, 193, *208*
Allen, G.W., 137, 138, 139, 140, 141, *150*
Alper, B., *108*
Amir, Menachem, 32, *109*
Anderson, H., 115, *119*
Angell, R.C., 115, *119*
Anthony, D., 172, *190*
Aquinas, T., 99, *108*
Argyle, M., *264*
Arndt, W.F., *188*
Asher, 200*n*
Augustine, St., *188*

B

Bailey, L.W., 142, *150*
Bainbridge, W.S., 111, 113, 116, 117, *119*, *120*
Baker, R.L., 183, *188*
Barker, E., 171, *188*
Barkley, B.J., 134, *150*
Barnes, T., 163, *188*
Bauer, W., 154
Beach, G.K., 24, 44, *109*
Becker, H., 124, *131*
Beckford, J., 169, 171, *188*
Bell, G.L., 133, *150*
Bell, R., 124, *131*
Bellah, R.N., 163, *188*
Beller, M., *188*
Bencheikh, El. H., 186, *188*
Benson, P.H., 193, *208*
Berman, H., 39, *109*
Bernard, 115
Bianchi, H., 47, 48, 76, 77, *109*
Billington, R., 168, *188*

Black, M., *110*
Blodgett, H.W., *150*
Bockle, F., *109*
Boettcher, R., 164, 167, *188*
Bradley, S., *150*
Bradly, M., 115, *119*
Brandon, T.S., Jr., 183, 185, 186, *188*
Breen, T.H., 4, 10, 11, *21*
Bromley, D.G., 167, 169, *188*
Bronner, A.F., 193, *209*
Brown, E.F., 133, 136, *150*
Brunner, E., *109*
Bryant, M.D., *188*
Buber, N., *264*
Burkett, S.R., 112, *119*
Burton, J., 50, 59, 59*n*, 65, *109*

C

Chadwick, B.A., 112, *119*, 193, *208*
Cheek, J.M., 142, *150*, *151*
Chenu, M.D., 187, *188*
Chorover, S., 171, *188*
Christensen, C.W., 133, *150*
Clark, J., 170, *188*
Cohn, H.H., 28, 31, 45, 51, 52, 61, 66, *109*
Cohn, N., 166, *188*
Colby, A., *264*
Conway, F., 171, *188*
Cooper, H.H.A., *110*
Cottrell, R., 180, *189*
Coulson, N.J., 52, 60, *109*
Cross, D.G., 143, *150*
Crutchfield, R., 117, *120*

D

Dale, F., 23, *109*
Davies, W.D., 38, 39, *109*
Davis, K., *208*
Davis, R.G., 193, 194, *209*
Delgago, R., 186, *189*

Subject Index